KT-366-138

STREET ETHNOGRAPHY

Selected Studies of Crime and Drug Use in Natural Settings

SAGE ANNUAL REVIEWS OF DRUG AND ALCOHOL ABUSE

Series Editor:

JAMES A. INCIARDI, *University of Delaware*

Editorial Advisory Board:

John C. Ball, *Temple University*

Barry S. Brown, *National Institute on Drug Abuse*

Carl D. Chambers, *Antioch College*

John J. Devlin, *Portage Program for Drug Dependencies, Montreal*

William C. Eckerman, *Research Triangle Institute*

Gilbert L. Geis, *University of California, Irvine*

Daniel Glaser, *University of Southern California*

Daniel J. Lettieri, *National Institute on Drug Abuse*

David F. Musto, *Yale University*

George Nash, *Westchester County Community Mental Health Center*

David M. Petersen, *Georgia State University*

Brian R. Russe, *University of Miami*

Frank R. Scarpitti, *University of Delaware*

Harvey A. Siegal, *Wright State University*

Richard C. Stephens, *University of Houston*

SAGE Annual Reviews of Drug and Alcohol Abuse

Volume 1

STREET ETHNOGRAPHY

Selected Studies of Crime and Drug Use in Natural Settings

ROBERT S. WEPPNER, Editor

SAGE PUBLICATIONS / Beverly Hills / London

UNIVERSITY COLLEGE

LIBRARY

CARDIFF

Copyright © 1977 by Sage Publications, Inc.

All rights reserved. No part of this book may be reproduced or utilized in any form or by any means, electronic or mechanical, including photocopying, recording, or by any information storage and retrieval system, without permission in writing from the publisher.

For information address:

SAGE PUBLICATIONS, INC.
275 South Beverly Drive
Beverly Hills, California 90212

SAGE PUBLICATIONS LTD
St George's House / 44 Hatton Garden
London EC1N 8ER

Printed in the United States of America

International Standard Book No. 0-8039-0808-3 (cloth)
International Standard Book No. 0-8039-0809-1 (paper)

Library of Congress Catalog Card No. 76-50446

FIRST PRINTING

CONTENTS

PREFACE TO THE SERIES

The excessive use of alcohol and the nonmedical use of drugs have long since been defined as social, medical, and legal problems in many nations around the world. Each of these phenomena not only reflects a long series of medical and social costs to individual users but, in addition, represents a considerable liability to society as a whole. Furthermore, the problems associated with the misuse of alcohol and drugs have traditionally been considered so dangerous and threatening to social stability that they have resulted in the structuring of an almost uncountable number of organizations and bureaucracies which alternatively focus on their study, management, treatment, and control.

Alcohol is, by far, the longest known and most widely used psychoactive substance. Evidence suggests that alcohol may have been produced by prehistoric man, and recorded history indicates that alcohol has continually played both symbolic and pharmacological roles in social, religious, and medical practices and customs for some six millennia. And while alcohol use has been long enduring and almost universal, so has been its misuse. Currently, as many as one hundred million Americans experience the effects of alcohol annually. These effects can vary with the quantity, frequency, and variability of use, and the excessive use of alcohol can result in direct influences on behavior and adverse reactions in the physical organism.

It is likely that the use of drugs, other than alcohol, also has its roots in the days of prehistoric man since so many varieties of psychomimetic drugs freely occur in nature. Yet the widespread problems associated with the use of drugs are of relatively recent definition, enduring for little more than a century in the United States. Opium was perhaps the first of the mind-altering drugs to receive significant notice, and its habit-forming nature was given national attention in August 1867, when Fitzhugh Ludlow commented in *Harper's Magazine:*

> The habit is gaining fearful ground among our professional men, the operatives in our mills, our weary serving women, our fagged clerks, our former liquor drunkards, our very day laborers, who a generation ago took gin. All our classes from the highest to the lowest are yearly increasing their consumption of the drug.

Although alcohol may represent the most persistent and prevalent substance of abuse, the problems associated with the misuse of other drugs may indeed be more complex. For during the 11 decades since Ludlow's comments on the opium habit, drug abuse has expanded to include synthetic narcotics, barbiturates, nonbarbiturate sedative-hypnotics, cocaine, amphetamines and other stimulants, major and minor tranquilizers, antidepressants, hallucinogens, nonnarcotic analgesics, solvents and inhalants, and numerous over-the-counter preparations. The majority of these substances reflect alternative behavioral effects and physical complications. And further, the interaction of these drugs, when taken in combination with one another or with alcohol, has produced additional avenues for social and medical concern.

Since the turn of the current century, the literature on drinking and drug-taking behavior and effects has been impressive, and extensive commentary on these phenomena has been offered by all of the clinical, professional, and academic disciplines. Our knowledge and insight have been increasing dramatically. Yet each new finding generates a body of new and more difficult questions; each new development in research strategy uncovers phenomenal problems previously untouched; and, with the resolution of old questions, the field of further inquiry expands. As such, we must continue to expand our knowledge base, asking new questions, seeking more appropriate answers, testing new methods and strategies for study, reexamining the discarded, and looking for the undiscovered.

Among the more enduring and elusive issues in the substance abuse field has been that of the relationship between drug use and criminal behavior. For the better part of the 20th century, both researchers and clinicians in the drug field as well as representatives of our government, mass media, and criminal justice agencies have repeatedly asked a variety of questions on this relationship. Is criminal behavior, first of all, antecedent to addiction, or is crime a phenomenon which appears subsequent to the onset of addiction? More specifically, is crime the result of or a response to a special set of life circumstances brought about by the addiction to narcotic drugs or the nonmedical use of nonaddicting drugs? Is drug use or addiction per se a deviant tendency characteristic of individuals already prone to offense behavior? And, finally, what about offense behavior? How many crimes do drug users actually commit? How many crimes must drug users commit in order to maintain their desired levels of drug experience? What kinds of offenses are committed by different types of drug users and addicts? What proportion of "street crime" are drug users responsible for? How much drug-related crime remains unrecorded in official criminal statistics?

The spectrum of concerns descriptive of the purported relationship between crime and drug use did not become entirely visible until after the passage of the Harrison Act in 1914, a revenue measure designed to make narcotics transferrals a matter of record. Yet even prior to this early piece of legislation, a body of attitudes regarding the use of drugs had been developing for decades prior to the beginning of the 1900s. Opium and its derivatives had been used as general remedies in this country since the early days of the American colonies, and its proliferation as a primary ingredient in patent medicines during the post-Civil War era made the drug available in uncontrolled amounts to hundreds of thousands of men, women, and children. Charles E. Terry and Mildred Pellens' *The Opium Problem* (1928), the classic contribution to epidemiological studies of drug use, documented how a noticeable portion of the medical profession in the 19th century viewed "opium eating" as a yielding to seductive pleasure. By the close of the 1880s attitudes had become even more potent. Dr. C.W. Earle, for example, expressed in the *Chicago Medical Review* that the opium habit, like alcohol use, constituted a vice; Constantin Schmitt suggested in 1889 that the condition was a psychopathic state; and Wilson and Eshner's 1896 edition of the *American Textbook of Applied Therapeutics* investigated the use of opium as a disease of both the mind and the body.

At a second level of observation, a portion of the police literature of the period also began to view opium use within a negative frame of reference. While the *use* of opium was not a crime per se, the operation of opium-smoking parlors was illegal in New York City, for example, and police activities that focused on closing such establishments further stigmatized the opium user. A.E. Costello's *Our Police Protectors* in 1884 and Thomas Byrnes's *The Professional Criminals of America* in 1886 and 1895, both authors being police administrators in New York, dramatized opium smoking and its consequences as being evil and associated such behavior with criminality.

The passage of the Harrison Act in 1914 generated the potential for applying a criminal label to every narcotic user in the nation. Under the interpretation of the new law, possession of a narcotic was seen as a criminal offense, and the drug became typically available only through nonlegal sources. Arrests became commonplace, and the drug taker as "criminal" was necessarily brought before the public eye.[1] By the 1920s, it was believed that perhaps 25% of all crimes were committed by addicts, the result of the alleged "maddening" effects of the drugs, and this belief has endured to the present day among some segments of society.

Research into the relationship between drugs and crime essentially began within a few years after the passage of the Harrison Act, and the major issue of concern was whether addicts had been criminals prior to their addiction or whether their criminality was the result of addiction. As the research became more formalized, it circumscribed four basic issues:

(1) that addicts ought to be the object of vigorous police activity, because the majority are members of a criminal element, and drug addiction is simply one of the later phases in their criminal careers;

(2) that addicts prey upon legitimate society, and the effects of their drugs do indeed predispose them to serious criminal transgressions;

(3) that addicts are essentially law-abiding citizens who are forced to steal in order to adequately support their drug habits;

(4) that addicts are not necessarily criminals, but they are forced to associate with an underworld element which tends to maintain control over the distribution of illicit drugs.

Parallel to the question of the relation of addiction to crime has been the notion that individuals dependent on narcotic drugs tend to commit specific types of crime. The literature of the 1920s through the 1950s reflected a diversity of opinions, suggesting on the one hand that addicts were predisposed to violent behavior and on the other that they were primarily property offenders. The more scientific community of the 1950s and 1960s conceded to the less violent orientation, but recent research has again suggested that addict crime has been becoming more aggressive—in the form of armed robbery and mugging.

Currently, with increasing rates of both crime and drug use, policy makers, legislators, and the general public have become more and more concerned over the possible relationships between these two phenomena, and our repository of knowledge in this behalf is seemingly based more on the conventional wisdom of suspicion and assumption than on concrete fact. In an effort to generate a better understanding of the crime-drugs issue, the National Institute on Drug Abuse created a Panel on Drug Use and Criminal Behavior during 1975 and 1976 to examine the state of our knowledge in this area and to make recommendations for further research. Within this same framework of inquiry, the National Institute also sponsored a two-day workshop in Miami, Florida, during 1976 for the purpose of examining how ethnographic field research techniques might be utilized for studying drug-related crime. This volume, *Street Ethnography: Selected Studies of Crime and Drug Use in Natural Settings,* edited by Robert S. Weppner, represents the contributions of that workshop. Professionals from diverse fields and with experience in ethnographic research were drawn together for input on the task at hand. While all of their contributions were not necessarily in the area of drug-crime, as can be noted in the contents of this volume, they nevertheless represented an exploration of techniques which were deemed useful for studying drugs and crime at the street level.

Finally, this volume also inaugurates a new series, the *Sage Annual Reviews of Drug and Alcohol Abuse.* Each volume will focus on a specific drug- or alcohol-related problem or issue, from a variety of unique frames of reference. An advisory board has been impaneled for the purpose of making recommendations in this behalf, and suggestions will also be welcomed from our readers.

James A. Inciardi
Newark, Delaware
December 1976

NOTE

1. For the most lucid and complete examination of the origins of narcotic control in the United States, see David F. Musto, M.D., *The American Disease* (New Haven, Conn.: Yale University Press, 1973).

FOREWORD

Ethnography is the science of cultural description. It involves the careful study of a specific cultural perspective on family life, hunting and fishing, curing of illnesses, belief in the supernatural, and hundreds of other aspects of human experience. Ethnographers describe particular ways of life among such groups as the Eskimo, the Kwakiutl, the Trobriand Islanders, the Bushmen, and the Pygmies. Their goal is to discover how each of these people define their world, how they routinely behave in everyday life, and how they make sense out of experience. Through a painstaking process of participant observation, one slowly comes to apprehend the insider's view of life and records it in a cultural description.

"Street ethnography" implies that the people who spend much of their lives on city streets have acquired a culture. At first glance, the ethnographic method, developed in remote tribal societies, may appear inappropriate to street life that involves crime and drug use. To someone like Bronislaw Malinowski, who wrote about the Trobriand Islanders in his *Crime and Custom in Savage Society* (1926), the concept of "street ethnography" might have seemed ambiguous or even contradictory. Although the need for ethnography in preliterate societies is readily apparent, of what value is this approach on the streets of Philadelphia, New York, or Seattle? The Trobriand Islanders speak a different language and live by strange, exotic customs. Can we say the same for the heroin addict, the pickpocket, the drunk, the prostitute, and the professional fence who live in the largest cities of our technological society? Since these people are part of American society, why not utilize more rigorous methods of survey research and laboratory experiments to understand their involvement in crime and drug use?

This book takes seriously the premise that complex societies are made up of many different cultures, subcultures, and cultural scenes. And each of these sociocultural worlds provides different ways of making sense out of life. The heroin addict does not view his behavior the same way the psychologist or suburban minister sees it. These people live in different cultural worlds. The pickpocket and the fence have acquired culturally specific perspectives on "crime" that contrast sharply with the perspective of the police officer or judge in the criminal court. Although these people may share the same geographical area of a city for part of each day, they live in different sociocultural worlds. If we are to understand such phenomena as crime and drug use, we must begin by describing their meanings from the various perspectives of the people involved.

Scholars in Western society frequently take their own perspective as the one which represents reality. In a classic article, "The Need for an Ethnomedical Science," Horacio Fabrega argued for the importance of a broader perspective in understanding disease. His comments could equally apply to other fields concerned with human problems besides medicine.

> In Western cultures, "disease" is what physicians and biologists study. The whole medical complex in Western nations, which includes knowledge, practices, organizations, and social roles, can be termed "biomedicine." Biomedicine thus constitutes our own culturally specific perspective about what disease is, and how medical treatment should be pursued; and like other medical systems, biomedicine is an interpretation which "makes sense" in light of cultural traditions and assumptions about reality. [1975:969]

All societies have knowledge, practices, and social roles related to disease. An ethnomedical science would build on these different systems to eventually develop a language for talking about "generic disease" in all cultures.

An ethnomedical science is only one area of study that seeks to take seriously the cultural variability of the human species. *Ethnopharmacology*, the study of specific cultural perspectives on drugs, has begun to develop and has important contributions to make to the study of drug use. Heroin and opium addicts, as well as those who use the various psychedelic drugs, have their own beliefs about the chemical substances they use. And these beliefs often contrast sharply with the perspective of professional phrmacologists. *Ethnocriminology*, a truly comparative study of criminal behavior, would build on the foundation of specific ethnographic studies of crime in other cultures and the various meanings of criminal behavior within out own society. The list of topics might include *ethnogerontology*, *ethnobiology*, and *ethnopsychology*. Underlying each of these fields would be the ethnographic description of how various peoples understand and deal with crime, aging, biological processes, and human psychology.

This book, then, challenges the tacit assumption in much of the research on drug use and crime, that the various participants all share the same perspective. It challenges the assumption that one perspective—whether legal, medical, judicial, or psychological—is always the best way to understand criminal behavior and substance abuse. As such, it not only contributes to the understanding of specific groups involved in crime and drug problems but it calls for a reorientation in social science research. The ethnographic approach may at first appear to make such problems as drugs and crime appear more complex rather than less. I would argue that the tendency to oversimplify social and behavioral problems in our society to a limited number of "variables" has not been as fruitful as many social scientists hoped. While such research will surely continue to add to our understanding, we also need to turn our attention to the more basic task of ethnographic description.

Although ethnography is essential to building a truly comparative science of human behavior, it also has more immediate usefulness. Government policy cannot always wait for the slower pace of science. Those engaged in treatment programs for drug addicts or rehabilitation of criminals need to understand the people they deal with. Ethnographic studies of street cultures—and some of the best are presented and discussed in this volume—can provide policy makers and treatment personnel with another perspective, the insider's perspective. In some cases we may discover that "victimless crimes" are not the problem we thought they were. In other cases, the insights and understandings of addicts and criminals may lead to improved programs of treatment or more humanitarian policies.

We live in a multicultural society. As social scientists, we must take seriously the existence of a vast number of different socio-cultural systems. Nowhere is this more important than with problems of crime and drug use, and the chapters in this book go a long way in that direction.

James P. Spradley

REFERENCES

FABREGA, H., Jr. (1975). "The need for an ethnomedical science." Science, 189:969-975.
MALINOWSKI, B. (1926). Crime and custom in savage society. London: Routledge and Kegan Paul.

ACKNOWLEDGMENTS

This book is the result of the labors of a small group of young social scientists who have done rather nontraditional research. Yet their training and quest for understanding has carried them into rather exotic cultures within their own larger culture, and they have produced some exciting results.

Strong encouragement and support for their work has come largely from the efforts of one person, Eleanor Carroll of the National Institute on Drug Abuse. She has been a mentor, confidante, and hard taskmaster for most of us, and we are all indebted to her.

We are also indebted to Dr. Robert Shellow, visiting fellow at the National Institute on Drug Abuse, who expedited funding for the workshop from which these papers came and gave strong support to the collective effort.

Finally, Susan Dalton and Rita Margolis typed and retyped manuscripts cheerfully and really maintained the whole operation. Our thanks to them, and my special thanks to Genie Sue.

Robert S. Weppner
Coral Gables, Florida
December 1976

STREET ETHNOGRAPHY

Selected Studies of Crime and Drug Use in Natural Settings

1

STREET ETHNOGRAPHY
Problems and Prospects

ROBERT S. WEPPNER

The National Institute on Drug Abuse and one of its precursor agencies, the Division of Narcotic Addiction and Drug Abuse of the National Institute of Mental Health, have sponsored a number of research projects which either have been ethnographic in nature or have had ethnographic components connected to the projects. In the search for an understanding to drug use in a cross-cultural perspective, the institutes have sponsored cannabis studies in Africa, Yemen, and Colombia. Two others are well known, one in Jamaica (Rubin and Comitas, 1975) and one in Costa Rica, part of which is reported by William and Joan True in the present volume (Chapter 5). This interest in drug use has extended to Mexican Americans in Chicago, street addicts in Chicago (Hughes et al., 1971), American Indians in the Southwest, working class Italian youths in the northeastern United States (Feldman, 1974), the Irish and Italians in New York City, white and black prostitutes in Seattle (James, 1972, 1976), a tri-ethnic community in Miami comprising American-born blacks, Cubans, and whites (McBride, 1975; Cleckner, 1975; Weppner, 1976), and treatment milieus in Philadelphia (Soloway, n.d.), New Haven (Gould et al., 1974), and San Francisco (New-meyer and Johnson, 1976).

Given the fact that many federal agencies are currently interested in the social problems of drugs and crime and that traditionally used research strategies of retrospective survey or file searches have not completely answered questions relating drug abuse to crime, officials at the National Institute on Drug Abuse offered to sponsor a workshop in Miami in the spring of 1976 which would bring together social scientists who had used a different approach to studying drug abuse and crime. These social scientists had primarily used the ethnographic technique of participant observation. Further, most had done their work in city streets, the natural habitat of the drug abuser, but some had worked in other milieus such as hospitals (Michael H. Agar and Robert S. Weppner) and jails (James P. Spradley and Jennifer James). Some of the workshop participants had used life history techniques (Carl B. Klockars, 1974; Francis A.J. Ianni, 1972), and one had interviewed some 30 police chiefs in the United States as to their opinions concerning drug abuse (Wesley Pomeroy, 1974). Many of the participants had taken the lead of one of the participants, Edward Preble, who worked on the streets among drug abusers beginning in the 1950s. Another anthropologist who was a pioneer in street studies, Elliot Liebow, offered pertinent comments throughout the workshop.[1] Some selected papers from the workshop compose the corpus of this volume.

The Relationship Between Drug Use and Crime

There is one area of research in drug abuse which has been studied in depth, and yet tantalizing questions remain. That area is the relationship of crime to drug abuse. Although large samples of narcotic addicts have shown a high involvement in criminality (see Greenberg and Adler, 1974, for a summary of the studies), the problem of the actual monetary costs of drug abuse remains. By this is meant that crimes such as drug selling and prostitution are, as Schur (1965) has noted, "crimes without victims" and thus have no direct cost to society. Other crimes committed to support expensive drug habits such as mugging, breaking and entering, and armed robbery are unresearched, although Inciardi and Chambers (1972) have stated that only one crime in 120 committed by drug addicts is cleared by arrest.

Most often, information about the criminality of drug abuse is obtained from retrospective survey questionnaires collected in some intervention agency context. These data are subject to retrospective distortion, lying, boasting, or any number of other biases. Weppner has noted (1973) the tendency of hospitalized narcotic addicts to elaborate on their life-styles. Such a tendency often occurs in an attempt to establish a "rep in the joint," but it may be checked out as described below in the discussion on methodology.

Given the knowledge that much drug addiction is supported by illegal activities, it still remains for researchers to devise techniques in which to document in what proportions "victimless" and "victim" crimes occur in a drug abuser's daily life. Until now, traditional survey and secondary data researchers have given less than complete answers. As a result, ethnography, the direct observation of behavior in natural settings by the researcher, may offer an alternative, or at least a very effective supplemental, approach. It is not suggested that the ethnographer must participate in criminal activity of drug abusers or even be a witness to it to obtain these data. What is suggested is that ethnography and its many forms of participant observation (Adams and Preiss, 1960; McCall and Simmons, 1969) can be used along with other research methodologies such as survey research or official record searches in a convergent strategy to provide some answers to issues, which will be described below.

STREET ETHNOGRAPHY

Ethnography as a method in the study of illicit drug use and/or crime has been a little used but potentially very effective tool. Two of the first anthropological studies in the field, Preble and Casey (1969) and Agar (1973), have shown that an ethnographical perspective of drug addiction—and, more specifically, heroin addiction—can lend in-depth knowledge of what it is to be a heroin addict from the addict's point of view. In addition, these and other excellent studies of other social scientists using the ethnographic method have pointed out various cultural features of what it is to be a heroin addict on the street. Sutter (1966), for example, produced a classic study on status and role among all types of drug users, but focused mainly on the "righteous dope fiend." Feldman (1968) worked on the socialization of black youngsters into the world of heroin users and later produced a short volume on problems of the ethnographer as a participant observer in the streets (1974). Recently, Gould, Walker, Crane, and Lidz (1974) produced an exceptional ethnography of the street addict's world. Giving in to their sociological training, however, they eschewed the "methodological naiveté that characterized many participant observation types of studies" (1974:xiii). Instead, they preferred a somewhat more rigorous if loose form of stratified sampling "to ensure contact with as wide a variety of heroin users as possible" (1974:xxi). What emerged was an informative "perspective *of* action" (italics theirs) of the actors in the heroin world. The value of their study is that it integrates the interaction of addicts, police, defense and prosecuting attorneys, probation officers, and treatment personnel into a somewhat unified whole of countervailing perspectives.

Other ethnographic studies have been carried out in Chicago by Hughes and Jaffe (1971) and Hughes et al. (1971) which have employed "indigenous observers," as Andrew L. Walker and Charles W. Lidz refer to their trained fieldworkers in the present volume (Chapter 4). Hughes et al. described a heroin copping community, that is, a heroin distribution site—its social structure, roles, and interaction patterns of dealers, users, and others in the setting. Overall, however, there has been little attention paid to street studies of deviance or crime by other than the contributors to the present volume and the other participants at the workshop. One notable exception is a completely sociologically oriented collection of ethnographic studies of deviance. Douglas (1972) presented a reader which presented methodological and ethical issues concerned with ethnographic research in deviance. The present papers, however, represent a new trend in which anthropologists can lend their disciplinary interests to the study of deviance and crime.

The street ethnographers in this volume have made a decision to work in the urban environments of North America. For sociologists, this is not a new direction, but for anthropologists it is. The question may arise among potential street ethnographers (it did not arise at the workshop proceedings reported herein): why bother to work in such surroundings? Such a question is moot if part of social science's task is a commitment to bringing an understanding of divergent life-styles.

First of all, we must make a decision on whom we wish to work with. Work with overclass deviants (as opposed to underclass deviants, as discussed by Harvey A. Siegal in Chapter 3) is not exactly new (Sutherland, 1949), but it may be more difficult than gaining access to groups of individuals who are different from the average American culture bearers. These individuals are by definition deviant even if their deviance amounts to nothing more than being poor. Because of their state, poor people, junkies, and prostitutes have accepted the questioning of social workers, law enforcement personnel, and social scientists much more readily than the overclass would. Gulick (1973) suggests, in a rather facile way, that the reason that anthropologists do not study the middle class is that "most of them are emotional refugees from this very culture" (p. 1012) and, if they do so, "they must overcome their prejudices, such as the general apathy to the middle class" (p. 1021). This statement may stir some anthropologists to indignation and yet stimulate others to justify ideologically the intellectual status quo.

The question of "studying up" (Nader, 1972)—that is, studying the overclass—may not be so much one of access as much as one of difficulty. The social scientist can gain access to just about any community, from industries (Roethlisberger and Dickson, 1939; Argyris, 1957) to the many small-town communities (Lynd and Lynd, 1929, Warner, 1941) et cetera, but it may be easier to gain access to a poolroom hustler, an addict, or a pickpocket, once you obtain your first entrée and "snowball" it to others (Polsky, 1969). Researching corporate theft by corporate officials could be done by life histories or participant observation, but it would take a large amount of resources and time. It is doubtful that an ethnographer could have uncovered the details behind the Watergate burglary, not because of lack of know-how, but because he or she would probably lack the resources to fly from coast to coast following leads. Thus the ethnographer chooses a group and gets on "one side or the other," as Becker (1967) puts it. And this does not involve romanticizing the group or necessarily taking their side because of "liberal or leftist leanings," as Douglas characterizes "a very important and influential minority of American sociologists (1972:23). It may well reflect the application of professional social scientific training to groups of natives who have hitherto been neglected because, at best, we have been unaware of research possibilities in our own backyard or, at worst, anthropologists have run out of exotic cultures as Franz Boas predicted they might some fifty years ago.

Anthropology and Criminology

Some anthropologists have been interested in cross-cultural law and litigation[2] but generally have contributed little to criminology, the attempt to discover underlying processes for criminal behavior. In the early 1930s, one anthropologist, A.E. Hooton, seemingly attempted to resurrect Cesare Lombroso's work.[3] Hooton produced two massive efforts (1939a, 1939b) in which he attempted to predict criminality by body type. By taking anthropomorphic measurements of incarcerated criminals and noncriminal civilians, he sought to prove that crime had biological as well as socioeconomic correlates. After determining that his criminal samples were on the whole younger than the civilian control group, weighed less, and had significant differences in chest breadth, head circumference, upper face height, nose height, and ear length (he neglected *social* correlates altogether), he made the unfortunate statement (1939a:309):

> Criminals are organically inferior. Crime is the resultant of the impact of environment upon low grade human organisms. It follows that the elimination of crime can be effected only by extirpation of the physically, mentally and morally unfit, or by their complete segregation in a socially aseptic environment.

Such a simplistic answer to crime brought an immediate response from Robert K. Merton and Ashley Montagu. In a bitingly sarcastic critique, they replied (1940:391-392):

It hardly comes as an unheralded discovery that the age-group of maximum criminality is in the young-adult period and that this age-group varies with the type of offense. The study of crime statistics had long ago led to this finding.

At this unfortunate juncture, no other anthropologists undertook the study of crime or criminal behavior per se in North America for another quarter of a century. It was at this time that ethnographers began to study the criminal process, if only collaterally to their main area of interest. Spradley's ethnography (1970) of public intoxication was a rigorous attempt to define the cognitive world of skid row alcoholics and their interaction with the Seattle criminal justice system, for, at that time, public intoxication was a crime. It was partly due to Spradley's efforts that much behavior has been, in the current parlance of substance abuse, "decriminalized." Spradley, in another article (1973:23), made the point that

Crime is only one form of social behavior, and it is intimately linked to many other forms. A fundamental premise of anthropology is that *social behavior* is culturally constituted. When an individual commits a crime, he does so in terms of the cultural meanings he has acquired.

Although one might see in this statement a rephrasing of the sociological theory of differential association (Sutherland and Cressey, 1974, passim), Spradley reminded the reader that policemen and judges also act in accordance with different sets of cultural rules. One fact is quite obvious in his article. Even though it is entitled "The Ethnography of Crime in American Society," anthropological references to crime studies are sparse or nonexistent.

Other street ethnographies, such as those of Hannerz (1969), Liebow (1967), and Keiser (1969), deal with crime or criminal acts only in passing, although Keiser's editing of Williamson's life story (1966) brings out the importance of criminal activities in many of the inhabitants of underclass urban areas. More direct ethnographic statements of crime and/or drug use have been Sutter's (1966) and James's (1976) contributions to readers in criminology. The classic study of William F. Whyte (1943), however, does describe the influence of racketeers on the Cornerville Social and Athletic Club.

Research in deviance and crime remained the province of sociologists, but, even so, many of them have used ethnographic methods to conduct their research. Becker (1963) used participant observation to research marijuana use, and some contributions in his reader (1964) were ethnographic, as are Douglas' (1972) collection of studies done among drug users, criminals, homosexuals, and other deviants. These studies are often unidimensional, however. That is, they do not attempt what the anthropological ethnographer calls the holistic approach: the interrelations of actors of different classes and statuses, the cultural perceptions of these actors, and the ecological milieus in which the activities occur. But Becker and Douglas do point out methodological and ethical difficulties of research into activities which usually occur in an urban context.

One well-known sociologist-ethnographer, Ned Polsky (1969), conducted deviance research among hustlers and poolroom players for many years. His book was sharply critical of criminologists who study crime from afar. He stated:

> Most sociologists find it too difficult or distasteful to get near adult criminals except in jails or other anti-crime settings, such as the courts and probation and parole systems. [p. 111]

Elsewhere he stated:

> The main obstacle to studying criminals in the field, according to Sutherland and Cressey, lies in the fact that the researcher must associate with them *as* one of them. . . . On the contrary, in doing field research on criminals, you damned well better not pretend to *be* one of them, because they will test this claim out and one of two things will happen: either you will, as Sutherland and Cressey indicate, get sucked into "participant" observation of the sort you would rather not undertake, or you will be exposed, with still greater negative consequences. [p. 117; italics added]

These comments may reflect the reluctance of sociologists to perform such participant observation studies altogether, whereas the reluctance in the past on the part of anthropologists may be due partly to Polsky's observations, but also to a lack of background in areas such as deviance theory and criminology.

Urban Anthropology and Street Ethnography

Several compilations of studies done in urban contexts have appeared over the years, and it is not the intention here to try to recount the history of urban studies from Weber and Tönnies through the Chicago school of urban sociology to present ethnographic efforts. The history of such efforts can be found in White and Weaver (1972) and Gulick (1973). Other reviews have been those of Despres (1968), Eddy (1968), and Kushner (1970). Throughout these reviews, there seems to be a dispute as to what to call ethnographic research in the cities. Some prefer "urban anthropology," others the "anthropology of complex societies." In many instances attempts to objectively define what is "urban" occurs. Gulick (1973) devotes well over one-fourth of his review to this problem.

Street ethnography is a loose term which has been applied conventionally among its practitioners to denote their activities. However, the street is where most addicts, prostitutes, hustlers, and pickpockets are found. The street provides the ability to mix with other passersby and thus achieve anonymity (Hughes et al., 1971; Weppner, 1973). No attempt will be made here to empirically define what "street" is, for such an effort would be as futile as past attempts to define what "urban" means, as Fischer notes (1975), although it is quite true that there are different degrees and kinds of "urbanism." The reader will learn that the street activity of the subjects in such studies occurs in the central and usually run-down parts of the larger cities. Edward Preble and Thomas Miller, James A. Inciardi, William R. and Joan H. True, and Harvey W. Feldman all allude to this fact in this volume. In addition, it may often, but not always, involve the observation of deviants or deviance. The contributors in this volume all deal with deviant groups or individuals, as does Douglas' (1972) group of readings. Street ethnography need not deal with deviants *only*. For example, it may be open to question as to just how deviant Liebow's (1967) group was, especially in the context of its own milieu. Deviance is a term imposed by the dominant culture anyway, and, as Quinney (1970) argued, this is how "crime is created." The nature of ethnographic participant observation attempts to remain value-free and to report the data with as little judgmental interpretation as possible.

Also, street ethnography is nothing more or nothing less than another "recent contribution to urban anthropology," as Weaver and White (1972:113) characterized studies of American Indians in the city environment. Gulick (1973), in his discussion of urban anthropology and urban sociology, noted that urban studies have usually been of migrants and their adjustment to city life, of the disadvantaged, and of ethnic groups. He indicates that

> Urban anthropology is not a subdiscipline in the sense of intellectual system and coherence that the term implies. Rather, it consists of a number of new directions that some anthropologists are taking. [p. 980]

Thus street ethnography is a new direction, especially for anthropologists. In noting the need for North American urban research into the problems caused by "loss of community," Gulick stated:

> My personal preference is for research that will elucidate the lives of particular people and at the same time help us to find cures for our present national agonies. [p. 1011]

No one would argue that street ethnography alone aspires to such noble motives, but it is cogent that federal agencies have sponsored such research in attempts to understand disturbing cultural phenomena such as crime and drug use. (This fact is addressed further below in a discussion of ethics.)

METHODOLOGY

If urban sociology and urban anthropology suffer from a lack of theoretical direction, as Fischer (1975) indicated, they also suffer from methodological problems. The problems of the ethnography of drugs and crime range from the risk to the researcher to the adequacy of data. Very briefly, some methodological issues can be listed:

(1) Can entrée into a street scene be facilitated by the training and payment of indigenous observers to perform such ethnographies?

(2) In a comparison of ethnography with other social research methods and strategies, how representative, generalizable, and valid are the respective data?

(3) To what extent does the observer's presence affect the behavior of the observed?

(4) What risks are there to the ethnographers from arrest by police, from being robbed or otherwise harmed by informants, or from the possible observation of crimes?

Reciprocity and Indigenous Observers

Early in the workshop, the question arose as to whether informants should be paid or not. The question of reciprocity is certainly not new. Wax addressed the issue in 1952, arguing that the ethnographer must give something of himself to get something in return (1960). However, some of the participants contended that attempting to help their subjects by lending them money, trying to get them jobs, appearing in court for them, and performing other services was too exhausting. It was easier to pay them, and indeed Andrew L. Walker and Charles W. Lidz's paper in this volume (Chapter 4) shows the benefits of paid informants. On the other hand, the papers by James A. Inciardi, Irving Soloway and James Walters, and Carl B. Klockars (Chapters 2, 7, and 9) show that payment is unnecessary, while Michael H. Agar argued in the workshop that payment never needs to be made. In this same kind of argument, Henslin (1972) noted that paying an informant might bias the information. He argued that it is better to know the motivation of the informant, and he went on to say:

> Deviants cooperate and give me research data, and I, on my part, give them such things as friends, attention, understanding, acceptance, a sympathetic ear, anonymity, insight, satisfaction of curiosity, fulfillment of altruistic needs, self-aggrandizement, the chance to cooperate with that magical thing called "science," fulfillment of obligations incurred within a friendship network, and/or an opportunity to establish obligations that their friend must repay at some future date. [p. 67]

Thus the first item of discussion in the workshop had the participants divided as to whether or not payment should be made to informants, and both positions have support in the published literature. This issue of payment appeared to be as situationally specific as the issue of ethics later proved to be. For example, Wax (1960) noted, "The gifts which a field worker repays the efforts of his informants will, of course, vary with each investigational situation," and she went on to discuss such "gifts" as relieving boredom or loneliness, giving support in grievances, or just assuming a learner stance (or, as Michael H. Agar notes in Chapter 6, a "one-down position").

In my work with narcotic addicts, I found that, once they come to trust you, they then are flattered by your interest and readily assume a teaching role (Weppner, 1973). But one must remember that an essential part of their life is the hustle, an often illegal endeavor. Indeed, part of their status on the street is determined by how good hustlers they are. As a result, I ended up bringing gifts of food, books, and items of clothes for my informants. I also bought "original" paintings which I later found to be tracings with the aid of an opaque projector and poorly made leather goods which my informants had made.[4] In this regard, one wonders if Wax's statement did not refer to a simpler and less materialistic group, for it certainly seems inapplicable to most of the subjects in this volume. Of course, Inciardi's pickpockets and Klockars' "fence" may be the exception to this statement, but the fact remains that the situation is variable, as Jennifer James would certainly argue, when she mentioned that exhaustion quickly set in with the onslaught of reciprocity demanded by her "natives."[5]

In the Trues' paper, however, reciprocity in its best sense is evidenced, in that all of the field workers gave money and exchanged favors with the informants and even acted as brokers with such institutions as the Ministry of Police.

Data Representativeness, Validity, and Generalizability

Another issue that was addressed early in the workshop was that of an epistemological nature. Agar argued that we must account for variability among informants and that we must also be able to account for shared meaning as he has done (1973). Spradley felt that the informant must define the sampling frame, just as he had noted earlier:

> Because the ethnographer seeks to discover the meaning which people attach to their experience, he must take great care not to pre-define the population he studies. [1973:25]

In this regard, Irwin (1972:131), in his participant observation study of criminals, felt that the ethnographer must develop theory from the categories of meaning discovered through participant observation rather than simply rely on verifying a preconceived theory.

James argued that, because of the subjective nature of street ethnography, one should use such additional measures as psychological testing and record searches. She also specified the need for combining these techniques into a convergent strategy for the validation of ethnographic observations. Walker and his colleagues (Gould et al., 1974) used sampling techniques, as mentioned earlier, as well as record searches. Preble and Miller certainly indicate some strength that a street ethnography could have over the officially published evaluation statistics of governmentally sanctioned agencies. In their paper (Chapter 10), they note the glowing reports of methadone maintenance program successes, when, in fact, on-the-scene observation shows a very different effect of methadone on the street addict's life. Herein lies a very positive aspect of research such as Preble and Miller's. Other nonethnographic reports have either sharply criticized the official evaluations of methadone maintenance programs (Maddux and Bowen, 1972) or supported Preble and Miller's contentions (Weppner and Stephens, 1973). In any event, such critiques have been largely ignored by methadone advocates. But Preble and Miller do note a recent apologia by the founders of methadone maintenance, blaming large-scale failures of the program on "government interference."

As for the question of generalizability of data, Inciardi's study (Chapter 2) may come the closest to being a description of a whole society, because of its diminishing numbers. He constructs a typology of a professional criminal, the "class cannon," from the categories of meaning of his informants themselves. By constructing a culture-historical approach to his definition, he places then in the perspective of time and place. He describes them as having common territories, argot, ideologies, and knowledge. Their recruitment is controlled, and they have a complex set of business maxims and a code of ethics.

Thus there seems to be less intracultural variation among pickpockets than among the youthful street drug users that Feldman describes (in Chapter 11) or among drug users in general, as Sutter pointed out (1966). The question of generalizability is always a problem which may be insolvable in pluralistic urban societies. One should keep in mind, however, Pelto's cautionary note that anthropologists seldom make a study of an entire society. Usually it is one community, which well may be atypical because it is remote and thus more "pure" or, even conversely, because it may be more accessible (1970:214-216).

The Effect of the Observer's Presence

It may be seen that many of the methodological issues are not mutually exclusive, nor are they exhaustive. The issue of being or avoiding the appearance of being a "spy," as Freilich labors over (1970), was not important to the workshop participants because they all had followed Polsky's dictum reported earlier, that it is better not to pretend to be "one of" your study group. The best and most obvious method to gain entrée to whatever group you wish to study is to tell them who you are and what you want to do. In no case was any covert research conducted by the authors of the present papers. For example, Inciardi was tested occasionally, but eventually became known as being "all right." In fact, he was awarded a "moniker" or nickname, which was a measure of status in the street and also a strong indication of acceptance.

Inciardi does point out a painful episode in which he hailed an informant while the latter was tailing a mark and the informant lost his "take off." What is instructive from the papers is that no informant changed his behavior in order to impress the ethnographer, although Soloway's unfortunate brush with an armed robbery may be interpreted in various ways. It may have been a test of what Soloway would do in the situation, but, as he and James agreed in the discussion of their papers, the ethnographer can set the limits to which he or she will go in advance of any interaction and the informant will almost always honor the contract.

Then, too, by a number of internal validity checks, the ethnographer can determine if he is obtaining reliable and valid data. Klockars, for example, used the technique of rechecking pertinent parts of his informant's life story and discussing discrepancies with him. Agar and Weppner found at the U.S. Public Health Service hospital in Lexington, Kentucky, that the "grapevine," that informal communication device used in the street, is a very good way to check whether or not the informant's report is true. This is a variation of what Douglas (1972:29) called "the member test," the use of former members of the group or other insiders. In some cases, Preble had to rely on the grapevine, especially in those cases in which the particular informant was inaccessible or dead from an overdose of drugs. This kind of triangulation—the use of other informants and, as James suggested earlier, official records and other tests—does produce checks on the truthfulness of the informant and the effect of the ethnographer on the informant's information.

Most of the workshop participants would agree with Irwin when he spoke of his research with criminals:

What we really mean by "participating" is being present to hear a lot of informal talk. Most data—histories, biographies, descriptions of events, meanings, concepts, patterns and categories—exist in and are conveyed to us through the informal talk of the subjects being studied. This is true because the structures and meanings that order a group's activities are constituted by their statements to each other—that is, by their on-going descriptions, discussions, and disputes. [1972:118]

Thus the fact that participant observation does not require being at the scene of reported behavior (in most cases, members of the group being studied would not want an outsider around to "mess up the action" anyway) and the availability of validity checks help to insure accurate portrayals of behavior.

Risks to the Ethnographer

As the workshop proceeded with its discussions, it became obvious that various topics overlapped with other substantive issues and areas. Although the first part of the sessions was reserved for methodological considerations, the effect of ethnographic research on policy determination arose. Fortunately, that issue, though closely tied to what ethnography can and cannot do, may be deferred to a later point in this present discussion. Less clear cut, however, were questions which arose in the method of street ethnography and the ethics connected with it. Thus questions arose as to the culpability of the ethnographer if he or she were inadvertently involved in some illegal activities. After Soloway presented his paper, he and Walters both confessed that they did not know to what extent they had violated the law. This led them to investigate the criminal code of their state thoroughly, and, to their relief, they found that no laws had been violated by the ethnographer after the alleged armed robbery.

As the two attorneys present agreed, there was no "misprison of a felony," although they agreed that the law might vary from state to state. Other protections do exist to assure the confidentiality and anonymity of informants. One recent legal provision is that contained in Public Law 92-255, the omnibus bill which, among other things, provided for the establishment of the National Institute on Drug Abuse. The pertinent provision for the street ethnographer is the one that holds that the research records of patients *while in treatment* for drug abuse may be granted immunity from subpeona. This permission must be obtained, in advance, from the director of the Drug Enforcement Agency. In theory, it might protect the drug researcher if he stays within the guidelines. There are, however, no other grants of immunity or privileged communication such as those afforded a lawyer and his client.

If this fact is considered, one might take into account Polsky's comment that the participant observer may have to take risks:

> If one is effectively to study adult criminals in their natural settings, he must make the moral decision that in some ways he will break the law himself. He need not be a "participant" observer and commit the criminal acts under study, yet he has to witness such acts or be taken into confidence about them and not blow the whistle. That is, the investigator has to decide that when necessary he will "obstruct justice" or have "guilty knowledge" or be an "accessory" before or after the fact, in the full legal sense of those terms. [1969:133-134]

How does this square with Irwin's comment about the hearsay nature of street research, quoted earlier? It is a difficult question to answer, although a major part of street ethnography does involve listening to hearsay and trying to make sure it is valid. Such a problem led Agar to question whether the information that he obtained on the streets of New York was any more valid than the data that he elicited in the "joint" at Lexington, Kentucky. Certainly the latter fieldwork was less risk producing, although even in that context the ethnographer may constantly witness infractions of institutional rules, as did Caudill (1958) and Goffman (1961). He then becomes caught in a role bind, just as he would in the street if he were to witness an individual being victimized.

Hypothetical moral and ethical situations are a bad substitute for actual situations. The workshop panelists agreed that, if they were called to testify in the prosecution of an informant, they must come forth with whatever information they have, but it probably would be hearsay anyway if the research bargain were reached (see below). Some panelists advocated looking into the local criminal codes before undertaking such research, but the practicality of that procedure is open to question. Another suggestion made by Spradley was to consult an attorney beforehand, especially before publishing, to protect the researcher from libel.

One possible approach to these legal and ethical dilemmas might be this: First of all, the assumption is made that you have identified yourself and identified why you are interested in the particular cultural phenomenon (as Klockars, Inciardi, and Feldman did). The second assumption is that you have gained rapport and enough trust with your informants so that you can make an agreement beforehand—that you are not what your informants are and that you do not wish to engage in activities that could be damaging to yourself. James was quite adamant in the discussions that you first of all should know who you yourself are and keep that distinction between you, the researcher, and the observed informants. One has to establish beforehand to what limits one will participate, observe, and listen.

All of this boils down to the fact that the street ethnographer should know whether or not he could possibly go "native," that is, drop old cultural values and roles and adopt those of the study group. It is quite unnecessary to take drugs in order to understand addiction or "the life" as the street addict refers to his activities. At one time, I was confronted by a heroin addict who accused me of not being able to understand heroin addiction because I had never "shot" heroin. At the time I was unable to make a rejoinder to the man, but later I was comforted with the thought that a toxicologist does not have to sample poisons to understand their pharmacology. There surely are drug researchers who have sampled opiates, but it is probably more for personal rather than professional reasons.

If this discussion leaves the impression that there are no clear-cut answers to the handling of risks involved in street ethnography, then we were in no better a position than Carey when he reported (1972:78):

> The fact that there are few convictions of researchers and no arrests at all in this kind of research situation was something we took into account. We still felt it necessary to allocate a certain amount of money for bail on the chance that we might be arrested. We also noted that in only a few states is it required that felonies be reported, so that we were unlikely to be

accused of having guilty knowledge. Although we came to no clear decision on what we would do if we were subpoenaed to testify, we probably would have tried to invoke the Fifth Amendment if such a situation had developed.

Let us turn to Polsky again for some words of advice about where the real risk may lie. They are perhaps somewhat disquieting, but they may approach the truth very closely:

> But if one refuses to be a sociologist of the jailhouse or court system, takes Malinowski to heart, and goes out into the field, there is risk involved. At least I have found this so in my experience. It is the sort of risk that writers of criminology texts, for all their eagerness to put down field work, surprisingly don't mention: most of the danger for the field worker comes not from the cannibals and headhunters but from the colonial officials. [Polsky, 1969:141]

Much of this kind of problem can be avoided in advance by approaching the proper local officials and stating the purpose of one's work. If the local criminal justice system objects, then it is not worth the bother. But local law enforcement systems are surprisingly open to research, even of themselves. Banton (1964) and Rubenstein (1973) have studied police forces; Klockars is presently doing so in Delaware; and Wesley Pomeroy, Chief of Police in Berkeley, California, stated in the workshop that he would welcome ethnographic research (with some qualification):

> First, it should be recognized that researchers and police chiefs have almost nothing in common—ideologically, functionally, or philosophically. They almost never perceive themselves as peers and have enormous difficulty in understanding anything the other says or intends.
>
> . . . It is essential that mutual trust be developed between the police chiefs and the researchers. This cannot be achieved unless there is honest discussion about what each other's agenda really is. The police chief must understand that the researcher needs to publish and make his work generally known. At the same time, there has to be a realization by the researcher that his need to publish may cut across the police chief's need to survive and thrive politically. They both need openly to acknowledge and discuss the risks and gains implicit in the relationship.

. . . I would also like for our relationship to include your sticking around after you make your study, for the implementation phase. I would like you not just to write a report and skip town, leaving it to me and my people to pick up the pieces or live with whatever consequences may come of your recommendations.[6]

In conclusion, Polsky may offer some help in the methodological and ethical problems connected with street ethnography. He listed some points which might make the potential street ethnographer less intrusive and threatening to a potential deviant informant, and the points are worth noting. They are paraphrased and summarized here (1969:120-129):

(1) Don't contaminate the criminal's environment with gadgets (tape recorder, questionnaire form).

(2) The absolute "first rule": initially keep your eyes and ears open *but keep your mouth shut.*

(3) Once you learn the group's special language (the argot), do not try to use it.

(4) Build a sample by "snowballing"; that is, get one criminal who will vouch for you.

(5) Once you establish a relationship with an informant, "let him know what you do for a living and let him know why."

(6) In studying a criminal, you must "realize that he will be studying you," and you must "let him study you. Don't evade . . . questions . . . about your personal life."

(7) "You must draw the line, to yourself and to the criminal." To the extent that you are unwilling to witness criminal acts your "personal moral code of course compromises" your "scientific role—but not, I think, irreparably."

(8) Keep faith. In reporting your research, you must "sometimes write of certain things more vaguely and skimpily" than you might prefer.

(9) "Letting criminals know where you draw the line of course depends on knowing this yourself. If you aren't sure, the criminal may . . . maneuver you into an accomplice role."

(10) Although you "mustn't pretend to be 'one of them,' it is equally important that you don't stick out like a sore thumb in the criminal's natural environment."

(11) "A final rule is to have a few unbreakable rules."

In reading the articles in the present volume, one can see that most if not all of the street ethnographers have followed Polsky's dicta.

OTHER IMPORTANT ETHICAL ISSUES

Just as the proceeding section considered, among other things, how a street ethnographer working with deviant groups can protect himself against risks involved in street research, we must also consider the questions of how informants are to be protected.

Reciprocity—or research bargains and payments between the researcher and his informants—takes on new dimensions in today's increased ethical scrutiny, both by peer review groups (university ethics committees) and by such federal organizations as the Department of Health, Education, and Welfare and the National Commission for the Protection of Human Subjects of Biomedical and Behavioral Research. As any peer review committee knows, no one can be paid to waive one's civil rights—an important one being the right to privacy.

One of the rules promulgated by federal agencies for sponsored research is that the potential research subject understand the intention of the research and sign an "informed consent" form, which incidentally must specify that the subject may withdraw from the research project at any time. These federal requirements present two problems in street research. One is, how does a researcher obtain the signature of an informant who may be engaged in activities which are not socially sanctioned and may wish to remain anonymous? And, second, how does a researcher in natural surroundings obtain informed consent from other individuals whose activities he might observe but who are unaware of his presence? A very strict interpretation of the Health, Education, and Welfare guidelines could make street research impossible. By the same token, the ability of informants to withdraw at any time could seriously affect the work of those scientists for whom random sampling is essential.

These federal rules have ostensibly been formulated to prevent further scandals emerging such as the Tuskeegee syphilis or the Willowbrook hepatitis experiments (Barber, 1976) and to actually protect human subjects from physical or psychological damages. But an underlying purpose that has emerged is also to protect the individual researchers or their institutions from legal suits. If the street ethnographer inadvertently or purposefully identifies an informant in any way, that informant may have a legal cause of action, regardless if he or she were paid in advance.

Unfortunately, the participants at the workshop, like those at the 1976 American Sociological Association meetings in New York, were more successful in bringing up issues than in resolving them. One issue was raised that the street ethnographer is both citizen and scientist. If this is the case, then he or she may be placed in a moral dilemma when the public good outweighs the private good of the cherished informant.

If the ethnographer spends so much time gaining entrée and rapport, can he stand by when he knows a crime is to be committed? The answer is, obviously not. But in less clear-cut situations, even Max Weber's value-free social science may fall flat. Trying to strike a bargain with the informant in the first place so that the researcher will not be placed in such a dilemma is part of the answer, but not all.

The Effect of Federal Sponsorship on Research

Some social scientists may view funding from agencies whose primary mission is to eradicate drug use, eliminate crime, and/or cope with overwhelming social problems as having ominous implications. Their reaction stems from a fear that they will be required to "expose" their informants or otherwise compromise their life-styles by making them more vulnerable. Here again, are we going to be forced to compartmentalize our scientific objectivity from our personal obligations to our subjects? When the participants in the workshop were told that the Drug Enforcement Agency might fund ethnographer field stations if such stations supplied periodic reports on the types of drugs being used on the street and delivered other unspecified data, the initial reactions of the panelists ran from uneasiness to horror. Operating from hypothetical standpoints, the participants took three positions: some argued that such research was unethical; some felt that the ethics were situationally specific to the situation; and some felt that it was nobody's business but the investigator's as to what is ethical. There was agreement that no funding agency should ever contract for the ethnographer's raw data and that information-gathering requirements must be reviewed in detail by the potential field station operators. In short, the participants did not reject the idea, but they were terrifically sensitized to falling into research comparable to that of the Camelot affair.

On the other hand, Alvin Gouldner (1968), in his rejoinder to Howard Becker's rather benign article (1967), raised some serious questions about the relationship of the researcher to his funding agencies and the resultant effect upon the individuals being studied:

> The funding agencies of social science today, whether government agencies or massive private foundations, are essentially the welfare state's purchasing agents for market research; they are the instrumentalities of this new reform movement. The new underdog sociology propounded by Becker is, then, a standpoint that possesses a remarkably convenient combination of properties: it enables the sociologist to befriend the very small underdogs in local settings, to reject the standpoint of the "middle dog" respectables and notables who manage local caretaking establishments, while, at the same time, to make and remain friends with the really top dogs in Washington agencies of New York foundations. [p. 110]

Gouldner was attempting to answer Becker's question as to whose side social scientists are on, as we will see below.

Advocacy

The well-known exchange between Becker and Gouldner as to whether sociologists (and it is applicable to anthropologists as well) should take sides remains unresolved. Gouldner criticized Becker for having almost maudlin sympathy toward the underdog, whom he said Becker characterized as more "sinned against, than sinning," and Gouldner elsewhere stated (1968:103):

I fear that the myth of a value-free social science is about to be supplanted by still another myth, and that the once glib acceptance of the value-free doctrine is about to be superseded by a new but no less glib rejection of it.

In answering Becker, he stated that we are on "our own side" and further stated that these social scientists identify more with deviant than respectable society. In summarizing what he called a bleak hypothesis, he further stated (Gouldner, 1968:108):

Sociologists with liberal ideologies will more likely adopt underdog perspectives when they experience these as compatible with the pursuit of their own career interests.

Perhaps some of this is true, but as Klockars and James argue forcefully in the present volume, the street ethnographer is committed to his subjects in more ways than he might be if he were to do research with an exotic foreign culture. In the latter case, it is all too easy to pack up the field station and leave forever. James feels that "anthropologists have rarely been around to witness the social consequences of their research." But as ethnographers start to work within their own cultural settings, as sociologists have been doing, they must take responsibility for their research and their writings and for their effect upon the study groups. Preble and Casey (1969) started ethnographic research among narcotic addicts which presented an entirely different social scientific view of what it is to be an addict. Their research pointed out the need for understanding this group if any effective treatment is to come about. In the same way, James's research with prostitutes indicates the need for reform of prostitution laws.

In a certain regard, advocacy is necessary because, if ethnographers such as those included herein do produce some social change, in a very literal sense they cannot leave the country and leave the uprising to the officials. Perhaps they work with their groups out of self-interest, as Gouldner suggests, but a certain measure of advocacy must occur or the ethnographer may soon become "burned out" by the sometimes intense nature of street ethnography.

CONCLUSION

The papers presented in this volume present the experiences of sociologists and anthropologists who have engaged in a similar kind of research activity, that of street ethnography. Most of the social scientists have worked with deviant groups in the United States, and they have recorded their experiences in as objective a manner as possible. Not all of their work is value-free, but that may be an illusory goal anyway, especially when the ethnographer is working with culture bearers who have much in common with him or her but have different orientations and adaptations to a very complex pluralistic society.

The issues raised by their papers may provide some insights for other ethnographers who are presently engaged in such research or for those who may be so inclined. The issues are not exhaustive, and many have not been discussed in this introduction. It is left to the reader to find out how one gains rapport with and entrée into a street culture; and Inciardi, Walker and Lidz, and Klockars describe the process, one that may often be quite fortuitous. For example, Inciardi was a parole officer and became acquainted with his pickpocket contact in that way. He "snowballed" this contact into a larger sample. It is also left to the reader to weigh the issues of how does the street ethnographer define his group. Such issues are presented by Siegal, who approaches an almost theoretical level.

On the whole, the issues here have been methodological and ethical, and many have not been clear-cut. Questions have arisen and gone unanswered as to ethical issues in this kind of street research. Certainly street ethnography could become more difficult as more restrictions are placed upon it, but, until now, no protection for informants has been established. At the present time, the guidelines of the U.S. Department of Health, Education, and Welfare are oriented more along biomedical lines than along behavioral or social scientific lines. They are still unevenly applied from region to region and from peer review committee to peer review committee. No precedents set down by various committees seem to be followed in a consistent manner. Until we see a broadening of the conceptual bases underpinning the guidelines and see them made as flexible as possible while still providing protection for informants, street ethnography may be difficult to perform. At the present time, the National Committee for Protection of Subjects in Biomedical and Behavioral Research is attempting to arrive at guidelines which will accommodate the interests of both the researched and the researcher.

All the participants in the workshop reported herein agreed that the risks to the street ethnographer from his informants or others on the street had been minimal. There was a consensus that more of a threat existed from official and governmental agencies, but this threat was more hypothetical than not. As one of the participants who was also a police chief noted, there are ways of working within the system and still performing the type of research that one wishes. What it amounts to is the establishment of rapport and trust with the "colonial officials" just as one would do with the "natives." Granted, anthropologists who work with underclass groups are often characterized as alienated from middle-class society, and sociologists who do the same thing are often characterized as deviant, altruistic, or just romantic; but the truth is that street ethnographers do face challenges that are not often faced by behavioral researchers further removed from their subjects.

Ethnographic research requires stamina and the ability to sell oneself and one's ideas to two groups that are much more wary of outsiders than many. The political ramifications for the official agencies and the personal and/or legal consequences for the informant group are large but not insuperable obstacles. It is hoped that the experiences set forth in the present volume may provide a guide for more street ethnography. For the ethnographer, it would do well to remember that some of the best cross-cultural comparisons for understanding behavior may exist at his own doorstep.

NOTES

1. The workshop was held at Key Biscayne, Florida, on May 6-7, 1976, under the auspices of the University of Miami's Division of Addiction Sciences and the Research Triangle Institute of North Carolina, with the support of the National Institute on Drug Abuse. Overall, the participants and observers came from divergent backgrounds. Over half were anthropologists (13), and the others consisted of six sociologists, two psychologists, one economist, and one law enforcement official. (The law enforcement official—a chief of

police—and one of the psychologists are attorneys.) Two of the participants had also been Drug Abuse Council Fellows in Washington, D.C. (Harvey Feldman and Wesley Pomeroy). The participants and observers are listed below:

Anthropologists

MICHAEL H. AGAR, Ph.D., University of Houston
ELEANOR CARROLL, M.A., National Institute on Drug Abuse
PATRICIA J. CLECKNER, Ph.D., Miami, Florida
FRANCIS A.J. IANNI, Ph.D., Columbia University
JENNIFER JAMES, Ph.D., University of Washington
ELLIOT LIEBOW, Ph.D., National Institute of Mental Health
BELA MADAY, Ph.D., National Institute of Mental Health
EDWARD PREBLE, M.A., New York School of Psychiatry
IRVING SOLOWAY, Ph.D., Medical College of Pennsylvania
JAMES P. SPRADLEY, Ph.D., Macalester College
WILLIAM R. TRUE, Ph.D., University of Miami
JAMES WALTERS, Graduate Student, Medical College of Pennsylvania
ROBERT S. WEPPNER, Ph.D., University of Miami *(Moderator)*

Sociologists

HARVEY W. FELDMAN, Ph.D., St. Louis University
JAMES A. INCIARDI, Ph.D., University of Delaware
CARL B. KLOCKARS, Ph.D., Beaver College, Pennsylvania
ROBERT SHELLOW, Ph.D., Visiting Fellow, National Institute on Drug Abuse
  (Co-moderator)
HARVEY A. SIEGAL, Ph.D., Wright State University
ANDREW L. WALKER, Ph.D., Stephens College

Psychologists

MARTIN KURKE, Ph.D., J.D., Drug Enforcement Administration
DEREK V. ROEMER, Ph.D., Baltimore Community Mental Health Center

Economist

FRED GOLDMAN, Ph.D., Columbia University

Law Enforcement Official

WESLEY POMEROY, J.D., Chief of Police, Berkeley, California

Other Observers

WILLIAM C. ECKERMAN, Ph.D., Research Triangle Institute
ROBERT HUBBARD, Ph.D., Research Triangle Institute
THOMAS MILLER, New York State Office of Drug Abuse Services
VALLEY RACHEL, Research Triangle Institute
JOAN TRUE, Ph.D.

2. Others have studied non-Western crime and jurisprudence to provide a cross-cultural comparison. Some examples are Bohannon (1957), Gluckman (1965), Hoebel (1954), and Nader (1969).

3. Cesare Lombroso may be considered an early physical anthropologist who tried to apply "constitutional" theories to criminal behavior. Although his theories were discredited, he conducted several symposia in "criminal anthropology," and his method of scientific enquiry led to the modern school of criminology. Inciardi and Siegal (1976) refer to him as the "father of criminology." For additional information, see Wolfgang's (1961) historical footnote on Lombroso.

4. One of the first things I learned was not to refer to my addict subjects as my "informants." The first time I did so, after a shocked reaction, my "main back man" told me, "Hey, dig this man, don't go calling me no *informer!*"

5. Many of these uncited quotes or reactions were taken from my edited version of the transcripts of the two-day workshop. In the first session, Feldman made the comment, "I didn't know I was a street ethnographer until somebody told me I was." One finds little consensus wherever one turns in any type of research.

6. These quotes are taken from the unpublished workshop proceedings.

REFERENCES

ADAMS, R.N., and PREISS, J.J. (eds., 1960). Human organization research. Homewood, Ill.: Dorsey.

AGAR, M.H. (1973). Ripping and running: A formal ethnography of urban heroin addicts. New York: Seminar.

ARGYRIS, C. (1957). Personality and organization. New York: Harper and Row.

BANTON, M. (1964). The policeman in the community. London: Tavistock.

BARBER, B. (1976). "The ethics of experimentation with human subjects." Scientific American, 234(2):25-31.

BECKER, H.S. (1963). Outsiders: Studies in the sociology of deviance. New York: Free Press.

——— (1964). The other side: Perspectives on deviance. New York: Free Press.

——— (1967). "Whose side are we on?" Social Problems, 14(winter):239-247.

BOHANNON, P. (1957). Justice and judgment among the Tiv. London: Oxford University Press.

CAREY, J.T. (1972). "Problems of access and risk in observing drug scenes." In J.D. Douglas (ed.), Research on deviance. New York: Random House.

CAUDILL, W. (1958). The psychiatric hospital as a small society. Cambridge: Harvard University Press.

CLECKNER, P.J. (1975). "Intracultural variation as a key to drug use in the United States." Paper presented at the meeting of the American Anthropological Association, San Francisco.

DOUGLAS, J. (ed., 1972). Research on deviance. New York: Random House.

EDDY, E.M. (ed., 1968). Urban anthropology: Research perspectives and strategies. Athens: University of Georgia Press.

FELDMAN, H.W. (1968). "Ideological supports to becoming a heroin addict." Journal of Health and Social Behavior, 9:131-139.

——— (1974). Street status and the drug researcher: Issues in participant observation. Washington, D.C.: Drug Abuse Council.

FISCHER, C.S. (1975). "The study of urban community and personality." In A. Inkeles, J. Coleman, and N. Smelser (eds.), Annual reviews of sociology. Palo Alto, Calif.: Annual Reviews.

FREILICH, M.L. (ed., 1970). Marginal natives: Anthropologists at work. New York: Harper and Row.

GLUCKMAN, M. (1965). The ideas of Barotse jurisprudence. New Haven: Yale University Press.

GOFFMAN, E. (1961). Asylums. New York: Basic Books.

GOULD, L., WALKER, A., CRANE, L., and LIDZ, C. (1974). Connections: Notes from the heroin world. New Haven: Yale University Press.

GOULDNER, A.W. (1968). "The sociologist as partisan: Sociology and the welfare state." American Sociologist, 3(May):103-116.

GREENBERG, S.W., and ADLER, F. (1974). "Crime and addiction: An empirical analysis of the literature, 1920-1973." Contemporary Drug Problems, (summer):221-270.

GULICK, J. (1973). "Urban anthropology." In J.J. Honigman (ed.), Handbook of social and cultural anthropology. Chicago: Rand McNally.

HANNERZ, U. (1969). Soulside: Inquiries into ghetto culture and community. New York: Columbia University Press.

HENSLIN, J.M. (1972). "Studying deviance in four settings: Research experiences with cabbies, suicides, drug users, and abortionees." In J.D. Douglas (ed.), Research on deviance. New York: Random House.

HOEBEL, E.A. (1954). The law of primitive man: A study in comparative legal dynamics. Cambridge, Mass.: Harvard University Press.

HOOTON, E.A. (1939a). Crime and the man. Cambridge, Mass.: Harvard University Press.

——— (1939b). The American criminal: An anthropological study. Cambridge, Mass.: Harvard University Press.

HUGHES, P.H., and JAFFE, J.H. (1971). "The heroin copping area: A location for epidemiologic study and intervention activity." Archives of General Psychiatry, 24:394-401.

HUGHES, P.H., et al. (1971). "The social structure of a heroin copping community." American Journal of Psychiatry, 128(5):551-558.

IANNI, F.A.J. (1972). A family business: Kinship and social control in organized crime. New York: Russell Sage-Basic Books.

INCIARDI, J.A., and CHAMBERS, C.D. (1972). "Unreported criminal involvement of narcotics addicts." Journal of Drug Issues, (spring):57-64.

INCIARDI, J.A., and SIEGAL, H. (1976). Crime: Emerging issues. New York: Praeger.

IRWIN, J. (1972). "Participant observation of criminals." In J.D. Douglas (ed.), Research on deviance. New York: Random House.

JAMES, J. (1972). "On the block: Urban perspectives." Urban Anthropology, 1:125-140.

——— (1976). "Prostitution." In E. Sagarin (ed.), Society and deviance. Morristown, N.J.: General Learning Press.

KEISER, R.L. (1969). The vice lords: Warriors of the streets. New York: Holt, Rinehart and Winston.

KLOCKARS, C. (1974). The professional fence. New York: Free Press.

KUSHNER, G. (1970). "The anthropology of complex societies." In B.J. Siegel (ed.), Biennial review of anthropology: 1969. Stanford, Calif.: Stanford University Press.

LIEBOW, E. (1967). Tally's corner: A study of Negro street-corner men. Boston: Little, Brown.

LYND, R.S., and LYND, H.M. (1929). Middletown. New York: Harcourt, Brace.
MADDUX, J.F., and BOWEN, C. (1972). "Critique of success with Methadone mainte-nance." American Journal of Psychiatry, 129(4):440-446.
McBRIDE, D.C. (1975). "Research objectives and progress of the center for theoretical and empirical research on drug abuse." Paper presented at the meeting of the American Sociological Association, San Francisco.
McCALL, G.J., and SIMMONS, J.L. (1969). Issues in participant observation. Reading, Mass.: Addison-Wesley.
MERTON, R.K., and MONTAGU, A.M.F. (1940). "Crime and the anthropologist." American Anthropologist, 42:384-408.
NADER, L. (1969). Law in culture and society. Chicago: Aldine.
––– (1972). "Up the anthropologist–Perspectives gained from studying up." In D. Hymes (ed.), Reinventing anthropology. New York: Pantheon.
NEWMEYER, J.A., and JOHNSON, G.R. (1976). "The heroin epidemic in San Francisco: Estimates of incidence and prevalence." International Journal of the Addictions, 11(3):417-438.
PELTO, P. (1970). Anthropological research: The structure of inquiry. New York: Harper and Row.
POLSKY, N. (1969). Hustlers, beats, and others. Garden City, N.Y.: Anchor Books.
POMEROY, W. (1974). Police chiefs discuss drug abuse. Washington, D.C.: Drug Abuse Council.
PREBLE, E., and CASEY, J.J., Jr. (1969). "Taking care of business: The heroin user's life on the street." International Journal of the Addictions, 4:1-24.
QUINNEY, R. (1970). The social reality of crime. Boston: Little, Brown.
ROETHLISBERGER, F.J., and DICKSON, W.J. (1939). Management and the worker. Cambridge, Mass.: Harvard University Press.
RUBENSTEIN, J. (1973). City police. New York: Farrar, Straus and Giroux.
RUBIN, V., and COMITAS, L. (1975). Ganja in Jamaica. The Hague: Mouton.
SCHUR, E. (1965). Crimes without victims. Englewood Cliffs, N.J.: Prentice-Hall.
SOLOWAY, I. (n.d.). "Ethnographic component in a Philadelphia treatment program" (personal communication).
SPRADLEY, J.P. (1970). You owe yourself a drunk: An ethnography of urban nomads. Boston: Little, Brown.
––– (1973). "The ethnography of crime in American society." In L. Nader and T.W. Maretzki (eds.), Cultural illness and health: Essays in human adaptation (Anthropo-logical studies no. 9). Washington, D.C.: American Anthropological Association.
SUTHERLAND, E.H. (1949). White collar crime. New York: Holt, Rinehart and Winston.
SUTHERLAND, E.H., and CRESSEY, D. (1974). Criminology. Philadelphia: Lippincott.
SUTTER, A.G. (1966). "The world of the righteous dope fiend." Issues in Criminology, 2(2):177-222.
WARNER, W.L. (ed., 1941). Yankee city. New Haven, Conn.: Yale University Press.
WAX, R.H. (1960). "Reciprocity in field work." In R.N. Adams and J.S. Preiss (eds.), Human organization research: Field relations and techniques. Homewood, Ill.: Dorsey.
WEAVER, T., and WHITE, D. (1972). "Anthropological approaches to urban and complex society." In T. Weaver and D. White (eds.), The anthropology of urban environments (Society for Applied Anthropology monograph no. 11). Washington, D.C.: Society for Applied Anthropology.

WEPPNER, R.S. (1973). "An anthropological view of the street addict's world." Human Organization, 32(2):111-121.

––– (1976). "The use of street ethnographies: The experiences of the Miami Center Grant for Social Studies in Drug Abuse." Paper presented at the meeting of the Society for Applied Anthropology, St. Louis.

WEPPNER, R.S., and STEPHENS, R. (1973). "The illicit use and diversion of Methadone as related by hospitalized addicts." Journal of Drug Issues, 3(1):42-47.

WEPPNER, R.S., STEPHENS, R., and CONRAD, H.T. (1972). "Methadone: Some aspects of its legal and illegal use." American Journal of Psychiatry, 129(4):451-455.

WHITE, D., and WEAVER, T. (1972). "Sociological contributions to an urban anthropology." In T. Weaver and D. White (eds.), The anthropology of urban environments (Society for Applied Anthropology monograph no. 11). Washington, D.C.: Society for Applied Anthropology.

WHYTE, W.F. (1943). Street corner society. Chicago: University of Chicago Press.

WILLIAMSON, H. (1966). Hustler! The autobiography of a thief (R.L. Keiser, ed.). New York: Doubleday.

WOLFGANG, M.E. (1961). "Pioneers in criminology: Cesare Lombroso, 1835-1909." Criminal Law, Criminology, and Police Science, 52:361-391.

–

PART I

METHODOLOGY AND THEORY

2

IN SEARCH OF THE CLASS CANNON
A Field Study of Professional Pickpockets

JAMES A. INCIARDI

When Thomas Bartholomew Moran died in 1971 at the Miami Rescue Mission, he was a vagrant, and his pockets were empty—an ironic ending to a life spent emptying the pockets of others. Yet, in spite of this dismal ceremony of his death, he had been considered by some as the dean of American pickpockets. Moran's career in crime began in 1906 in Kansas City when, at age 14, he would walk through crowded stores opening ladies' purses and removing small change. Known as "moll-buzzing," this practice was looked down upon by the professionals in his field, but, by 1912, Moran had graduated to the more complex problems of stealing from male victims. Ultimately, he polished his approaches to picking pockets to the point where he could remove a diamond pin from a garment, a watch from a wrist, and a wallet from a suit coat or pants pocket, all without his victim knowing that a theft was taking place.[1]

Thomas Bartholomew Moran was a "cannon," or pickpocket, and a "class cannon" as well—a designation which typified him as an old-line professional with the skill and daring to devote a lifetime to stealing from the pockets of live victims. The term "cannon" is said to be a corruption of the Jewish *gonnif,* meaning thief. "Cannon" was allegedly abbreviated to "gun," followed by "cannon" as the designation for a "big gun" or experienced thief or pickpocket. The term seems to have first appeared in criminal slang shortly after the turn of the 20th century and endured through the 1950s (see Partridge, 1961:103; Sutherland, 1937:44; Wentworth and Flexner, 1960:87).

While "cannon" is rarely used within the underworld today, "class cannon" still has some currency within the old-line pickpocketing fraternity. It is a term which reflects the expert pickpocket's conception of his occupation. He works at picking pockets as a business; it is his living; and he is recognized and accepted by other pickpockets as having "class"—the expertise of a professional. Class cannon implies achievement in the art of picking pockets and a total commitment to a way of life. The class cannon sees himself as separate and apart from the amateur pickpocket, and he looks down upon nonmembers of his fraternity, as one informant told me:

> Class cannon means experience, skill, connections, and a sense for knowing when to steal and when not to steal. . . . It means that the cannon is part of your life. . . . It means that you're not one of those amateurs who spend their time *grinding up nickels and dimes* [ineptly stealing for low stakes] .

The class cannon has endured for many centuries, yet, as a criminological phenomenon, he is beginning to pass from the American crime scene. In this behalf, the following commentary offers some observations of the class cannon through history, with a search for the remnants of his criminal culture in the contemporary urban world. Specifically, the cannon is first viewed within the wider spectrum of professional theft, followed by notes on the persistence and decline of his social organization and occupational structure during the last hundred years. Finally, in an effort to examine a portion of the "hangers-on" in his dying profession, 20 active class cannons were located and interviewed. A description of these individuals is offered, with a discussion of the problems associated with locating, observing, and communicating with them within a field setting.[2]

THE PROFESSIONAL THIEF AND THE CLASS CANNON

The professional thief has been described as a highly specialized, nonviolent criminal who makes a regular business of stealing (Sutherland, 1937). Crime is his occupation and means of livelihood, and, as such, he devotes his entire working time and energy to stealing. He operates with proficiency and has a body of skills and knowledge that is utilized in the planning and execution of his work. The professional thief is a graduate of a developmental process that includes the acquisition of specialized attitudes, knowledge, skills, and experience. He makes crime his way of life, organizing his life around criminal pursuit and developing a philosophy regarding his activities and profession. He identifies himself with the world of crime, and there he is a member of an exclusive fraternity that extends friendship, understanding, sympathy, congeniality, security, recognition, and respect. Finally, the professional thief is able to steal for long periods of time without extended terms of incarceration. He commits crimes in a manner that reduces the risks of apprehension, and he is able to effectively deal with agents of various forces of social control. The more typical forms of professional theft include shoplifting, safe and house burglary, forgery and counterfeiting, extortion, sneak theft, confidence swindling, and, importantly, *pickpocketing.*

Professional theft emerged as an outgrowth of the disintegration of the feudal order in Europe during 1350-1550, and its evolution was hastened by the mobility and economic changes resulting from that disintegration. It appeared among English-speaking peoples during the Elizabethan period and later in the United States during the early 19th century. Historical documentation verifies that professional theft has remained relatively unchanged for centuries and that the types of crime, techniques, skills, attitudes and philosophies, interactional setting, patterns of recruitment and training, exit paths, style of life, and to some extent the argot of 20th century professional thieves are characteristically like those of professionals of previous epochs.[3]

Among the rogues and vagabonds, thieves and sharpers who swelled the criminal classes of London, Exeter, Norwich, and Bristol during the early years of Shakespeare's youth, the pickpocket was conspicuously evident. As early as 1591, the art of picking pockets was described to reflect a refined pattern of criminal expertise:

> The nip and the foist, although their subject is one which they work on, that is, a well-lined purse, yet their manner is different, for the nip useth his knife, and the foist his hand; the one cutting the purse, the other drawing the pocket. . . . Their chief walks is St. Paul's, Westminster, the Exchange, plays, bear-garden, running at tilt, the Lord Mayor's day, any festival meetings, frays, shootings, or great fairs. To be short, wheresoever is any extraordinary resort of people, there the nip and the foist have fittest opportunity to show their juggling agility.

> Commonly, where they spy a farmer or merchant whom they suspect to be well moneyed, they follow him hard until they see him draw his purse, then spying in what place he puts it up, the stall, or shadow, being with the foist or nip, meets the man at some strait turn, and jostles him so hard that the man, marvelling, and perhaps quarrelling with him, the whilst the foist hath his purse, and bids him farewell. . . . But suppose that the foist is smoked, and the man misseth his purse, and apprehendeth him for it, then straight, he either conveyeth it to his stall, or else droppeth the bung, and with a great brave he defyeth his accuser; and though the purse be found at his feet, yet because he hath it not about him, he comes not within compass of life. [Greene, 1591] [4]

Elizabethan literature highlighted the way of life of the pickpocket and closely observed the nature of his trade, and, although there have since been minor modifications in technique made necessary by changing clothing fashions, the pickpocket of centuries ago differs little from his contemporary counterpart.[5]

The process of pickpocketing typically includes (1) the selection of a victim, (2) the locating of the money or valuables on the victim's person, (3) the maneuvering of the victim into the proper position, (4) the act of theft, and (5) the passing of the stolen property.

Professional pickpockets generally work in "mobs" of two, three, or four, with each member playing a specific role in the total operation, and they seek only those victims who appear to have enough money to make the theft worthwhile. This ability to select the proper victim ("mark") is in many ways an occupational intuition and is based on many years of experience.[6] This adroitness is not infallible, however, as one pickpocket operating outside of Miami's jai alai fronton recently indicated:

> First there's the theory and then comes the real world. The theory is the intuition and the sense that tells you who to stroke. The guy with the cash has a certain look about him . . . an expression, the way he walks, how he wears his clothes, and carries himself. The real world is that 75% of the time you're wrong. . . . You get more of the $5 ones than the fifties.

When a victim has been selected, the money is then located on his person by feeling his pockets ("fanning"). With mobs of two or more members, the operation is done by one called the "tool" or "dip," while another (the "stall") closely watches the victim's movements. (The operation is not necessary if the location of the wallet or other valuables—the "loot"—is known.) The stall then maneuvers the victim into the proper position, and the tool removes the wallet, and the success of the operation rests on the stall's distractions, the tool's dexterity, and their combined teamwork. Finally, the loot may be passed to a third or fourth mob member (or the wallet or pocketbook may be passed for emptying—"cleaning"—and dis-carding—"dropping"—so that the tool will be free of the stolen property in the event that he is suspected by the victim or the police).

Although most class cannons generally work within the security and efficient structure of a mob, some do prefer to operate on their own. A pickpocket encountered at the Miami Beach Convention Hall during a 1976 performance of the Ringling Brothers and Barnum and Bailey circus commented:

> I've always worked alone . . . at least for the last 20-odd years anyway. I'm a whole mob in one. . . . The risks are greater, but then so are the rewards.

Pickpockets thrive in crowds, a situation similar to that of the Elizabethan "foists" who operated on the streets and in the ale houses of 16th century London. The modern class cannon generally focuses on the crowded areas which would specifically draw victims with money in their possession—amusement centers, public gambling attractions, shopping areas, and transportation depots.

Finally, like other professional thieves, class pickpockets maintain a unique style of life quite unlike that of members of the wider society and other criminal cultures as well. Briefly, their habitat is within the regions of vice and crime, the amusement centers, and the rooming-house and skid-row districts. Central to their habitat is a system of hangouts where interaction with other thieves is extensive. Yet they have no fixed abode, living only in transient settings in the vicinity of their hangouts. Their communication is usually verbal, characterized by a complex system of argot transmitted through face-to-face interaction and an underworld grapevine. Class cannons are members of a fraternity—a tightly interlocked group of criminal specialists who share common territories, ideologies, and knowledge. Recruitment into the ranks of this fraternity is generally controlled by its membership, and the training lasts many years during which the pickpocket acquires knowledge and skills and a consciousness of the dangers of stealing. Pickpockets, as part of their tutelage, develop the ability to remain immune from incarceration by learning the techniques and sources for "fixing" arrests and pending court appearances. Within the world of the old-line professionals, there is a status hierarchy, a complex set of business maxims and rules, and a code of ethics. And, finally, class cannons maintain an elaborate system of rationalizations employed to justify their antisocial behavior; that is, they redefine their actions as parallel to the dishonest practices of businessmen and law enforcement agents, and they devalue their victims by suggesting that the latter could easily absorb their losses. In sum, the fraternity of pickpockets (and other professional thieves as well) reflects a highly complex subculture. It is one characterized by shared attitudes, values, rules, codes, interactional settings, and criminal action patterns, all affected by the nature of the relationship between the underworld and the norms and behavior systems of the upper world.[7]

THE PASSING OF THE CLASS CANNON

The profession of picking pockets has seemingly been unmolested by changes in technology, fashion, and systems of money distribution. Despite the widespread use of checks, credit cards, and charge accounts, many victims with money in their pockets continue to be available, and the pickpocket's techniques of theft have consequently survived for generations and centuries. Yet evidence suggests that the profession has experienced severe declines during recent decades. Maurer (1964:171) estimated that in 1945 there were some five to six thousand class cannons operating in the United States, with a reduction to about one thousand by 1955. By 1965, according to one expert pickpocket from New York City's Times Square, the total number suffered even further reduction:

> Most of the ones left are old timers, and I say that there are probably no more than six or seven hundred in the whole country—if that much. There are plenty of amateurs, young ones, old ones, prostitutes, addicts, but they were never associated with the old time mobs. [Inciardi, 1975:21]

Similarly, a member of the Pickpocket and Confidence Squad of the New York City Police Department indicated during the following year:

> You see very few of the real experts these days. They have either quit, died, or are in jail, and they are rarely replaced. Most of the newer boys are from Harlem, and you can spot them a block away. [Inciardi, 1975:21]

In January 1974, a 72-year-old retired pickpocket working as a part-time clerk at a Miami Beach retirement hotel told me:

> Gone forever are the times of the pants pocket *gonnif.* I've seen less and less of them since the start of the 1950s. . . . An estimate? Who knows. . . . When I packed it in four years ago we had maybe six hundred. Now . . . probably less, I'm sure.

And in 1976, a 62-year-old cannon operating in downtown Miami stated:

> Each year you'll see about 50 of us pass through Miami; . . . it's been a tradition. You go up to New York and Philly in the summer, and to

Chicago in the fall, and you see the same guys most of the time. . . . I'd say if you put all of us together you couldn't fill an old-time mickelodeon[8] . . . maybe three hundred, maybe four.

The decline of the class cannon has seemingly been the result of a process which began as far distant as the turn of the 20th century. The pickpocket, as part of the professional underworld, had enjoyed the security of a criminal life style that was for the most part immune from the forces of social control. This immunity perpetuated contact among members of the profession, permitting the development of a subculture aimed at maintaining a low level of social visibility. An intricate network of relationships and linguistic constructions developed for the purpose of keeping out "outsiders" —amateur criminals—and a code of ethics was constructed for internal social control. A dissemination of information regarding case fixing and untrustworthy members of the profession developed to maintain a defense system against the infiltration of any representative of the wider social world. As such, this specialized segment of the underworld operated within a "functional superstructure" of isolation, protection, and group support (see Inciardi, 1975:75-82).

The process which caused the decline of professional pickpockets was one that served to erode the foundation of this superstructure. Since the turn of the century, the increased cooperative relationships between local, state, and federal law enforcement groups, as well as growths in the technology of communication systems, combined to impinge upon the almost unlimited security that had been enjoyed by interstate fugitives. Fingerprinting, begun in this country in 1903, rapidly emerged as a totally infallible means of personal identification. Federal legislation relative to interstate flight and the habitual offender laws served to create preliminary obstacles to case fixing, and the bureaucratization of many police and court systems made the fixing of cases even more difficult.

The convergence of these and other factors not only reduced the number of active professional pickpockets but, in doing so, also weakened the stability of the profession as a long-term economic pursuit, thus creating significant shortages in the number of potential recruits. With only a few new recruits to a career that was rapidly becoming more visible, the subculture began to atrophy, leaving behind only the seasoned old-timers who had no other profession to turn to, yet had enough accumulated expertise to survive. In this behalf, one hanger-on to the profession stated in 1972:

> Tougher and tougher things have been getting lately. It's still easy to steal, but it's the *fixing* that's tougher. You can't do it as often as before, and if you can, it costs a fortune. . . . Things just aren't that profitable no more and the newcomers realize it.

IN SEARCH OF THE CLASS CANNON

The literature on pickpockets—and, specifically, professional pickpockets or class cannons—is severely incomplete, and empirical data on this fraternity of specialized thieves is even more critically limited. The richest body of information on this colorful group of criminal entrepreneurs was generated during the latter part of the 19th century, and this was compiled by journalists and the police in New York City. In 1868, for example, Edward Winslow Martin's *Secrets of the Great City* offered a brief yet highly descriptive portrait of pickpocket operations in New York, with summary data on who they were, where they operated, and how they were integrated as a group. Several years later, Edward Crapsey's *The Nether Side of New York* (1872) provided statistical data on their numbers, arrest rates, and conviction rates. In 1886 and 1895, Thomas Byrnes' *Professional Criminals of America,* published in two editions, provided descriptive information on pickpocketing in general, combined with career histories of the 71 major cannons operating in New York City during that period. Within a more scientific frame of reference, we are limited to the works of Edwin H. Sutherland's *The Professional Thief* (1937) and David W. Maurer's *Whiz Mob* (1964). Sutherland's work, while representing a landmark study of the professional thief, reflects little specifically related to the pickpocket. Furthermore, his data were drawn primarily from the experiences of one criminal, supplemented by parallel commentary offered by a small group of incarcerated thieves whom

Sutherland relied upon for validating the descriptions provided by his chief informant. Maurer's *Whiz Mob* is thorough and extensive, but it too has its limitations. First, Maurer was a linguist and a professor of American speech, and his study of pickpockets was an attempt to view their behavior pattern through their technical argot. As a result, while his work represents the most thorough examination of pickpockets ever undertaken, it lacks much of the discrete data necessary for constructing a comprehensive reflection of the social organization, occupational structure, and style of life of a deviant group. Furthermore, Maurer never fully described the sources of his information, in terms of how many pickpockets and thieves he interviewed, or whether they were active, retired, or incarcerated criminals.

Given the situation that professional pickpockets are seemingly passing into obscurity, my intent in studying them was designed to compile an empirical data base on the characteristics of the thieves themselves before all of the remaining practitioners in this dying profession ultimately disappeared. As such, my primary interest was the pickpocket, and my secondary concern was his profession. What follows is a discussion of how I gained access to this fraternity of thieves, the problems associated with studying them in a field setting, and a brief description of my findings. It might be noted here that all names, places, dates, and events are real and that no attempt has been made to disguise the identity of the various phenomena. This has been done to satisfy the interests of myself and some of my colleagues who have an historical orientation and who have an insatiable desire to relate given criminological events to the social, demographic, and organizational structures of the communities in which they occurred. At the same time, my informants are nevertheless protected in that, for the most part, they were known to me only by their underworld "monikers" (nicknames), very few of which have ever reached police files. Furthermore, the pickpockets mentioned in this essay were willing to have their monikers used, and the information reported here does not relate specific thieves to specific thefts and, hence, could be interpreted in a court of law only as hearsay evidence.

My initial glimpse of the professional underworld occurred in 1962 shortly after I received my first case load with the New York State Division of Parole. One of the parolees under my supervision was an individual known to his friends as Socks, and an overview of his criminal history suggested that he was a confirmed and hardened offender upon whom any efforts at rehabilitation and change would have been futile. Socks had been born in 1908 in Berlin, Ohio, a small town some 30 miles west of Cleveland. His criminal record spanned more than a third of a century, and reflected a total of 45 arrests for shoplifting, auto theft, house burglary, and bank burglary. The amazing thing about Socks's career in crime was that, with almost four dozen arrests, he had been convicted on only six occasions and his total time served in prison was less than half a decade. I was advised by a senior colleague that Socks was a professional thief, that his only trade was stealing, that it was best to just leave him alone since he had only a few months of parole time to do, and that for further information I ought to consult Sutherland's work. I read Sutherland's description of the professional thief with considerable astonishment, but my efforts to learn more about that segment of the underworld from Socks proved futile.

Two years later, in 1964, I began to come in contact with other professional thieves who had suffered serious "falls" (arrests) and had worked their way out of prison into a parole setting. During the following years I developed trusting relationships with several pickpockets, burglars, and shoplifters, and these contacts provided me with contemporary data on professional theft which ultimately led to the publication of *Careers in Crime* (Inciardi, 1975).

My intimate knowledge of the contemporary world of the class cannon came later, although my entry into that subculture actually began a decade ago and followed a rather circuitous route. During the years 1966 through 1968 I was supervising a seasoned professional pickpocket who had received a 1½- to 3-year indeterminate sentence for the possession of heroin. This pickpocket was known in the underworld as Crying Phil, and, when questioned as to how he earned such a name, he stated:

I've been called that name for the better part of twenty years. Some son-of-a-bitch cop in the 71st [Precinct, New York] called me that and it got on my *Yellow Sheet* [criminal history sheet]. Since then, everyone called me that. [Inciardi, 1975:57]

When I met Phil it was just after New Year's Day in 1966. He had just finished serving one year in New York's Green Haven Prison with two years of parole in front of him. Shortly after our first meeting, Phil inquired as to whether he could obtain an out-of-state pass to spend the remainder of the winter in South Florida, for his parents had a small condominium on Miami Beach. The Florida Probation and Parole authorities agreed to assume supervision of the case for a maximum of three months, and Phil journeyed south. After two winter seasons with this arrangement, Phil and I went our separate ways: he had finished his parole term, and I had accepted a research position with another New York State agency. That was in early 1968.

In October 1971 I became a resident of the state of Florida, and several months later, while enjoying the atmosphere of my new environment, I visited the Dade County Youth Fair. The Youth Fair is an annual event in Miami. It resembles the typical state fair, composed of livestock, truck-farming, and other 4-H type exhibits, public safety displays, and science projects prepared by the county's elementary, middle, and high school students. In addition, the fair has a huge midway usually provided by one of the carnival truck shows, such as Deggeller Brothers or Amusements of America, and attracts well over a hundred thousand visitors during its 10-day date.

While viewing one of the midway attractions, I became uneasy about the pressing crowd and decided to move my wallet from my back to my front pocket. As I grasped my wallet I found someone else's fingers touching it, and, upon turning quickly to confront the thief, I found myself face-to-face with a smiling Crying Phil. This would not have been the first time he had picked my pocket, for as a parolee, he would find it amusing to remove articles from my person and desk during an interview and then to return them, finding a bit of mirth in my embarrassment. Phil explained that except for the winter of 1965 when he was serving his term in Green Haven Prison, he had wintered in Florida every year since 1950. His purpose was to steal from the tourists, and he had done this even during the two seasons while he was under parole supervision. Phil introduced me to three other pickpockets who had been operating in the Miami area at that time, and these provided me with further information as to how the area was used by class cannons from various parts of the nation.

It seems that Miami and Miami Beach (as well as other areas in greater Dade County) have been a haven for numerous seasoned pickpockets for more than half a century. They travel primarily from New York, Philadelphia, Chicago, St. Louis, and other cities in the Northeast and Midwest to victimize the Northern winter tourists. The Miami area provides these cannons with a large transient population of highly mobile wealth in a carefree carnival atmosphere and within a safe, anonymous setting. As one pickpocket suggested:

> First, Miami gets us too out of the frozen North. Second, the tourist who comes here has money, and he comes here to spend it; . . . we just help him to better pass it around the community. Third, he's on vacation and isn't thinking much about being taken.

Or similarly, as Phil himself stated:

> It's easy to catch them off guard. . . . All they're thinking about is where to spend their money next. . . . Also, down here they don't have friends who are cops or lawyers or judges who can put on extra pressure.

Since my reunion with Crying Phil in early 1972, I have spoken with dozens of pickpockets who come to Miami during the winter season. They have reported a variety of locations where many "marks" can be easily beaten—the race tracks, the jai alai fronton, the Miami Beach Convention Hall, and the crowded streets of downtown Miami and Miami Beach. Some cannons also work the airport, the small auditoriums throughout the county, as well as attractions in other parts of South Florida such as Disney World and the vacation communities along Florida's Gulf Coast from Sarasota to Tampa.[9]

While most pickpockets will frequent the racetracks and the crowded streets, each one seems to have a set of preferences. One individual, known to the profession as Bat Masterson—named as such because he claimed to be a relative of William Barclay Masterson, the one-time legendary friend of Wyatt Earp and later U.S. Marshal of the southern district of New York State—was a patron of Miami's Orange Bowl:

> You see, I'm a real super fan as they say here in Miami. For the last 10 years I've always gone to Super Bowl city—wherever it was. Super Bowl X here in Miami this year was the best ever. . . . I first beat the scalpers to the tune of 20 tickets, and then the crowd for over three hundred dollars. [10]

Crying Phil found the Miami jai alai fronton to be an especially lucrative location:

> Jai alai is a good spot. There's plenty of people, plenty of action, and plenty of money. When a player scores a point and everyone yells and jumps, that's the time for a hit. [11]

Locating and interviewing a sample of pickpockets large enough to compile some general data on the personal characteristics of members of a fraternity of thieves that is seemingly in the process of decay was a burdensome task. For the data that is reported later in this essay, the process was initiated by Phil, my primary informant. He introduced me to a pickpocket mob of three individuals who had arrived in Miami during December 1975. These, in turn, introduced me to two others, creating an ever-widening circle of contacts until, by April 1976, I had contacted and interviewed a total of 20. But the process was not one of simple introductions and setting up of interviews. Class cannons are a highly suspicious group and a highly mobile group who work and communicate on their own terms. Although they were ultimately willing to cooperate with my research, they were never willing to go out of their way to do so.

The first problem to be overcome was their suspicions of me. Who was I and what did I want? Phil vouched for me with the initial contacts, explaining, in so many words, that my interest was in researching deviant life-styles, that I could be trusted, and that once their identities and places of operation were known to me I would not identify them to local police. This ice-breaking mechanism served as a satisfactory introduction to segments of the wintering cannon fraternity, but it was significantly extended by the fortuitous arrest of Crying Phil for petit larceny. Phil called me, requesting that I put up $50 for his cash bail, which I did immediately. Once on the street, Phil spread through the local grapevine that I had helped him and that I was "right" (trustworthy) and sympathetic to the profession). This strengthened my credibility, and within the local transient fraternity I became known as Jungle Jim.[12]

In spite of having the credentials of being Jungle Jim (the "right" researcher), the actual maneuver of locating a pickpocket for interview was rather complex. First of all, while the "winter season" is defined as Thanksgiving through Easter, no individual cannon remains in Miami for its full term. "It's dangerous," they say, for after five to eight weeks they may become too familiar-looking in any particular area. As a result, those with whom I had the closest associations were not always available to make new introductions for me. Furthermore, since a pickpocket usually did not decide upon where his day's activity would be until the morning of the given day, I could not anticipate exactly where to locate anyone of them. And finally, while a few had fixed residences where I might visit,[13] most did not or were reluctant to provide me with such information.

Under these circumstances, my procedure involved cruising and loitering in and around their working habitats until I spotted one that I knew. This meant spending many hours of many days and nights drifting along the streets of south Miami Beach, or visiting the various racetracks and other amusement centers. When I finally recognized a pickpocket that I had met previously, I would make the appropriate introduction and ask if he knew of any other cannons working in the immediate vicinity. In about one out of every 10 instances I would receive an introduction combined with some comment as to my status of being "right."[14]

In studying the class cannon in a field setting, one of the difficulties I had to overcome involved certain aspects of my own personal clumsiness as an observer. I learned quickly, for example, never to interrupt a pickpocket during the course of his work. On one occasion, while loitering on Miami Beach's Collins Avenue looking for pickpockets, I observed one that I knew walking alone along the other side of the street. I crossed the traffic to greet him, only to have him ignore me and turn his back and walk away. Later that day I met him again, and on this second occasion he annoyingly explained that he had been following a "mark" whom he had observed leaving a drug store stuffing money into his wallet. I had broken the thief's concentration, and he could no longer pursue his victim. From that point on, when recognizing a pickpocket already known to me, I would observe him for a time and from a considerable distance until I was confident that he was not "tracking a mark." This practice provided me with numerous opportunities for observing the operations of both individual cannons and cannon mobs. I also learned never to conspicuoulsy watch a cannon while he was working. Pickpockets dislike being watched, even by those who may be "right," because they become uneasy and clumsy and feel conspicuous.

My personal interactions with active class cannons in a field setting were circumscribed by an additional set of problems—those involving demeanor and comportment. More specifically, those concerning my dress and speech.

In terms of dress, the pickpocket is somewhat of a chameleon in that he tends to remain inconspicuous, blending in with those around him. While he generally does not have the social or educational background necessary for coalescing with a country club set, he can nevertheless adjust his attire and manner for most situations. In Miami, he will appear at the racetrack as a New York tourist, dressed in bermuda shorts, flowered shirt, white shoes, and perhaps even a straw hat; or he will appear on Miami Beach's south end as a pensioner—tired, slow-moving, and somewhat disheveled. In my interactions with the pickpocket, it was necessary to anticipate the circumstances in which such interactions were likely to take place. Attire that was in direct contrast with the pickpocket's set and setting would have been deemed obvious and unnatural by him, and hence communication would be short. And while I was not seemingly required to outfit myself as he might, a business suit was out of order, whereas "shirt-sleeve attire" was preferred.

As Polsky (1969:109-143) has noted, speech is important when communicating with criminals. Researchers cannot appear as complete "squares," nor should they overuse what they believe to be the appropriate jargon or argot. Rather, I learned that simple language that reflected a basic understanding of their profession and the problems associated with it was the most comfortably received.

The final problem encountered was one which generally besets most anthropological and ethnographic investigations—the mechanics of recording data. Most pickpockets will openly refuse to allow the use of tape recorders and interview schedules. This puts pressure on the observer-interviewer to record notes and reconstruct quotations within minutes after an interview. This was only a limited problem in my research since the interactional setting allowed frequent yet inconspicuous interruptions. With many interviews being undertaken at racetracks and the jai alai games, several alleged visits to the betting windows during the course of one interview permitted me to record most of what I had seen and heard. Among those pickpockets whom I knew well and at times when interviewing was taking place in a private setting, tape recorders and interview schedules could be used.

A BRIEF PORTRAIT OF THE CLASS CANNON

My investigation of the transient class cannons who frequent South Florida during the winter months endured from December 1975 through April 1976. A total of 20 of these seasoned old professionals were contacted, and extensive data were collected on their personal histories, criminal careers, mob operations, life-styles, and argot. Although the extent of my contacts varied with each informant, an informal interview instrument was constructed to uniformly collect basic information on the entire sample. The content of this instrument was committed to memory and filled out immediately after the interview. A portion of these data are briefly described below.

As indicated in Table 1, the class cannons interviewed were an older group for the most part, ranging in age from 39 to 76, with a mean age of 56 years. While they were born in numerous parts of the nation and several had been European immigrants, more than half

Table 1. PERSONAL CHARACTERISTICS

Case	Age	Place of Birth	Years of School	Trade
1	74	Chicago, Ill	none	none
2	68	Britt, Iowa	none	none
3	54	Philadelphia, Pa.	10	laborer
4	47	Sacramento, Calif.	13	mechanic
5	42	Ogden, Utah	8	none
6	62	Berlin, Germany	10	factory worker
7	60	New York, N.Y.	16	cab driver
8	39	Salt Lake City, Utah	13	cab driver
9	57	Philadelphia, Pa.	7	none
10	61	New York, N.Y.	8	plumber's helper
11	41	New York, N.Y.	16	none
12	40	Peoria, Ill.	16	none
13	51	Jackson, Miss.	6	truck driver
14	76	New York, N.Y.	none	none
15	50	San Francisco, Calif.	12	waiter
16	62	Brooklyn, N.Y.	14	typesetter
17	66	Portland, Maine	14	bartender
18	52	Dublin, Ireland	8	bricklayer
19	56	London, England	9	veterinarian's assistant
20	66	New York, N.Y.	none	machine operator

had originated in large urban centers and 30% were from New York City. Their level of education was generally low. More than half had less than a high school education, and as many as four reported having no formal schooling at all. The mean level of education for the group was nine years. While the majority reported having some kind of trade, some 35% reported having no trade, one indicated semiprofessional training as a veterinarian's assistant, and the remainder reflected skilled-unskilled laborer or service trades.

All the class cannons who were interviewed had reportedly extensive criminal histories. As suggested in Table 2, their mean age of first arrest was 13.6 years, and 85% of the group were under age 20 at the time of this initial arrest. These onset arrests, as indicated, generally involved nonviolent activities, with 70% reflecting direct acquisitive property crimes. The rate of arrest within this group was high, with the number of arrests reflecting a mean of approximately 43 and with pickpocketing arrests reflecting a mean of some 29. In general, and not surprisingly, the older the pickpocket the longer was his arrest history.

Table 2. ARREST HISTORIES

Case	Age 1st Arrest	Offense 1st Arrest	Total Arrests	Total Arrests for Picking Pockets
1	8	Breaking and entering	82*	36*
2	10	Breaking and entering	100*	25*
3	17	Auto theft	16	10
4	16	Statutory rape	27	20
5	8	Purse snatching	36*	29*
6	23	Petit larceny	65	60*
7	17	Grand larceny	40	39
8	11	Vandalism	6	--
9	15	Shoplifting	30	29
10	11	Breaking and entering	42	38
11	20	Breaking and entering	11	--
12	10	Petit larceny	30*	15*
13	10	Auto theft	20	19
14	12	Burglary	66	40
15	25	Homicide	11	10
16	12	Shoplifting	100*	90*
17	16	Bank robbery	45	40
18	10	Burglary	20	10
19	10	Arson	18	15
20	10	Petit larceny	100*	50*

*These figures are estimations.

Most class cannons, as indicated in Table 3, worked in mobs of two or more: 20% worked in mobs of three, 55% in mobs of two, and 25% worked alone. The individual's average annual income from picking pockets was reported at just over $23,000, with $9,200 indicated as the average *seasonal* income while in Miami, and $2,750 for any one winter month. Interestingly, class cannons who worked in mobs reported lower annual incomes (X = $19,600) than those who worked alone (X = $34,000). This is necessarily the result of a mob's equal splitting of the proceeds of their thefts, while the loner requires no such sharing practices. It might be noted, however, that a class cannon's spendable income is reportedly half of his overall earnings. With their high incidence of arrest, the major portion of their incomes is spent on attorney's fees and case fixing.

Finally, these data relate that the class cannon's career in pickpocketing is relatively long, ranging from 15 years to as long as 60 years. The average career for this sample was some 30 years. Most

Table 3. PICKPOCKETING CHARACTERISTICS

Case	Size of Mob	Length of Career (years)	Annual Income	Seasonal Income	This Season (1 month)
1	2	36	$ 5,000	$ 4,000	$1,000
2	2	41	5,000	4,000	1,000
3	2	31	12,000	5,000	2,000
4	1	17	25,000	10,000	3,500
5	3	15	20,000	10,000	2,500
6	3	30	20,000	10,000	2,500
7	3	26	20,000	10,000	2,500
8	2	16	12,000	2,000	1,000
9	1	37	50,000	25,000	5,000
10	2	44	15,000	2,000	2,000
11	2	16	15,000	2,000	1,000
12	2	20	40,000	10,000	5,000
13	2	34	25,000	5,000	1,000
14	2	60	20,000	5,000	2,000
15	1	20	40,000	20,000	5,000
16	1	40	35,000	20,000	3,000
17	3	26	25,000	10,000	3,000
18	2	24	30,000	10,000	5,000
19	2	16	30,000	10,000	3,000
20	1	44	20,000	10,000	4,000

had turned to picking pockets on a full-time basis by age 30 (75%), with the mean age of career commitment at 27 years.

EPILOGUE

In retrospect, this essay has provided an overview of professional pickpocketing, with some brief ethnographic and empirical notes on a small sample of this variety of career offender. Importantly, it has been demonstrated that, although class cannons are few in number, are not readily visible to the wider society, and have developed a behavior system in crime so well structured that they are able to steal for long periods of time without experiencing extended terms of incarceration, the ethnographer can nevertheless locate them within a community, study their criminal occupation, and observe their deviant activity. The method of study utilized here could be modified to apply to other deviant life-styles. In applying this technique, the observer-researcher would attempt to understand the phenomena under study, locate the initiating informants within the deviant community, and establish a demeanor that would not be threatening to the target group.

NOTES

1. The materials on Thomas Bartholomew Moran were gathered by me and by Wendy Ross, a staff writer of the *Miami Herald,* and are partially reported in Ross (1976).

2. The quotations offered in this essay have been drawn from field studies of professional thieves undertaken in New York City during 1968-1970 and reported in Inciardi (1975) and from my communications with pickpockets in South Florida during 1972-1976.

3. For a documented description of the history, social organization, and occupational structure of professional theft, see Inciardi (1975).

4. This excerpt, taken from Robert Greene's *The Second and Last Part of Conny-Catching,* comes from a collection of Tudor and early Stuart tracts, pamphlets, and ballads which describe the life and times of the Elizabethan vagabonds and thieves. The majority of these rogue pamphlets have been reprinted in Viles and Furnivall (1880), Wheatley and Cunningham (1891), Chandler (1907), and Judges (1930), and their historical reliability has been examined by Aydelotte (1913:76-78, 114-139) and Inciardi (1975:146-147).

5. Beyond minor changes in argot, past discussions of pickpocketing by numerous observers in the United States and Great Britain show little variation from the recent depth analysis by Maurer (1964). See, for example, Mayhew (1862), Martin (1868), Crapsey (1872), Buel (1891), Byrnes (1895), Willard (1900), Hapgood (1903), Felstead (1923), Dearden (1925), O'Connor (1928), Ingram (1930), Sutherland (1937), Dressler (1951), Campion (1957), and Varna (1957).

6. Although some of the argot of the pickpocket is mentioned here, it is reported for illustrative purposes only. David Maurer's *Whiz Mob* (1964) represents the most complete study of pickpocket argot ever undertaken, and it reflects the period 1945-1955. I have noted some changes since Maurer's time, but these will be treated in a separate report.

7. The style of life and occupational structure of the professional pickpocket is discussed only briefly here, for it has been discussed at length elsewhere. See, for example, Sutherland (1937), Maurer (1964), and Inciardi (1975).

8. While most of us think of a nickelodeon as a jukebox, the old-time nickelodeon referred to here was actually a small movie house charging an admission price of five cents.

9. The racetracks are by far the more popular of locations, and Dade County has numerous horse and dog tracks including Biscayne Dog Track, Calder Race Course, Fabulous Flagler Kennel Club, Gulfstream Park, Hialeah, and Miami Beach Kennel Club. In addition, pickpockets are also attracted to the neighboring Hollywood Dog Track and Pompano Park Harness Raceway.

10. It might be noted here that after the 1976 Super Bowl in Miami, some 28 wallets were reported stolen and 36 empty wallets were found by Orange Bowl clean-up crews (Ross, 1976).

11. Complementing Phil's words, the jai alai's head usher told me, "Every Friday and Saturday night, in season, there's at least 14,000 people crowded in, and over half a million dollars is bet, . . . so there's plenty of money there. Every weekend there were empty wallets turned in to me."

12. The meaning of this "moniker" eluded me at first, but I later realized its connotation when a pickpocket referred to South Florida as "the jungle."

13. The Holiday Inn at Homestead, Florida, some 25 miles southwest of Miami at the beginning of the Florida Keys, was the headquarters of one three-man troupe. The Hotel Tamiami, in downtown Miami's small skid-row area, was used by a two-man mob.

14. I was never able to figure out whether these pickpockets had some coded mechanism for testifying to my "right" status, for I could perceive it in neither their facial expressions, nor their intonations, nor their argot. The possibility of such a coding scheme occurred to me since it does exist in other criminal groups. Within certain segments of the Italian underworld, for example, when an outsider who *cannot* be trusted is introduced to the group, he is referenced as *questo e un amico mio* ("this is a friend of mine"); if he *can* be trusted, he is referred to as *questo e un amico nostro* ("this is a friend of ours").

REFERENCES

AYDELOTTE, F. (1913). Elizabethan rogues and vagabonds. Oxford: Clarendon.

BUEL, J.W. (1891). Sunlight and shadow of America's great cities. Philadelphia: West Philadelphia Publishing.

BYRNES, T. (1886). Professional criminals of America. New York: G.W. Dillingham.

––– (1895). Professional criminals of America. New York: G.W. Dillingham.

CAMPION, D. (1957). Crooks are human too. Englewood Cliffs, N.J.: Prentice-Hall.

CHANDLER, F.W. (1907). The literature of roguery. Boston: Houghton Mifflin.

CRAPSEY, E. (1872). The nether side of New York. New York: Sheldon.

DEARDEN, R.L. (1925). The autobiography of a crook. New York: Dial.

DRESSLER, D. (1951). Parole chief. New York: Dutton.

FELSTEAD, S.T. (1923). The underworld of London. New York: Fox, Duffield.

GREENE, R. (1591). The second and last part of conny-catching. London.

HAPGOOD, H. (1903). The autobiography of a thief. New York: Fox, Duffield.

INCIARDI, J.A. (1975). Careers in crime. Chicago: Rand McNally.

INGRAM, G. (1930). Hell's Kitchen. London: Herbert Jenkins.

JUDGES, A.V. (ed., 1930). The Elizabethan underworld. London: George Routledge.

MARTIN, E.W. (1868). Secrets of the great city. Philadelphia: National.

MAURER, D.W. (1964). Whiz mob: A correlation of the technical argot of pickpockets with their behavior pattern. New Haven, Conn.: College and University Press.

MAYHEW, H. (1862). London labour and the London poor: Vol. 4, Those that will not work, comprising prostitutes, thieves, swindlers and beggars, by several contributors. London.

O'CONNOR, J. (1928). Broadway racketeers. New York: Horace Liveright.

PARTRIDGE, E. (1961). Dictionary of slang and unconventional English. New York: Macmillan.

POLSKY, N. (1969). Hustlers, beats and others. Garden City, N.Y.: Doubleday.

ROSS, W. (1976). "Pickpockets: The passing of the old pro." Miami Herald, March 21, pp. G1-4.

SUTHERLAND, E.H. (1937). The professional thief. Chicago: University of Chicago Press.

VARNA, A. (1957). World underworld. London: Museum Press.

VILES, E., and FURNIVALL, F.J. (eds., 1880). The rogues and vagabonds of Shakespeare's youth. London: N. Truber.

WENTWORTH, H., and FLEXNER, S.B. (eds., 1960). Dictionary of American slang. New York: Crowell.

WHEATLEY, H.B., and CUNNINGHAM, P. (1891). London life, past and present (Vol. 3). London: John Murray.

WILLARD, J.F., pseud. Josiah Flynt (1900). Notes of an itinerant policeman. Boston: L.C. Page.

3

GETTIN' IT TOGETHER

Some Theoretical Considerations on Urban Ethnography
Among Underclass Peoples

HARVEY A. SIEGAL

Ethnographic studies of drug abuse and its concomitant life-styles
have suffered from the same difficulty that has troubled all urban
ethnography. Although many excellent studies and monographs have
been produced, little real understanding of the problems and
prospects of the ethnographic method in social research has been
communicated to the larger scientific community. Ethnographers
have had difficulty explaining precisely what they do. For this
reason, ethnography has taken somewhat a backseat to other analytic
frameworks.

These issues became painfully apparent to me when I undertook a
long-term ethnographic study of the slum and welfare hotels and
single-room-occupancy (SRO) tenements in New York City. I
quickly discovered that I needed to do more than simply "make like
an anthropologist" to produce findings that would make any sense
out of the peoples under study. Concepts such as "community" and
"boundaries," which are easily bandied about by both social
scientists and lay policy planners, took on real significance when I
was confronted with an increasingly large and heterogeneous urban

area. "Methodology" took on a new meaning for me. It quickly became necessary to set forth some sort of schema or paradigm into which the social world I was studying might be ordered. Methodology, in this sense, is very much like theory; it is a way of illuminating and interrelating selected aspects or components of a problem. If this can be done successfully, not only does it make possible the collection of relevant and meaningful data, but it also allows for their integration into some kind of system that reflects both the common-sense, everyday understanding of the studied peoples and the larger social science enterprise. The findings of such a study can have a wealth of uses ranging from direct planning and intervention on the very practical level to greater understanding of certain societal processes on the more abstract level.

The paper to follow discusses some of the methodological difficulties encountered in doing ethnography in an urban setting with a primarily "deviant" population; I shall attempt to develop a number of concepts that are immediately relevant to urban ethnography conducted on underclass peoples. The fact that most of the people studied were committed (or addicted) to the use of some chemical substance (primarily alcohol) made, I believe, little difference to the study. The problems of doing restrictive ethnography (i.e., ethnography limited to a specific population) in an urban area would be the same for a nonaddicted population.

THE ORIGINAL RESEARCH:
SLUM/WELFARE HOTELS AND SRO TENEMENTS

The study concerned the life of those people who were the more or less permanent residents of the slum/welfare hotels and SRO tenements found on Manhattan's Upper West Side. The study was actually conducted from 1970 through 1972 when I lived in a number of welfare hotels in this Upper West Side area. Following that experience, I was able to replicate parts of the original SRO study in some 20 cities across the nation. This experience provided unique opportunity to "field-test" continually the methodological frame of reference against a number of widely varying conditions.

The common denominator was the studied people: in all cases they represented rootless, alienated, and unhealthy people living outside the expected ghetto skid row, or institutional setting. Almost all of them were socially terminal individuals—i.e., individuals forgotten by the rest of society—with little hope of ever taking a place in it again. For example, more than three-fourths of the people in the surveyed hotels were long-term welfare recipients. Also, a disproportionate percentage of the population studied were nonwhite, and, in addition, the population tended to be advanced in age, most having already exceeded middle age.

The question arises: how does this population persist in an area that lacks the institutional support system which normally accompanies an underclass population in a skid-row or ghetto setting? I examined the ecology and morphology of Manhattan's Upper West Side to see how such an area might accommodate an underclass population. The scene and its setting proved *not* to be markedly dissimilar to other areas of the country, where in city after city a closely related ecological constellation could be documented.

In Manhattan, the first residents of the Upper West Side were white Anglo-Saxon Protestants who built for their families the elegant brownstone buildings lining the east-west cross streets. Before long, however, the Jews, Germans, and Irish, successful in business, began arriving from further downtown. To accommodate families from these groups, large "greystones," multistory apartment buildings, were constructed along with six-story tenements for their less successful countrymen. Greystone buildings were generally quite large, each unit containing seven or more rooms. The arrival of the immigrant groups initiated the exodus of the original WASP population. As they left, their brownstones were sold and altered to accommodate a larger number of people per unit. Late in the 1930s, however, the first real suburban push was felt. As the number of immigrant families grew, many left the area for the safer open spaces of the suburbs.

Early in the 1940s, with the entrance of the United States into the Second World War, a tremendous housing demand was created both by servicemen and by civilian defense-industries workers who came to the metropolitan area eager to fill the manpower vacuum created by the armed services draft. Landlords responded by further subdividing existing housing. The brownstones were divided from three-story, two- and three-family units into two "studio apartments" on the first and second floors, a basement "studio" and four or five "furnished rooms" (with neither cooking facilities nor a private bath for each room) on the third floor. The apartments of the greystones were divided into six or seven single-room occupancies (SROs). Each of these SRO units kept the original kitchen and bathroom facility; now, a single stove, refrigerator, sink, toilet and bath served a minimum of seven separate rooms. Often, in the early days of SRO housing, an entire family would utilize a single SRO apartment, with family members sleeping in shifts. Many hotels in the area responded to the increased demand for dormitory-like housing in the same way; suites were divided, and former elegance and service were sacrificed in the interest of greater profit.

The termination of the war and the demobilization of the military and defense industries engendered yet another shift in the population of the SRO tenements, hotels, and brownstone rooming houses. This last phase, with its roots in the early 1950s endures to the present. In part, the Upper West Side population came to include the remainder of the Jewish, German, and Irish ethnics who made the area their home until the war. Many of those who did not move out of the area—who were either too weak, too old, too sick, or too frightened to leave—found that the only available housing was in these buildings. Others, recently arrived from the South and without employment or financial resources, were placed by the Department of Welfare in such housing because it was inexpensive. Newly released prisoners or state mental patients found that this was the only type of housing available to them. Still others, who wished to live alone and unnoticed. found that living in these hotels satisfied their needs.

What all of these persons seemed to share was their marginality in relation to the mainstream of the life of the city and the nation; they were as effectively isolated as those in the ghettos. Yet the ghetto, because of its social isolation, contains within itself an almost complete way of life. Deprived of many of the institutional supports available to the middle and upper classes, the people of the ghetto necessarily evolved their own patterns. The people living in the hotels and rooming houses, however, found themselves confronted by a very different situation. They were a marginal, predominantly lower-class group residing in very dense enclaves, nestled check-by-jowl with people of a much higher social class. They were poor people, seemingly isolated from the usual sustaining complex of indigenous institutions. It is this dimension of apparent isolation that must be considered in constructing an ethnography of peoples of this kind.

While early writing on such populations is clear in its suggestion of social disorganization and atomism, more recent studies have documented the existence of complex and all-encompassing forms of organization. What was needed was a methodological framework or perspective that could readily look beyond the initial stress and confusion to the forms, patterns, and functions of the organization. To accomplish this, it was necessary to examine the concepts that are routinely employed in studies of underclass life. These concepts had to be examined so that it might become possible to employ parts of them in visualizing the emerging social forms and behavioral patterns.

The focus of the methodology was necessarily on eliciting information on the social construction of the world of single-room occupancies. In a larger sense, though, the methodology had to address the problems of investigating a population which is materially poor yet living in a money-oriented society, is often committed to or regularly engaged in activities that are considered illegal or deviant, appears to be marooned in a single spot in the social structure, and yet manages to build a viable, integrated social system. Attention was directed to the rules constructed, the patterns of social interaction that evolved, and the ways in which this community is able to sustain itself in its larger social environment. More specifically, this methodology examined the ways in which people without either the material supports so significant in the larger culture or access to the informal institutional arrangements such as could be found within the ecological area in which the poor are normally contained satisfy the broad and diverse needs upon which everyday life is dependent. The methodology concerned itself with ways of defining and categorizing the activity of persons in an ongoing system small enough to be viewed as a discrete entity.

THEORY AND METHODOLOGY

A scientific theory is a way of organizing the world. It is a way of seeing the similarities in seemingly disparate impressions so that a unified picture or model emerges. Methodology is the dynamic aspect of theory which helps select and organize the key impressions or data. In the ethnographic research conducted on these slum hotels or SROs, three major theoretical threads quickly appeared. They are the concepts of (1) "community," (2) "a culture of povery," and (3) "deviance."

The SRO world may be seen as a "community." In micro terms, each building is an isolated "community" in which one may equate its rooms to houses and its halls to streets; the entire system is bounded by the walls of the building. In macro terms, the SRO community is a set of buildings spread throughout a geographical area. Members of this community are able to move from unit to unit and possess a certain amount of knowledge about the various buildings that constitute the community. What is indicated, then, is some sociological definition of "community" that allows the incorporation of both perspectives.

Since the SRO community is composed overwhelmingly of poor people and because they, for the most part, have been destitute for a considerable length of time—in many cases, from birth—the concept of a "culture of poverty" becomes theoretically relevant. This perspective makes it possible to see the poor as distinguished from other Americans by more than the mere fact of their indigence.

Because many SRO inhabitants regularly practice or are committed to patterns of behavior that are generally considered to be deviant or illegal, it is necessary to admit some theoretical conception of "deviant behavior." The behavior of these people must be considered within the context of the SRO world. In order to understand the complexity of the behavior, a theoretical approach that makes it possible to see such behavioral patterns problematically, thereby focusing attention on their situational aspects, was developed. This orientation completely eschewed any atomistic approach to deviance, focusing instead on the member in his natural habitat, asking what he does, how he does it, who he does it with, and how it came to be so.

One might suggest that some comprehension of these three central concepts—community, a culture of poverty, and deviance—is in some way necessary to any study of underclass life. Furthermore, any methodology that is to be employed must be capable of bringing forth data that are relevant to these central theoretical threads. Much research can be easily scored because the larger theoretical threads have never been adequately identified and therefore the derivative methodology appears at best murky and directionless. Below I shall briefly examine the three major theoretical threads to determine their utility for doing ethnographic research on underclass peoples. I shall then present the operationalization of these concepts into a methodology.

Community

In any study of underclass life involving the consideration of deviant behavior, the notion of a "community" is crucial. The concept of community goes hand in hand with the concept of culture. Culture must have some structural or organizational base, and this is provided by community. In trying to derive a workable definition of "community," however, sociologists have experienced more than a modicum of disagreement. Several writers have surveyed the literature and have conlcuded that the areas of agreement concerning the concept are almost negligble. (See, for instance, Hollingshead, 1948; Simpson, 1965; Sutton et al., 1960; Hillery, 1955, 1959.) One writer, in fact, has pointed out that the only idea on which there is complete agreement is that community has something to do with people (Hillery, 1955).

Although the concept is rather ambiguous, it is essential for understanding the behavior of underclass people living in the slum hotels and SRO tenements. Let us examine some of the ways in which the phenomenon is typically seen, in order to determine how best to derive a workable concept of community. Such a concept would necessarily have to address the special social and ecological problems inherent in any urban ethnography.

A community might be described most simply as "a collection of people occupying a more or less clearly defined area," along with the institutions in that area (Park, 1952). This definition is, however, too simplistic to be fruitfully employed in most studies of underclass life in urban areas. A dynamic approach–that is, one capable of viewing community from an interactional perspective–is necessary. Such a perspective can locate and identify a community within a dense urban setting (dense in terms of both people and institutions) and can consider factors like "social space," "social control," and "social differentiation" as resources that are regularly manipulated by persons living within a given locale. In this regard, community becomes a type of problem-solving device for people confronted by the exigencies of an indifferent or even hostile physical and social environment. Such a dynamic definition of community is especially relevant in the case of urban areas that are densely settled by socially isolated yet coterminously residing groups.

Morris Freilich is an anthropologist who has turned from the institutional conception of community, so popular in American sociology, to one that considers social interaction as its pivotal variable. In his view, a community is a type of interactional system possessing the following characteristics:

> Each community is unique (1) in terms of using a set of geographical points (centers) as loci of interaction, (2) in having a given set of interactional groups meeting at such centers, and (3) developing a local-interaction culture based on information collected at such centers *and* distributed primarily to members of the community. [Freilich, 1963]

Geographically, the community is a set of centers related to each other by being used regularly by a unique set of associational groups. Socially, these associational groups use the given set of interrelated centers more often than they use any other set of centers.

Another interactional approach to community has been suggested by Richard DuWars. He has proposed that a community be viewed in terms of the similarity in the way that members of a group (and perhaps, in a larger sense, the group) come to define situations. He argues that:

> the basic social process is that of evaluative interaction; that social units are distinguished by the kinds of situations which they evaluate; and the

defined response of similar units to the same type of situation distinguishes each unit from others in the category. . . . Whatever the breakdown the kind of situation attended by the unit is the first distinguishing feature of the unit. . . . If communities, our social unit in this instance, do have characteristic individuality indicated by their value systems that arise as the community members interact to define recurring life situations, then two very similar communities can be distinguished by their separate definitions of the same event. [DuWars, 1962]

Because of the unusual problems presented by a study of underclass peoples residing in a heterogeneous urban area, I found it necessary in my SRO research to employ an interactionist definition of community. In a study of hotels and tenements which are scattered over the entire Upper West Side of Manhattan, the concept of community defined in terms of "place" is meaningless. To simply label each building as a "community" and stop the analysis there entirely begs the question. One must consider whether each building is, in fact, a meaningful social unit. Institutional services, as utilized by underclass peoples, are neither of their own creation nor for their exclusive use, nor are they controlled and/or operated by the population they serve. Moreover, in most cases (significantly, for hospital care) the SRO residents have to leave the geographic bounds of their area in order to obtain the desired service.

In my SRO research, it was also useful to employ an ecological perspective—one which envisions the single slum hotel or SRO tenement as a component of a larger community. This perspective made possible the study of the larger SRO community in a holistic fashion. Robert Redfield's discussion of the "little community as an ecological system" (1953) sheds light on this ecological approach. In his work on the small, technologically backward villages of the Yucatan peninsula, the interrelationships of man and nature are defined by the ecological system. The ecological system is not a static one; rather, its organization responds to both external and internal changes. In urban ethnography this concept sensitizes one to the regular, temporal transformation of the system. In this sense, the system is like a dramatic or literary composition; there is a cycle (usually annual) in which there is a cast, a prologue, a development, and a denouement or conclusion. In each cycle, the community lives the play, but its last act in any one cycle may be different from the last act in the next (Redfield, 1953).

The concepts of the ecological system and ecological time are particularly relevant to research on underclass urban communities. For example, given the realities of the American political scene, much of what happens to an underclass population lies outside its control. People who are unorganized and effectively disenfranchised have little influence over politicians and bureaucrats sensitive to the needs and wishes of a different segment of the population. Housing ordinances, zoning regulations, delivery of vital services, and police activity all strongly affect the quality of underclass life, yet the underclass (or deviant) community has about as much control over these factors as the Central American Indians have over the amount of rain that falls on their crops.

In describing and categorizing the regularly occurring events over which the community has little or no control, the concept of "ecological time" is useful. For example, although few members of the SRO community participate in the electoral process and even fewer look to it for solutions to their problems, the period preceding elections precipitates major alterations in activity for many persons in the community. Persons engaged in illegal occupations or those whose life-styles depend on illegal goods find operation much more difficult before election time when promises have been made to "clean up the streets" by removing undesirable (i.e., deviant) individuals.

In describing some of the life-styles of members of an underclass community, the concept of ecological time is equally useful. An addict's life-style is very amenable to such analysis. A complete cycle evolves around the regular acquisition of his drugs; definable parts of the cycle are the strategies that must be employed to "cop" or secure drugs and the various ploys needed to assure their enjoyment free from fear of apprehension or harassment. The concept calls attention, as well, to the variations in the availability of illegal drugs. During "panics," for example, when drugs are scarce, drastic disruptions or alterations in the addict's daily routine necessarily occur. The concept of ecology, then, can be very useful in the study of both the underclass community and its members' specialized life-styles.

The Culture of Poverty

Since the Great Society years of the 1960s, the notion of a "culture of poverty" has become part of not only the sociological idiom but the rhetoric of reform and revolution as well. The poor—especially the hard-core or "disreputable" poor—have become radically distinguished from the larger body of Americans. For this core group, poverty is a way of life, and a culture has evolved to provide some assistance in satisfying individual needs. Like "community," culture is a problem-solving device. This quality of culture—its ability to provide a collective solution to individual problems—is the one that is most sociologically interesting.

From this perspective, such writers as Everett C. Hughes see culture evolving as a sharing of symbols and meaning leading to a common understanding of an environment. Members of a given culture know what can be done and when and how it is appropriate to do it. Hughes observes that

> Whenever some group of people have a bit of common life with a modicum of isolation from other people, a common corner of society, common problems and perhaps a couple of common enemies, their culture grows. It may be the fantastic culture of the unfortunate who, having become addicted to the use of heroin, share a forbidden pleasure, a tragedy and a battle against the conventional world. It may be the culture of a pair of infants who, in coping with the same all-powerful and arbitrary parents, build up a language and a set of customs of their own which persists even when they are as big and powerful as the parents. It may be the culture of a group of students who, ambitious to become physicians, find themselves faced with the same cadavers, quizzes, puzzling patients, instructors and deans. . . . Where people who engage in deviant activities have the opportunity to interact with one another, they are likely to develop a culture built around the problems rising out of the differences between their definition held by other members of the society. [Becker, 1963]

The underclass welfare hotel and SRO tenements provide just such a fertile ground necessary for the flowering of culture. The common set of problems necessary for the genesis of culture are present. For example, a problem which results from the crowded living conditions and poor construction of the SRO units is that residents frequently find themselves hearing—often through thin partitions—information not intended for their ears. In response to this common problem, SRO residents have learned when and what to "hear." They have evolved a tacit set of rules which help them to ignore certain information and to interact in accordance with this pose of ignorance.

Contributing to the construction of this shared life-style are the special ecological problems imposed by the location of the welfare hotels in the midst of affluent residential areas. The culture of poverty provides some of the necessary information to sustain moneyless people in a money-oriented world. Oscar Lewis, the anthropologist who is perhaps most closely identified with the concept, suggested that the culture of poverty is

> both an adaption and a reaction of the poor to their marginal position in a class-stratified, highly individuated, capitalistic society. It represents an effort to cope with feelings of hopelessness and despair which develop from the realization of the improbability of achieving success in terms of the values and goals of the larger society.... [One must try] to understand poverty and its associated traits as a culture ... with its own structure and rationale, as a way of life which is passed down from generation [to generation].... This view directs attention to the fact that the culture of poverty in modern nations is not only a matter of economic deprivation, of disorganization or of the absence of something. It is also something positive and provides some rewards without which the poor could hardly carry on. [Lewis, 1965]

This view sensitizes the researcher to the nature of a community subjected to material deprivation, to the relationship between this subculture and the larger society, and to the attitudes, values, and character structure of the indigent individual.

Lewis cautioned us not to romanticize the idea of living within a culture of poverty and not to regard the poor as modern-day noble savages. Rather, the concept of a culture of poverty should call attention to the adaptive functions of human beings and to their ability to create a design for living, with a ready-made set of solutions for human problems. This is not, however, a statement of value; it does not imply that the poor are poor because they wish to be and if choice were possible would cling to the status quo. Instead, poverty (and all that it implies) should be treated as an ecological condition within which people will naturally invent the behavioral and social patterns that make life livable.

Deviance

Some workable sociological statement about the concept of social deviance is needed. Writers have experimented with a large number of definitions, each emphasizing different facets of the phenomenon. Some writers treat deviant behavior as simply another type of goal-directed activity essentially indistinguishable from legitimate enterprise. This nonnormative orientation is not a radically new way of looking at deviance. Edwin Sutherland (1973), for example, in reconstructing the biography of Chic Conwell, discussed the life and work of this professional thief in wholly occupational terms. Ned Polsky (1964), writing on the pool hustler, described a way of life very similar to any other profession. And Donald Ball (1967), describing the operation of an illegal abortion clinic, depicted a functioning organization in such ordinary occupational terms that there was almost no way to distinguish it, sociologically, from a legitimate medical practice. These are but a few examples of an orientation that stresses the similarity of deviant and legitimate careers and searches for the cultural and social supports that provide the underpinnings of any social activity.

The deviant (like everyone else) regularly does what he has to do to satisfy the demands made upon him by his needs and, in the process, organizes his activities into a recognizable daily round. In a larger sense, too, certain forms of deviant activity appear to parallel legitimate careers, progressing through such observable steps as entry, apprenticeship, and retirement (Hirschi, 1962).

It would be naive, however, to assume that, except for their being "high" on dope or inebriated regularly, addicts, alcoholics, street-walkers, and others are in no way "different" from other members of society. There is, after all, a dimension which separates the "real" deviants from "the rest of us." Kai Erikson (1964) recognized this dimension and stressed its positive function. He viewed the "differentness" of deviant behavior as vital to the ongoing operation of society. In his view, the social system, despite its apparent abstractness, is organized around the movements of persons joined together in regular social relations. For such a system, the only material defining its boundaries is the behavior of its participants. However, often the kinds of behavior which best perform this function are deviant, since they represent the most extreme sort of conduct to be found within the experience of the group. Erikson (1964:122ff.) defined deviance as

> conduct which is generally thought to require the attention of social control agencies—that is, conduct about which "something should be done." Deviance is not a property inherent in certain forms of behavior. It is a property conferred on these forms by the audience which directly or indirectly witnesses them.

In this view, then, deviance is any behavior which is perceived by various persons as threatening to the social system (i.e., the group or society) of which they consider themselves to be members. Transactions taking place between the deviant member on the one side and the agencies of control on the other are boundary-maintaining mechanisms. They mark the extreme limits to which a norm has jurisdiction and, in this way, attest to the amount of variability permitted within the system. Without such limitation the system is in danger of disintegration. Each time that the group censures some act of deviance, it affirms the authority of the violated norm and declares again the normative boundaries of the group. In short, Erikson's contention is that "deviance" cannot be dismissed simply as behavior which disrupts stability in society, but may itself be, in controlled quantities, an important condition for preserving stability.

Central to this conception of deviance is the actual or potential response of the social-control agents and/or agencies. Thus, some writers are beginning to discuss deviant behavior which depends upon the *probability* of a response from the agents of social control. In this regard, Edwin Lemert pointed out that with repetitive, persistent deviation or invidious differentiation something happens inside the skin of the deviating person. Something gets built into the psyche or nervous system as a result of social penalties, or "degradation ceremonies," or as a consequence of having been made the subject of "treatment" or "rehabilitation." The individual's perception of values, means, and estimates of their costs undergoes revision in such ways that symbols which serve to limit the choices of most people produce little or no response in him, or else engender responses contrary to those sought by others. [Lemert, 1964]

Lemert's perspective directs one's attention to those situations in which persons caught in a network of conflicting claims or values choose behavioral solutions which carry risks of stigmatization. A response from the agents of social control becomes one possible outcome of their action, though it is not inevitable. Attention, then, must be directed not only to the person's act but also to *the resources (symbolic and otherwise) that he has at his disposal to either disguise the deviation, by maintaining an adequate cover, or manage the agents of social control delegated to regulate him and his activities.* With this in mind, it is possible to examine the varied and often profound differences between those persons actually "committed" to a deviant career and those persons who only occasionally find themselves transgressing.

In an investigation of deviant behavior, the researcher must consider the entire social process involved in the creation and maintenance of deviant life-styles. His analysis must progress beyond a member's immediate act and examine the larger organization of the behavior; he must not lose sight of situational aspects helping to shape the interaction. Lemert's perspective is particularly helpful in this regard.

The argument for seeing community, culture, and deviance in dynamic terms is clear: traditional space-and-institution-bound conceptions cannot make sense out of the complex urban scene; they must be eschewed in favor of those that emphasize fluidity and continuity. Fluidity and continuity are the central ideas of this perspective. The social organization is not merely an external environment; it is a sociopsychological overlay. The following section considers the methodology through which this social organization can be studied.

THE METHODOLOGICAL FRAMEWORK

For urban ethnography, a methodology is needed which considers the widest range of data, neither doing violence to the worlds of the peoples studied nor falling into the trap of producing soft science or journalism. Such an outlook is emerging from a perspective labeled "naturalism" or "naturalistic behavioralism." Norman Denzin (1971:166-167) has provided a concise statement of this perspective, suggesting that it is

> the studied commitment to actively enter the world of native people and to render those worlds understandable from the standpoint of a theory that is grounded in the *behaviors, languages, definitions, attitudes,* and *feeling* [sic] of those studied. . . . Naturalistic behaviorism aims for viable social theory. . . . This version of behaviorism recognizes that humans have social selves and as such act in ways that reflect their unfolding definitions of the situation. . . . The Naturalistic employs any and all sociological methods, whether these be secondary analyses of quantitative data, limited surveys, unobtrusive measures, participant observation, document analysis, or life history constructions. He will admit into his analyses any and all data that are ethically available.

Urban ethnography involving peoples who might be considered in some way as deviant needs both the breadth and discipline brought by naturalism. From the standpoint of this naturalistic methodology, social organization is conceived as a real framework inside of which the acting units (both people and groups) develop their action. Both the framework and the acting units are real and warrant consideration. By simultaneously considering the acting unit, the larger social stage or platform, the member's methods of dealing with others perceived as similar to himself, and representatives of the larger world outside who confront him in many aspects of his daily round, the ethnographer can develop a portrait of an underclass world that is reasonably complete.

William F. Whyte, in the now classic *Street Corner Society* (1955), called for visualizing a complex, heterogeneous social area in organizational terms. His research was premised on the idea that, although an outside observer first perceived the area as "socially disorganized," it was anything but that. There were rules that could be distinguished if the "proper" observations were made. Whyte discovered that a sociometric orientation made it possible to describe and analyze the entire range of social relationships found in a street corner group. Further, by including a more macroscopic approach, the relationship of the group to the larger social setting within which it operated could also be studied. This latter phase of the research described the self-perceptions of the larger community, the interaction of the various voluntary associations, and the images that community members carried of the outside world.

Similar to *Street Corner Society*, yet different for its methodology, is Elliott Liebow's *Tally's Corner* (1967). Liebow was confronted not by a well-defined associational group such as the Nortons (the name of the gang that Whyte studied) but by a loosely integrated group of black men who spent the larger part of their time loitering on a street corner in the heart of Washington, D.C.'s black ghetto. Since the problems were different (phenomena that figured so importantly in Whyte's analysis—such as leadership—were not to be found on Tally's corner), the methodological appraoch that served so well in *Street Corner Society* proved inapplicable. To overcome these obstacles, Liebow turned to a more anthropological approach. Such an approach both identifies and describes the major elements in the group's daily life. In this way, the group's structure is divided into a number of analytically separable systems. The combination and interaction of the several subsystems contributes to the maintenance of the group. This type of ethnographic research derives its organization from the situations and rules that are themselves meaningful to the involved people. *Tally's Corner*, for instance, is organized so that each of the social categories employed by the street corner men—such as "Men and Jobs," "Lovers and Exploiters," "Friends and Networks"—is represented, described, and analyzed.

The strength of this approach lies in its ability to recognize the social categories and classifications that are themselves meaningful to the population under study. This dynamic method also has the ability to capture the process of social interaction as it is happening. The researcher accomplishes this by catching the process of interpretation through which they [the persons under study] construct their actions. . . . To catch the process, the student must take the role of the acting unit whose behavior he is studying. Since the interpretation is being made by the acting unit in terms of objects designated and appraised, meanings required, and decisions made, the process has to be seen from the standpoint of the acting unit. . . . To try to catch the interpretive process by remaining as aloof as a so-called "objective" observer and refusing to take the role of this acting unit is to risk the worst kind of subjectivism—the interpretation with his own surmises in place of catching the process as it occurs in the experience of the acting unit which uses it. [Blumer, 1962]

In my SRO research, I employed just such a participant methodology. I lived in a number of the hotels under study and altered my daily life-style so as to mirror, as closely as possible, the lives of the SRO residents. At one time I even confined myself to my hotel room for several weeks, so that, with a grocery messenger as my only human contact, I could experience the loneliness—the extreme isolation—of an SRO "shut-in." This participant methodology significantly aided me in gaining the confidence of the underclass population under study—a population normally suspicious of academic observers.

The methodological frame suggested here utilizes the strongest parts of each tradition. From Liebow and others committed to entering the worlds of the studied peoples, we recognize that the study must organize itself around the social categories, classifications, and common-sense meanings evolved by the participating member. Yet, drawing from Whyte's experience, we find it necessary to consider the more or less objective indicators of underlying conditions. What emerges is a methodology which can consider the consequences of forces such as "culture," "social structure," and "social control" without losing sight of human beings as acting agents—people who are continually responding to their own and each other's behavior and who are responding not simply to the actual behavior but as much to the meanings and definitions that are attached to any social situation or interaction. This methodological synthesis rests upon the assumption that there are discontinuities within the social structure. Reliance on any single methodological approach will, therefore, render whole areas of behavior invisible.

The methodology I am suggesting provides the researcher with an understanding of the symbolic universe in which the group member operates, the process through which commonly held meanings or definitions become attached to actions (or objects and situations), and the parameters and frameworks within which such action takes place. The ethnographic researcher must always bear in mind that it is his task to shed light on the ways of a people. It is people, and the world that they build, which concern him.

In applying this methodology to the study of specific groups, the ethnographer has two problems: (1) conceptually limiting the social world to manageable units of analysis and (2) developing the concepts necessary to examine each of these social units in holistic terms. In the study of a diffuse, sophisticated urban setting, it is difficult to delineate a unit of analysis that is at once independent and yet small enough to meet the requirements of the methodology and that can still be representative of the phenomena that one wishes to study.

Anthropologists who have undertaken studies in developed, industrialized cultures or sociologists who have employed anthropological methods in urban research have typically focused their observation on one of these five social units: (1) a *neighborhood,* as did Padilla (1958), Gans (1962), and Suttles (1969); (2) a *housing project,* as did Willmoth (1960) and Rainwater (1970); (3) a *gang or associational group,* as did Whyte (1955) and Liebow (1966); (4) a *community of deviants,* as did Lenznoff and Westley (1956), Reiss (1961), and Becker (1963); or (5) a *single family,* as did Lewis (1965).

Each of these, however, presents significant disadvantages as an object of study. Because the first unit, "the neighborhood," is often too large for complete study, one is often left wondering who actually served as informants for the research and how representative they were. Moreover, often it is the researcher who determines that his target area is a "neighborhood" or "community." This judgment begs the question of whether the area's inhabitants also see it as such. The housing project, on the other hand, which is certainly a more manageable unit in terms of size, is rarely a "naturally" occurring social entity. Tenants are usually admitted according to statutory regulations, which often involve criteria over which they have no control. (For example, in New York City an entire family can be disqualified if a single member has ever been convicted of a felony, even if that member is not living with the family.) Thus, it is problematic whether, considering the exclusionary criteria employed, the tenantry can be considered representative of anything but a rather narrowly defined statistical group. One could suggest that such a group is scarcely representative of the strata of the population that a study of underclass life is concerned with. The remaining three units (the gang, the community of deviants, and the single family) are eminently suited to study through participant methods. However, the exceedingly detailed data on only a single family makes it very difficult to extrapolate to a larger portion of the population. Also, the study of the gang and the deviant community provides a view of only a limited segment of the target population and is additionally suspect because it often restricts itself to but a single area of the persons' lives.

In my SRO study the entire hotel or tenement building was chosen as the unit of analysis. These buildings are not only suitable for study in terms of size but also, if carefully selected, capable of representing the whole of the target population. The need to observe several sites or locales was established early in the research. The slum hotel or SRO tenement is more than a building with rooms in it—it is a social system. Each building, because of the difference in tenant population, management personnel and policies, and other factors, has its own individual character. For example, when asked about a certain hotel, most people within the SRO community have some notion about it; certain buildings are known to be more violent than others, or "everyone knows" that narcotics are very easily accessible in some. In judging the buildings, tenants apply two major criteria: (1) appearance and facilities and (2) security. The latter, which often determines the physical condition of the building, is considered the more important of the two.

In studying the SRO community, one has to identify a set of boundaries that satisfied the requirements of the study's methodology without doing violence to the group's perception of the environment in which it operates. Sociologists have suggested a number of different approaches to the question of boundary definition. Some writers have conceptualized the process in terms of norms; a group's boundaries can be delineated by ascertaining where and when in social space the legitimacy of a specific norm subsides. This, then, marks the limit beyond which the normative force of the group does extend; people holding to other norms can be seen as members of other systems (Erikson, 1964). For others the question has been conceptualized in more simplistic terms: the group or little community is isolated in space (or time), and its boundaries are definitively marked geographically or in some other way signified by dimensions over which the group can exert no control.

Another approach to the problem of boundary definition utilizes the common-sense definitions held by the population under study. This approach is useful in understanding the ways in which people construct boundaries in a large, heterogeneous urban area—an area in which one finds overlapping use of the same geographical space by coterminously residing groups (Ross, 1962). With this perspective, the investigator can see how a person comes to define the area in which he operates as a "community" and thereby establishes some sense of territory, while not necessarily signifying any notion of "we-ness" or "consciousness of kind." Thus conceptualized, one is able to envision persons who perceive themselves as "members of a community" while not necessarily belonging to any group and interacting (in some cases) only minimally with those around them.

This perspective focuses attention on a specialized underclass community (in this case, SRO) by demonstrating how members restrict their daily round of interaction to places, persons, and institutions that are generally rejected by the coterminously residing middle and/or working class population. Knowledge of the community's boundaries and of the individual buildings which should be chosen as study sites derives from the limits indicated by the common-sense impressions of persons within the community. By utilizing this folk knowledge, one could construct a model defining some of the "stations" within the larger SRO world.

The recognition of such "stations" suggests the quality of social navigation—the ability to move about in a social milieu—and the significance of the various symbolic markets that delineate the important status positions in the milieu. The status represented by the different building units depends not on their geographical location but, as has been mentioned, primarily on the security afforded to their residents. In fact, groups or clusters of buildings that fall into separate status steps can be identified. Those highest on the scale are those most "closed"—i.e., those which make an effort to exclude "high risk" residents and which carefully control traffic into the buildings. Such units have elaborate security provisions, often including sign-in/sign-out policies. At the opposite extreme are the most "open" buildings; these each have more than one entrance and do little to control traffic into the building. Such units are often used for temporary refuge by purse snatchers and muggers who loiter in front of the hotel or tenement, waiting for a likely victim. Additionally, residents in such buildings are prey to criminals from outside who wait for the tenants to leave and then burgle their rooms. The most open buildings also employ no standards on accepting individuals; often, severely regressed alcoholics or addicts inhabit these units. Certain hotels and tenements are notorious among SRO people. Even those who have never been in such hotels as the Harvard or the Marseilles know the names and fear what they represent.

The more open SRO buildings house those individuals who have the least to hope for. These people are, indeed, socially terminal. The closed buildings, on the other hand, house a more upwardly mobile population; they contain many tenants who view these units simply as inexpensive temporary residences. Once one perceives the continuum along which these "stations" arrange themselves, the SRO community takes on a fuller character. A person enters this community (sometimes at birth, but not necessarily so), occupies several more or less well-defined status positions (usually accompanied by changes in physical situ), and ultimately exists (generally until death).

SUMMARY AND CONCLUSION

While the conduct of any ethnographic research will necessarily reflect the exigencies of the field situation, it is important to define the conceptual underpinnings of the work. This paper is an attempt at this. Several key concepts such as "community" and "deviance" are discussed, and it is argued that, to be methodologically effective, they must be translated into an interactionist context. The next step is a consideration of the implication of naturalism—specifically, naturalistic behaviorism—as a central organizing concept. The arguments conclude with an examination of how some of the key concepts might be operationalized for the study of urban underclass communities containing persons committed to patterns of behavior likely to be labeled as deviant.

This kind of conceptual analysis is needed to fully ground urban ethnography. Without a clear theoretical formulation, it is difficult to meaningfully relate any specific study to the larger body of social science knowledge. While I am not by any means advocating abandoning all previous urban ethnographies, the time for a self-conscious appraisal of our discipline, its assumptions and methods, is clearly at hand.

NOTE

1. The formulation of this section owes materially to a discussion of the problems of urban ethnography by Dr. Alan Harwood (1968).

REFERENCES

BALL, D. (1967). "Ethnography of an abortion clinic." Social Problems, 14:293-301.
BECKER, H.S. (1962). "Society as symbolic interaction." Pp. 188ff. in A. Rose (ed.), Human behavior and social process: An interactionist approach. Boston: Houghton Mifflin.
——— (1963). Outsiders. New York: Free Press.
BLUMER, H. (1962). "Society as symbolic interaction." In A. Rose (ed.), Human behavior and social process: An interactionist approach. Boston: Houghton Mifflin.
DENZIN, N. (1971). "The logic of naturalistic inquiry." Social Forces, 50:166-167.
DuWARS, R.E. (1962). "The definition of the situation as a community distinguishing characteristic." International Journal of Comparative Sociology, 3:263ff.
ERIKSON, K. (1964). "Notes on the sociology of deviance." Pp. 10-11 in H.S. Becker (ed.), The other side. New York: Free Press.
FREILICH, M. (1963). "Towards an operational definition of community." Rural Sociology, 28:122ff.
GANS, H. (1962). The urban villagers. New York: Free Press.

UNIVERSITY COLLEGE LIBRARY CARDIFF

HARWOOD, A. (1968). "Neighbor medical care demonstration." Unpublished manuscript, Bronx, New York.

HILLERY, G.A. (1955). "Definitions of community: Areas of agreement." Rural Sociology, 20(June):111-124.

——— (1959). "A critique of selected community concepts." Social Forces, 37(March): 236-242.

HIRSCHI, T. (1962). "The professional prostitute." Berkeley Journal of Sociology, 7:33-39.

HOLLINGSHEAD, B.A. (1948). "Community research: Development and present condition." American Sociological Review, 13:136-146.

LEMERT, E. (1964). "Social structure, social control and deviation." Pp. 81-82 in M.B. Clinard (ed.), Anomie and deviant behavior. New York: Macmillan.

LENZNOFF, M., and WESTLEY, W. (1956). "The homosexual community." Social Problems, 4:257-263.

LEWIS, O. (1965). La vida. New York: Vintage.

LIEBOW, E. (1967). Tally's corner. Boston: Little, Brown.

PADILLA, E. (1958). Up from Puerto Rico. New York: Columbia University Press.

PARK, R.E. (1952). Human communities. Glencoe, Ill.: Free Press.

POLSKY, N. (1964). "The hustler." Social Problems, 12(summer):3-15.

RAINWATER, L. (1970). Behind ghetto walls. Chicago: Aldine.

REDFIELD, R. (1953). The little community. Chicago: University of Chicago Press.

REISS, A.J. (1961). "The social integration of queers and peers." Social Problems, 9:102-120.

ROSS, L.H. (1962). "The local community: A survey approach." American Sociological Review, 27:75-84.

SIMPSON, R.L. (1965). "Sociology of the community: Current status and prospects." Rural Sociology, 30:127-149.

SUTHERLAND, E.H. (1973). The professional thief by a professional thief. Chicago: University of Chicago Press.

SUTTLES, G. (1969). The social order of the slum. Chicago: University of Chicago Press.

SUTTON, A., et al. (1960). "The concept of community." Rural Sociology, 25:197-203.

WHYTE, W.F. (1955). Street corner society (2nd ed.). Chicago: University of Chicago Press.

WILLMOTH, P. (1960). "Class and community at Dagenhom." Unpublished paper, Institute for Community Studies, London.

4

METHODOLOGICAL NOTES ON THE
EMPLOYMENT OF INDIGENOUS OBSERVERS

ANDREW L. WALKER and CHARLES W. LIDZ

The design of ethnographic research is itself an interesting sociological problem. The problem is multidimensional, involving the specificity of the ethnographer's goals, the complexity of the social system under analysis, the receptivity of the members to the researcher and his aims, the resources available to the researcher and the terms of their availability, the organization and size of the system to be studied, and a host of other subsidiary variables. The sheer complexity of these factors and their resistance to standardized categorization virtually guarantees the uniqueness of every ethnographic project—something, we believe, that most ethnographers relish.

The complexity and resistance to categorization of these "design parameters" have another, more troublesome consequence, however: it is difficult and perhaps impossible to devise and maintain a set of programmatic and evaluative guidelines for this kind of research

AUTHORS' NOTE: Work for this paper was partially funded by the National Institute of Mental Health, Narcotic Addict Treatment Program, grant no. 1H17MH16356.

(Cohen and Narroll, 1970). Perhaps over a lifetime an ethnographer may accumulate the personal wisdom to design infallible ethnographic research (provided he knows enough about the group to be studied in advance), but even then the road is long and rocky. Still, the recent increase in published discussions of the methodological problems of participant observation and ethnography indicates renewed interest in these problems; and, if not clear-cut guidelines, at least perhaps we are developing a list of matters that need consideration in planning and evaluating ethnographic research (McCall and Simons, 1969; Feldman, 1974). To contribut to this exchange, we wish herein to consider one available methodological technique: the employment of what are currently being called "indigenous observers."

At the heart of ethnographic research lies the need to collect the "stories" that subjects generate in the process of making sense of the world for practical purposes. No matter what the research design, these stories remain the basic data of ethnography, so any successful research design will seek to maximize the researcher's access to these stories. Depending on the factors mentioned above, though, a variety of alternative and complementary "routes" may be taken to these stories. The researcher may (for instance) simply locate himself at a communication node and share in the "news" circulating within the system; he may search out optimal informants; he may rigorously sample from the population in order to guarantee generalizability; and so on.

As the size and complexity of the system increases, though, the ability of the ethnographer personally to hear enough stories and to gain a representative sample of such stories decreases. Consequently, some ethnographic projects practically require the utilization of a research team, and once we start thinking in terms of a research team the idea of including people who have had direct experience with the social system rapidly comes to mind. Having such indigenous observers on staff gives the appearance of solving a series of practical and theoretical problems in this kind of research.

Another way of looking at the utilization of indigenous observers is to consider them not as a staff with practical experience with the phenomenon, but rather as part of the phenomenon who are paid to be part of the study. In this connection it is worth remembering that an ethnographic study is always a joint production of the ethnographer and his subjects, and there are inevitably gifts of one sort or another provided by the ethnographer to his subjects in return for cooperation. The question is whether or not this exchange relationship is best formalized into an employer-employee relationship.

However conceptualized, it seems fruitful to consider some of the problems of ethnographic research and the extent to which they can be solved through the employment of lay sociologists with an intimate familiarity with the phenomenon. However, first we will briefly describe our experience with indigenous observers.

A CASE STUDY OF THE
EMPLOYMENT OF INDIGENOUS OBSERVERS

In late 1968, the National Institute of Mental Health awarded a substantial grant to Herbert Kleber, M.D., for the establishment of an experimental drug abuse treatment center. Included in that grant were provisions for the creation and support of an "Epidemiology and Evaluation Unit" with a complex mandate, including that it assess "scientifically" the impact of this new treatment agency on the "drug problem" in the designated city. In order to fulfill that part of the grant, Kleber hired a research director, Leroy Gould, who was a sociologist primarily interested in matters of deviance and social control.

Gould decided to direct his attention to a study of the changes in the "system of heroin use and its control" in our target area, which he felt would satisfy the evaluation requirements of the grant. He hired the present authors, and, together, this staff of three sociologists (none of whom had previous experience in qualitative research) formed the professional core of the research unit. All three of us were familiar with and sympathetic to the methodological debates which deviance theory was generating in the 1960s, and we concluded that the object of our study could not be some "objective" drug problem, but rather a drug problem as it appeared to the various people who generated the events out of which the publicly certified drug problem was constituted (Walker and Lidz, 1974). The principal actors in those events were law enforcement personnel, medical personnel, and the illegal drug users, so our research strategy was to approach each of these "groups" separately and record their practical understandings of the system of heroin use and control.

In addition to these professional sociologists, the research unit also included several black ex-addicts. Their inclusion was not a carefully conceived research strategy, but rather a practical accommodation to mundane organizational options. That is, the first of these ex-addicts was one of several "star patients" in the methadone program. The directors of the various clinical programs were eager to use ex-addicts as "paraprofessional" clinicians and had offered this person a halftime position as a counselor. Since he was so verbally adept and willing to share his street experiences, his "remaining" halftime was offered to the research unit. This person was a very skilled negotiator, though, and managed to convince the research staff and the rest of the directors that it would be a good idea to employ his wife (who was also an ex-addict on the methadone program) as well. Thus we were essentially offered the services of two knowledgeable ex-addicts "for free," in that their appointment would not cost us any of our already allocated budgetary resources.

Since the research design was still flexible, there was no great difficulty in incorporating these two individuals into the staff. Andrew Walker had assumed responsibility for constructing an ethnography of the "streets," and his first thought was to use the two new "research associates" to cover the black heroin scene—a project that had been worrying him quite a bit. While he personally felt reasonably comfortable in interaction with "street blacks," early experience and outside advice had suggested that he was going to have a great deal of difficulty establishing the kind of rapport that traditional ethnography requires (Junker, 1960).

In addition, Walker was becoming increasingly interested in white heroin use, which was beginning to look significant in 1969. So with some relief, he turned the job of collecting data of black heroin use to his new associates. However, this produced new problems, even as it solved others.

First came the inevitable query: "What do you want us to do?" It rapidly became clear that our answer of "Go out and find out what is happening and come back and write it up" simply would not do. To begin with, they did not see why they had to gather data about something they had spent their whole lives doing. Second, their idea and Walker's idea of what were the relevant issues did not completely coincide. Thus there seemed to be a need for greater specificity. Walker settled the matter by asking them to do two things. First of all, the research unit was writing quite a few working papers then, not only about the streets but also about the cops and the clinic. He asked them both to read everyting that was circulating and to attend the criticism sessions. In this regard, Walker wanted both to expose them to "professional ethnography" and to use them as "lay experts" who could validate or invalidate our professional accounts of their life-world. Since we were concerned with uncovering the common-sense assumptions of the protagonists in the drug problem and since these two individuals were certified protagonists, we assumed that they were competent (if not final) judges of the adequacy of our efforts.

Second, Walker asked his associates to prepare their own accounts of the life-world of the black addict. Since the woman had worked as a prostitute and we were particularly interested in hustling, he asked her to start with a paper on prostitution; and since the man had been part of the drug scene in our area for over a decade, Walker asked him to start with a paper on the historical development of the current "street scene." Within a few months, the male associate had finished a historical piece that was interesting and informative, but largely unsubstantiated.

At our urging, his wife had followed a more acceptable methodology in interviewing a number of local prostitutes, but she found it almost impossible to integrate her material into a descriptive account. Like so many poor Americans, she had never learned to express herself well in writing, and she felt inadequate because the rest of the staff was so much more proficient with pen and paper. As a practical and expedient solution to this problem, we moved her desk into Walker's office, and he began to spend much more time with her, ostensibly helping her write her paper, but actually eliciting a verbal version of the same material. Of course, it took Walker a while to realize that this was what was going on, but eventually he started taking notes on their "office-mate" conversations. She understood that he was taking notes, but they never actually agreed to forgo the written report. In fact, just before her death, she finally finished the paper that she had started 18 months previously. During that period, though, she had given us a tremendous amount of data on the life-world of the addicted black woman. Those data did not come as either the polished papers and notes of an "assistant ethnographer" or the raw data of an informant, but rather as unstructured "oral reports."

Walker's relationship with her husband was considerably different. He was a reasonably proficient writer and very skilled verbally, which meant that we had no trouble obtaining interesting accounts from him. The problem with him was that the very skills which made him attractive as a researcher also made him attractive as a clinician and clinical administrator. Since our research was being carried out in the organizational context of a clinical program, he was often subject to conflicting demands from the clinical and research units. His background as a street junkie did not prepare him well to juggle organizational demands, and he found it difficult to apportion his time appropriately. In practice, this meant that he tended to disregard the need to collect data systematically, relying instead on his own experience and intuition for his data. We should emphasize that he was a very experienced and perceptive street addict, and his contributions were invaluable to us, but we were never really successful in getting him to concentrate on the routine work of *collecting* stories about the world.

Walker worked very closely and productively with these two people for about 18 months. Then the woman died suddenly, of asthma, and several months later her husband was appointed full-time assistant director of the methadone maintenance clinic. Replacing these two proved to be very difficult, largely for organizational reasons. The basic problem was that working for the research unit had become a very prestigious position, and the clinical directors were extremely anxious lest the "wrong" people be given this reward. Obviously, as far as the clinicians were concerned, the positions could not go to unreformed addicts. How would it look for a drug abuse clinic to employ an addict? That meant that the positions could go only to ex-addicts, and the only way to become an ex-addict is to enter a treatment program and be certified as an ex-addict by the clinicians in that program. But since our agency was the only legitimate agency in town, this meant that only members of our programs could be acceptable to the clinicians. Moreover, they could not permit the position to be offered to someone who had been "counterproductive" in a treatment program, so that further narrowed the field to those patients who had managed to please their clinical overseers.

Although we had significant reservations about these selection criteria, we looked carefully at all the candidates—and then rejected them all. After several months of wasting quite a bit of time on this matter, we finally found two acceptable candidates, one of whom was one of the leaders of the local "grass-roots" drug abuse referral agency which had been co-opted by Kleber's Drug Dependence Unit, and the other was one of the first "graduates" (and most vocal critic) of the methadone program who had taken a white-collar job with a private service agency. Both had been prominent local black addicts, both had been certified as ex-addicts, and both maintained extensive contacts with the current heroin scene.

In hiring these two individuals, we somehow managed to recreate the original situation of having one articulate associate who was too busy to put in the disciplined effort necessary for responsible research, and another associate who was tremendously interested in the work but could not express himself well in writing. So the patterns of utilization which had emerged with our first pair of associates continued with the second. From our articulate associate we received incisive and well-directed feedback and criticism, but very little original material. By the time he was hired, though, we had already completed two years of fieldwork and were beginning to put our material into coherent form, so his criticism was both welcome and appropriate.

Our relations with the other associate were more complicated, but more productive as well. This productivity seemed to depend on a close working relationship with Walker. Walker asked him to work on two papers: one on the heroin distribution system and the other on "hustling." Neither paper ever materialized, but he understood the need to find information rather than to make it up. So over the next two years he brought Walker into contact with a variety of dope dealers, hustlers, and other street types with whom Walker would never have been able to establish contact on his own. Perhaps because after several years of field research Walker was finally learning to manage his relations with black ex-addicts, his relations with this individual were the most satisfactory of all the research relationships. Walker was able to explain, without apology or embroidery, what he needed, and this associate was able to help him find it. Sometimes the associate conducted interviews in the field and gave Walker tape recordings; sometimes he brought Walker to addicts who would be fruitful sources; and many times he listened to and corrected our formulations of black addicts' conceptions of the world.

Shortly after this individual came to work with us, we began to organize our data into a body for publication. Because our data on the black heroin-using community had been collected so unsystematically (we estimated that there were perhaps 800 to 1,000 black regular users of heroin in our target area, and we had met perhaps 100), we were less than confident of our ability to portray their world adequately. This particular person supplied not only enough verbal material to cover at least the outline of that world but also enough independent corroboration to assure us of the validity of that information.

A parallel but somewhat different problem arose in the research on the legal control of drugs in the same project, which was Lidz's responsibility. Usually when one thinks about indigenous observers in ethnographic studies, one thinks about lower-class street people of the sort that we have been discussing. However, when Lidz began to observe the criminal courts, the police, and other aspects of the legal control of drugs, he found that there existed a whole frame of reference for these activities which was largely alien to him—namely, "the law." This problem is familiar to the anthropologist who goes into an alien society and spends years learning the language and culture of an alien tribe. While this problem was perhaps not quite so severe in our case,[1] the easiest solution seemed to be to hire one of the "natives"—namely, a certified lawyer—to help.

When the lawyer came to work with us, it rapidly became apparent that we had underestimated the complexity and peculiarity of doing ethnography. Although he understood the concept of fieldwork and the need to gather data, the procedures of *doing analysis* remained something of a mystery to him. He took it for granted that we had specialized knowledge of how to analyze data and never felt comfortable doing it himself. His own writing was done largely within the context of legal definitions of how the court was supposed to operate.

Like our street indigenous observers, the lawyer's special use to the research project was to offer up his own specialized knowledge when needed. He could relate our sociological formulations to the law and clarify the legal understanding which those we observed were employing. Yet he was never able to produce fully ethnographic accounts of the legal system, for he was not able to go beyond the formal and informal legal categories to the ethnographic categories of the life-world.

Before leaving this descriptive section, we should also mention that there were various other positions on the research staff which did not specifically involve the collection of ethnographic data. The research unit was also responsible for collecting and reporting various statistics on the operation of the clinic. Whenever possible, we filled these positions with "lay experts" about the streets, usually program members but in one case a nurse who had left a clinical position. For the most part, these lay experts were perfectly capable in these positions, and they were additional informal sources of ethnographic data. They read and criticized all of our writings and often went out of their way to supply us with additional information and contacts. While their utilization in this regard was anything but systematic, they added considerably to our data base.

THE FUNCTIONS OF INDIGENOUS OBSERVER STAFF

Having described our four-year experience with ex-addict and legally trained research associates, we will now analytically consider some of the ways in which indigenous observers can be utilized in ethnographic research. For convenience, we can consider four categories of function: informant, facilitator, ethnographer, and validator.

The Indigenous Observer as Informant

The function of the indigenous observer with which traditional ethnography is the most comfortable is that of informant. Informants do not have to understand the nature of the ethnographic enterprise. All that is necessary is that they trust the ethnographer sufficiently to "divulge their world" to him, that is, to explain the meaning of symbols, actions, and other objects in the culture of which they are a part and which the ethnographer is studying. Since it is the ethnographer's task to uncover that world, informants are absolutely essential to him. Ethnography conceives of the world as a subjective construct; hence, unless some of those with intimate knowledge of that world share their constructions with the researcher, he is lost and must attempt to infer "ordering categories" from observable events, which is definitely a dangerous procedure.

Fortunately, the operation of ordinary social interaction seems to require intersubjectivity. Thus competent members of a social system learn to share their understandings of the world with other members, and an interpersonally skilled ethnographer learns how to elicit these understandings without questioning their common-sense character. Still, it would be incredibly naive to believe that informants share their common sense with the ethnographer simply because intersubjectivity is part of the everyday world. Presumably there are many possible reasons for an informant to share his world with a researcher: religious duty, prestige, anticipated economic or political gain, proselytization, and so on. And it seems reasonable to assume that the reasons for an informant's cooperation will color the knowledge which is shared.

Since our project had the resources available, we tried to put as many people with this type of knowledge on the payroll as possible, on the theory that in contemporary America the idea of cooperative relations between employer and employee is well enough accepted that it would provide the common-sense grounding for long-term communicative relationships between ethnographers and informants. By contemporary standards, it also is a convenient solution to the ethical problems of eliciting information from subjects who do not know the purposes for which they are giving the information, since it gives the informants access to the "inner workings" of the ethnographic project. We will return to this point in the conclusion.

This is not to say that hiring informants is a perfect solution to the data-collection problem. Many potential informants are not interested in going to work for an ethnographic project, and, if the ethnographer relies solely on his employees, he will certainly get an incomplete and misleading view of the system that he is studying. Furthermore, the ethnographer must guard against the dangers of relying exclusively on his paid informants, who are much easier to find and cooperate more easily. This is a problem precisely because of the advantages of employee informants who are apt to be more productive and consistent than the unpaid variety.

Using the indigenous observer largely as a paid informant has serious limits. As Schutz (1967) and Garfinkel (1967) have noted, the accounts generated retrospectively are different from accounts generated in the process of an activity. Indeed, the knowledge that accounts of activities are "situated" is one of the strongest arguments for doing ethnography. The explanation that an addict gives for using heroin as he is cooking it up is markedly different from the explanation that he gives on an intake question when trying to get into a drug program. Likewise, one must suspect that the account that he will give sitting in an office over coffee with his "boss" will not be quite the same as an account "on the scene." Thus, while the use of indigenous observers as informants is very helpful in some ways, it also poses serious dangers.

The Indigenous Observer as Facilitator

In addition to supplying "raw data," the indigenous observer may also serve as an invaluable "social assistant" to the professional ethnographer (Cohen et al., 1970). As a practical expert on the system under study, the indigenous observer should be capable of teaching the ethnographer how to participate effectively in that system (if only as a role model). In a sense, the indigenous observer can be used as a socialization agent, teaching the ethnographer the "dos and don'ts" of the system, styles of dress and language, and the cast of major actors. In a closed and hostile system such as the drug-using subculture, and to a lesser extent the court system, the success of the ethnographer's project depends on his ability to fit into the system with minimal friction. Of course, the necessity for native assistance depends on the particular characteristics of the system and the ethnographer. For instance, because of his own background, Walker was prepared to mingle freely with white heroin users, but, without the help of his black research associates, he never would have been able to gain access to the black subculture.

In the court system which we studied, an ethnographer was an unknown role, but a lawyer working for another "agency" was not. As a credentialed member of the legal profession, our lawyer, in spite of the fact that previously he had not been a member of this specific legal community, fitted in quite well and served as both a role model and a legitimate introduction for our sociological observer. Although the problem of entrée was not nearly as serious in court as on the streets, the lawyer's credentials did help both observers.

An extension of this socialization function is the use of native associates to establish "credibility." Needless to say, in street society, a person's personal reputation is a critical matter. Ultimately that reputation will be based on performance, but, during periods of initial contact, a quasi-identity can be established through endorsement by accepted regulars. While Walker never asked his associates to endorse him on the streets, they realized that this was essential and provided unsolicited endorsements. In doing so, they were putting their own reputations on the line, and their trust was deeply appreciated.

This, of course, points to the importance of selecting the proper person to function as the indigenous observer. Although it has been observed that marginal men have a more insightful understanding of their social world, they are poor introductions. W.F. Whyte's famous study of Cornerville depended very largely on the willingness of an important local leader to vouch for him, as Whyte readily acknowledged (Whyte, 1955, Appendix). If access is needed, the individual who will establish the ethnographer's credentials must be well thought of by the other participants in the system.

The final and most specific sense of facilitation by indigenous observers is that they can arrange and manage interview situations which would be beyond the reach of even the most accomplished ethnographer. In the street observations, Walker was able to explain "holes" in his data to our research associates, and often they could set up interviews with persons who could supply appropriate material. Interviews of this sort were very pleasant and productive since the associate was usually present and could steer conversation to the relevant points. Because of this, in some ways our data from the black subculture were more complete than our data from the white subculture, since the white subculture was researched without any staff assistance. Likewise, the lawyer was able to facilitate data gathering in joint interviews by steering questions into legal areas that Lidz was not even aware existed.

The Indigenous Observer as Ethnographer

A third possibility for indigenous observers is to actually function as ethnographers on their own. If the purpose of ethnography is to capture the subjective but interpersonal world of a particular group, then why not hire one or more of the members of this group to produce these accounts? Would not this avoid the distortion introduced by a professional ethnographer? (Sutherland, 1937). Unfortunately, it was in this area that we had the most difficulty, and we suspect that the problems are nearly insurmountable. There seem to be two major areas of difficulty: the "impractical" nature of ethnography itself and, for the street ethnography, the level of written communication skills of most natives.

By far, we think the more difficult problem lies in the nature of ethnography. We have found it nearly impossible to tell any of our associates how to do an ethnography. In part this was due to our own uncertainties and the absence of clear-cut formulations of what ethnography is in the literature, but we believe that it had more to do with the necessarily practical orientation that indigenous observers bring into the research situation. After all, it was precisely because of their "practical" expertise in the social worlds that we were studying that we had hoped that they would be able to add to our work. But, because of this practical orientation, they had great difficulty understanding why anyone would want to describe the world "the way it appears to the participants." They could not see why any outsider would want such a description (cf. Manocchio and Dunn, 1970). If asked to describe the world as it "really is," they could do so (often with a passion); but, in doing so, they were functioning as informants rather than ethnographers since they always imbued their categories with an "objective" character. They could give cogent accounts of "how addicts relate to cops," "how people get into prostitution," or "the best way to defend a case involving illegal entry," but they always construed these accounts as the "inside story" which is objective, true, and incontestable (McCaghy et al., 1968). Clearly, accounts such as these can be the gist of ethnography, but, in and of themselves, from the ethnographers point of view, they are epistemologically presumptuous. Ethnography does not involve simply a presentation of the point of view of the subject. It must also place that account in perspective. The practical problem, which seemed to be almost unsolvable, became one of trying to make the indigenous observer aware of the subtleties of the matter without "putting him down" or discouraging further effort. In our experience, the lawyer was a slightly better ethnographer than the ex-addicts, but to him it did not seem to be a good use of his time either.

The second problem in using indigenous observers as native ethnographers, which did not apply to our legal associate or to all of our ex-addicts, is that the construction of sound ethnography requires a level and style of writing that is rare in most subcultures (cf. Campbell, 1955). This is not to say that addicts are all illiterate. To the contrary, we found various pieces of both prose and poetry which were striking in both content and style. But the enterprise of literal description seems to require both an extensive vocabulary and a great deal of literary discipline. While there are clearly people in the heroin subculture who have these skills and we employed two of them, they are in short supply and high demand. Those who possess these skills often seem to be ambitious to the point where they choose routes to success other than academic ethnography. So, unless an ethnographic project has the time and resources to train *and retain* native ethnographers, it seems impractical to count on them for this function.

The Indigenous Observer as Validator

A final function of indigenous observers, which we took quite seriously in our project, is the validation of the resulting ethnographic accounts. As we all know, no matter how closely the ethnographer works with his data, the resulting accounts will necessarily represent a synthesis of those data. The accounts go beyond the utterances of any particular subject and consequently become utterances of the ethnographer. Thus the validity of any ethnographic account is always problematic.

One conceivable way of validating an ethnographic account is to show the consistency of the components of that account with the data available to the writer, but this technique ignores the emergent characteristics of the entire account. We partially solved this problem by having our manuscripts reviewed exhaustively by our "lay experts." *Any* questions or qualifications that they had about the manuscripts were fully resolved before the material was released. Initially we feared that none of our accounts would be completely acceptable to the subjects, but, with a great deal of effort on both our and their parts, eventually we were all satisfied.

With regard to this particular problem, it was our experience that our staff associates were freer and more comfortable in their criticism than ordinary subjects in the target population. There seemed to be two reasons. First, in spite of the above-mentioned problems, our associates understood the nature of ethnography far better than "unaffiliated informants" and could consequently offer more germane suggestions. Second, "unaffiliated informants" seemed far less comfortable in taking issue with statements we made. That is, in the target population, there was a strong tendency to defer to the authority of the social scientist. They had (understandably) a great deal of trouble telling us "you're wrong." Since our research associates were well aware of the limitations of our data, they could point out our mistakes without appearing to insult us.

RESEARCH PROBLEMS GENERATED BY INDIGENOUS OBSERVERS

Having dwelt at some length on the potential benefits of employing indigenous observers, we would like to balance the discussion by raising some of the methodological problems which they are liable to generate. These problems seem to fall within three general categories: unfamiliarity wtih social scientific methodology, involvement in street politics, and the maintenance of intrastaff relations.

Methodological Naiveté

At the very beginning of this chapter, we suggested that professional ethnographers do not have a well-developed set of formal methodological rules. If this is so, then we should not be surprised that indigenous observers have trouble understanding such problems of data as validity, reliability, and generalizability. We found it extremely difficult to communicate the social scientist's concern for these matters to our associates.

As a result, most of our associates were haphazard in their data-collection techniques. In its most extreme form, this meant that they tended to rely on their own ideas and experiences for data, rather than search rigorously for those data in the target population. But, even when they realized the need to elicit the impressions of others, they relied heavily on their friends for information. Thus the information that they supplied actually reflected the conceptions that were shared by a narrow clique, rather than a distribution of beliefs characterizing the entire social system. This can be somewhat mitigated by employing experts who do not come from the local area. Our lawyer, drawn from another city, was less prone to this difficulty. Of course it is worth noting that trained ethnographers are not exempt from this problem. Everyone tends to feel that the people he or she likes are better sources, but at least a trained ethnographer understands the methodological problems involved.

Also, since our associates tended to think of their beliefs as objectively true, they underrepresented and even discounted contrary beliefs held by other members of the social system. They apparently felt that a presentation of those beliefs would undermine the veracity of their accounts and ultimately their own credibility. We tried to convince them that their credibility depended on the faithfulness with which they collected and reported data, not on the objective veracity of those data; but this distinction was largely lost in translation.

Professional Involvement in the Politics of the System Under Study

It is presumably a rare social system that can be characterized as conflict-free. Especially in groups that have to deal with scarce resources and intense external pressure, internal dissent and hostility are facts of life, and various factions coalesce in contention for real and symbolic rewards. In all the groups that we studied there was considerable distrust and hostility between factions. The introduction of a research project into a system of this sort is a significant political event, and the actions taken by the ethnographer will acquire significant political meaning (Kahn and Mann, 1952).

A skilled professional ethnographer working alone has enough problems avoiding identification with any particular faction and must carefully and evenly distribute his attention. When, however, a project employs members of the system, it almost necessarily becomes involved in the system's politics. In practical terms, this may involve pressure to protect certain subjects from external pressure, show preference for certain subjects, or degrade others. We can think of no particular guidelines for the ethnographer in this situation, except to suggest that some forethought will help. Once again, employing experts whose practical experience is not local helps, but, of course, one loses many advantages this way as well.

Of more concern to us are the methodological implications. The researcher's stock in trade is the free flow of information, and this is precisely what is restricted by these factional hostilities. By employing and thereby favoring members of one or more factions, the entire project becomes identified with those particular cliques. Unless remedial steps are taken, the resulting ethnography will reflect the biases of these cliques, not only because the indigenous observers will be inputting these biases but also because the professional ethnographers will not be able to establish satisfactory and productive relationships with the members of other contending factions. However, the researcher must avoid any tendency to disavow his relationship with his native associates, since that would leave him without any credentials at all (at least in the early stages of research). Thus the situation may become quite difficult, and the researcher must develop some procedures for minimizing the effects of partisan politics (Sellitz et al., 1961:214-215; Junker, 1960:36; Gold, 1958; Lofland, 1971:111).

Intrastaff Relationships

We raise the issue of intrastaff relationships with considerable hesitancy, since there are so many variables which come into play in the relationship within a research team. Some of our research associates "took us to the cleaners" for literally thousands of dollars, while others provided assistance and direction that was literally invaluable. Fortunately, we had sufficient financial and organizational resources that we could absorb our losses without seriously jeopardizing the overall project. Consequently, we never really had to confront our own organizational deficiencies.

It seems to us that most of these deficiencies stemmed from the dissimilarities between ethnography and any of the routine activities with which most of our associates were familiar. All of our ex-addict associates had survived and succeeded by mastering the "art of the hustle," which relies heavily on opportunism, deception, and self-reliance. Needless to say, these particular qualities are not all that beneficial to an ethnographic team. We honestly do not believe that our associates tried to deceive us (with perhaps one insignificant exception), but they were sometimes at a loss to figure out what was expected of them. The professionals on the staff made a determined effort to train them, but we felt it inadvisable to establish a strong teacher-student relationship, since we felt it inappropriate to "correct" their work. Similarly, we felt that emphasizing the authority inherent in the employer-employee relationship would only make us more susceptible to the "hustle." We *needed* our associates, and we let them know that.

CONCLUSION

At the very beginning of this essay, it was suggested that no two ethnographic projects will be the same since there are so many independent factors which determine both the design and the execution of projects. What would be appropriate for one project would be disastrous for another. Rather than trying to announce rules for how and when to employ indigenous observers, we have instead reported one case in which such paid lay experts were integral to the execution of the work. We also considered the potential contributions of indigenous observers to various phases of the ethnographic project. Finally, we suggested that the employment of indigenous observers may introduce additional complications to the research. These complications are sometimes difficult to fully anticipate, but the prudent ethnographer is well advised to think through and plan for both the theoretical and the practical ramifications.

One final point, which was mentioned above, concerns the ethics of employing local talent. In this regard, we observed that paid native associates were probably able to give a more meaningful informed consent than "unaffiliated informants." In a much larger sense, though, ethnographers (and *all* social scientists) are heavily in debt to their subjects. That debt is always acknowledged in the preface of published ethnographies, but far too few subjects ever read those acknowledgments, and, even then, they seem paltry to those who read them. We propose that the employment of native associates (at least in contemporary America) is a far more ethically satisfying response to that debt, since it offers the subjects several "things" which are more meaningful than "eternal gratitude."

First, the employment of native associates offers the subjects tangible evidence of *respect*. Rather than seeing a social system as a "vein of gold" to be mined by the professional, the employment of associates communicates the view that *any* ethnography is a joint production of the subjects and the professional. Of course employment per se is not a good and sufficient demonstration for every possible system that ethnographers might want to study, but it works well for the urban poor.

Second, the employment of native associates gives at least a few subjects a chance to improve their circumstances as a result of their work on the study. In contemporary America, poor (and discriminated-against) people are well aware that social scientists come into their community for a few months in order to write a book as a way of succeeding in the academy. They realize that much of the money spent "on the poor" is really spent paying (relatively) rich people to study the poor. The resulting bitterness is an impediment to the collection of suitable data, but the problem is moral as well as practical. While the employment of a few natives certainly is not a complete solution to this problem, it serves to communicate the ethnographer's concern for his obligation to his subjects.

NOTE

1. The similarity is, however, greater than it may appear at first glance. After all, it takes a law student three years of intensive study to become a certified lawyer. The law is complex, and Durkheim's (1947) analyses of social structure very largely amount to an analysis of formal law.

REFERENCES

CAMPBELL, D. (1955). "The informant in quantitative research." American Journal of Sociology, 60:339-342.
COHEN, R., LANGNESS, L.L., MIDDLETON, J., UCHENDU, V.C., and VANSTONE, J.W. (1970). "Entry into the field." In R. Narroll and R. Cohen (eds.), Handbook of method in cultural anthropology. New York: Columbia University Press.
COHEN, R., and NARROLL, R. (1970). "Introduction." In R. Narroll and R. Cohen (eds.), Handbook of method in cultural anthropology. New York: Columbia University Press.
DURKHEIM, E. (1947). The division of labor in society. New York: Free Press.
FELDMAN, H. (1974). Street status and the drug researcher: Issues in participant observation. Washington, D.C.: Drug Abuse Council.

GARFINKEL, H. (1967). Studies in ethnomethodology. Englewood Cliffs, N.J.: Prentice-Hall.

GOLD, R. (1958). "Roles in sociological field observation." Social Forces, 36:217-223.

JUNKER, B. (1960). Fieldwork: An introduction to the social sciences. Chicago: University of Chicago Press.

KAHN, R., and MANN, F. (1952). "Developing research partnerships." Journal of Social Issues, 8:4-10.

LOFLAND, J. (1971). Analysing social settings. Belmont, Calif.: Wadsworth.

MANOCCHIO, A., and DUNN, J. (1970). The time game: Two views of a prison. Beverly Hills, Calif.: Sage.

McCAGHY, C., SKIPPER, J., Jr., and LEFTON, M. (1968). In their own behalf: Voices from the margin. New York: Appleton-Century-Crofts.

McCALL, G., and SIMMONS, J.L. (eds., 1969). Issues in participant observation. Reading, Mass.: Addison-Wesley.

SCHUTZ, A. (1967). The phenomenology of the social world (G. Walsh and F. Lehnert, trans.). Evanston, Ill.: Northwestern University Press.

SELLITZ, C., JAHODA, M., DEUTSCH, M., and COOK, S. (1961). Research methods in social relations (rev. ed.). New York: Holt, Rinehart and Winston.

SUTHERLAND, E. (ed., 1937). The professional thief. Chicago: University of Chicago Press.

WALKER, A., and LIDZ, C. (1974). "Preface: Technical notes for social scientists." In Gould et al. (eds.), Connections: Notes from the heroin world. New Haven, Conn.: Yale University Press.

WHYTE, W.F. (1955). Street corner society: The social structure of an Italian slum (2nd ed.). Chicago: University of Chicago Press.

5

NETWORK ANALYSIS AS A
METHODOLOGICAL APPROACH TO THE STUDY OF
DRUG USE IN A LATIN CITY

WILLIAM R. TRUE and JOAN H. TRUE

As students of the use of hallucinogens in underdeveloped societies have long understood, drug use takes its form and assumes its meaning from the particular sociocultural context in which it occurs (Furst, 1972; Harner, 1973; Rubin and Comitas, 1975). Drug use, therefore, must be studied as a part of culture. Its physiological and psychological effects must be examined with reference to the context which provides the circumstances and the interpretations circumscribing the drug-using experience. As Goode points out, drug use "cannot be understood apart from the web of social relations in which it is implicated" (1969:55).

This was the perspective of researchers who conducted a two-year cross-cultural, transdisciplinary study on chronic marijuana use in San José, Costa Rica. Funded by the National Institute on Drug Abuse in 1973[1], this study called for extensive sociocultural and biomedical studies of a matched sample of 41 working class users of marijuana and 41 nonusers. The purpose of the research was to obtain in-depth data on the sociocultural context of chronic marijuana use (chronic use defined as 10 years or more of use), the effects of use on interpersonal relations, motivation, job perform-ance, and career development, as well as possible physiological effects as indicated by a complex battery of medical and neuro-psychological tests.

The sociocultural component of the project was, in effect, a study of Costa Rican society, with special reference to the drug theme about which other social phenomena were ordered when observed and recorded. The researchers examined marijuana use among working class men in San José, focusing on behavior characteristics of that stratum of Costa Rican society.

This research afforded an opportunity to refine and elaborate ethnographic procedures traditionally used by anthropologists. The analytical use of social networks as method and theory was particularly appropriate for the study and enabled us to cope with the complex, discontinuous urban environment of San José. Through repeated contact with certain key individuals whose personal networks were extensive, we were able to gain access to informal relational groupings from which we selected our sample. Our incorporation into these social networks enabled us later to obtain in-depth data on the dynamics of working class life in San José and the integral, functional nature of marijuana use in the lives of some of its members.

The responsibility for finding the sample population rested with the anthropologists who were to recruit potential participants from natural, ongoing social settings and enlist their voluntary cooperation for the two-year study.

The first year of the study was spent recruiting a base sample of 240 subjects from which the final matched sample would be selected; 84 of the original 240 were users, and 156 were nonusers. Twice as many nonusers were recruited to give the researchers considerable latitude in matching the controls with the users.

Once the 240 were recruited, the final sample were selected, a process lasting two months. Forty-one users were matched with 41 nonusers on a one-to-one basis using seven criteria: age, sex, marital status, education, occupation, alcohol consumption, and tobacco consumption.[2] The recruitment and selection of a single final sample for all phases of the study was central to the research design, providing cohesion in the comparative analysis of biomedical and sociocultural data. Thus, data could be interfaced from all phases of the study.

A network approach was used for the recruitment and selection of participants in order to gain entry into the social world of working class San José, permitting in the process a view of marijuana use as an everyday customary activity. The setting for the study was the capital city of Costa Rica, San José. Its urban environment defined the city as the residential base and social and economic world of the study's subjects.

SAN JOSE: AN OVERVIEW

San José is home to almost a half million residents and is located on the broad intramountain valley commonly referred to as the central plateau at an altitude of 1,160 meters (3,770 feet). Within 50 kilometers of San José are the other three major cities of Costa Rica. With the concentration of population and commercial activity, the area completely dominates the rest of the country.

This dominance, however, was not always the case. From its discovery by conquistador Juan de Cavallón in 1561 until relatively recent times, the central plateau was a rustic farming complex with only rudimentary village complexes. The Spanish found neither gold nor willing Indians to exploit, and the area was a colonial backwater which was utterly ignored. The nearly complete absence of colonial buildings today reflects the lack of attention given Costa Rica by the vice-royalty in Guatemala.

According to the Costa Rican Academy of Geography and History, San José was founded in 1737 (Academia de Geografía y Historia, 1952). By the end of the 18th century, the city had grown only to slightly under 5,000 inhabitants (Rodriguez and Teran, 1967:27). When independence from Spain was proclaimed in 1821, it took several months for word to reach Costa Rica from Guatemala, and belated celebrations were held in the villages on the plateau.

During the 19th century the internal municipal organization of

San José took place, with appropriate administrative units and utility services. The first census of the country in 1864 showed that San José had grown to slightly less than 9,000 residents. During the second half of the 19th century, the opening of the British market for coffee symbolized the first significant participation in world commerce on the part of Costa Rica. This discovery of economic potential was associated with the beginnings of the population growth which saw the central plateau intensively urbanized in the San José region during the first half of the 20th century. From 1927 to 1973, the city's population increased from 89,006 to 436,862 (Ministerio de Obras Públicas y Transportes, 1973:5).

This population increase has resulted in extensive development of residential areas near the center of the city. These areas grew in two surges. The first took place during the first two decades of this century, which saw the formation of the southern barrios from which many of our working class subjects were drawn. These neighborhoods were no more than a few miles from the center of town and were largely established in their present configurations by the early 1920s (Rodriguez and Teran, 1967:74). It is reported that during the early 1920s the density of housing had greatly increased, with some residences noticeably impoverished and the majority built contiguous with one another (Rodriguez and Teran, 1967:76). A second surge is reported for the late 1930s and 1940s, when a second set of sourthern working class barrios developed farther out than the first, and a complex of neighborhoods east of the center emerged. These recently formed zones also provided a number of subjects for the study. Working class men with jobs in the metropolitan area live with their families in these areas.

Construction of housing since the 1950s has also been intense, the most notable examples being the government housing authority projects south and west of the city's center. The government has been ambitious in providing housing and urban services to this new urban population, and although residents' expectations about the quality of services have exceeded actual accomplishment, vital services and transportation arteries have been established. Of particular note is the extensive system of bus routes which provides convenient, cheap transportation to the entire urban population.

Although rapid population growth has dramatically changed the physical configuration of the city, traditional patterns of traveling through the city via the heart of San José have not changed. All bus routes either feed into the Central Park facing the cathedral or to special shops within a few blocks. There is no interneighborhood service, unless the individual's stop happens to be on the route back to the center of town. Upon reaching the Central Park, a rider must switch to the appropriate bus to go back out to his destination. This centrality of interaction may be vividly witnessed at rush hour, when seemingly endless charges of exhaust-belching buses roar along the edges of the Central Park, unloading and loading at the same time, often in not more than a minute or two. Police are present, frantically blowing whistles to keep the buses from waiting too long to load. Waiting for the bus marked for their neighborhood, hundreds of passengers are watching the approaching buses.

The Central Park and its adjacent streets are the most dramatic of the interaction nodes we observed and are important for the concentration of activities engaged in by San José residents to be found in the immediate area. The simple confluence of activity through the park and its perimeters practically guarantees meeting an acquaintance. There are a number of individuals who are fixtures in the central area, including several different groupings of shoeshine boys, a couple of guards, traffic police, an evangelist, lottery salespersons, money changers, newspaper vendors, indigent beggars and musicians, car washers and self-appointed guardians, full-time loiterers, and, of course, full-time employees of the bars, restaurants, and commercial establishments. Many of these persons have assumed the role of information brokers, and often a message left with someone in the Central Park will be delivered the same day. Ringed around the park are the city's most popular movie theaters and several crowded all-night restaurants and bars. Within a couple of blocks, there are a number of dance halls where contact with prostitutes can be made.

Without walking more than two blocks from the Central Park, one can experience the extremes of San José life. The elegant Gran Hotel Costa Rica and National Theater provide stark contrast to the cheap bars and brothels only a few hundred yards away. This lack of discrete specialization of the central area of the city is evidence of its role in the lives of a wide range of San José residents and provides a point of reference and identification in a city where so much is occurring away from the center in the residential and industrial areas.

This change is occurring at a rapid rate and is most manifest in the ubiquitous construction of new residential and commercial buildings. Recent changes in the skyline of San José through commercial expansion are particularly radical when considered in the context of San José's rural roots and extremely late development. The shock of changes in the vertical profile of the city so impressed observers Rodriguez and Teran (1967:139) that they included a profile in their book, demonstrating the vertical distortions of San José of the construction of the Central Bank, the Gran Hotel Costa Rica, the Social Security Administration Building, and the Supreme Court. These buildings are all within a few blocks of the Central Park. Given the extensive urbanization in the surrounding areas of San José, the conversion of coffee farms into suburbs of the city, and the dramatic changes in the center, it may be said that San José has been completely transformed in the last quarter of a century.

ENTRY INTO WORKING CLASS SOCIAL NETWORKS

At the beginning of the study, we realized that the subjects needed for the project would neither form a separate entity nor be conveniently located in one particular place. It was expected that recruitment of the sample would be with people dispersed throughout the city.

The most urgent initial problem was how to establish contact with users of an illegal drug residing in the metropolitan area of over 438,000 inhabitants. This search was hampered by the users' skills of evasion which had become refined as pressure from the police had alerted them to the dangers of conspicuous drug consumption and the risks of careless social contacts with strangers who might be masking their true identity. For, indeed, the penalty for use of marijuana or suspected sale was severe, with periods of incarceration for from six months to several years not uncommon.

Our initial probings at locating subjects were based on the assumption that social networks, once tapped, would lead us to a corps of subjects meeting the criteria needed. These initial probings were tentative, frustrating, and generally unsuccessful attempts to identify productive spots where initial progress on the problem of sample identification could be begun.

Gradually we discovered sites in working class areas where drug users and nonusers met for social interchange. These centers of interaction included a park corner, a bar, a particular street corner, a shoeshop, and an athletic field. To gain entry into these social circles, we frequented these places, making ourselves visible, answering questions, and chatting with persons who happened by.

Given the sensitive nature of the research and the presence of a large and obvious police force devoted to narcotics enforcement, our presence in the working class areas was at first very suspect. In order to win legitimacy, we had to establish outselves with a core group of men who could be convinced that we were not INTERPOL officers and who would vouch for us as research proceeded.

To facilitate this, we cultivated contacts met in a bar known as a center of drug activity in one of the working class neighborhoods where we hoped to recruit many of our subjects. This bar was a hangout for drug traffickers, fences for stolen goods, those who were looking for these services, plus a corps of very loyal drinkers. The police were regular visitors. We hung around this bar for about two months, meeting many consumers of marijuana. The researchers' first impressions of users were very distorted as a result of this experience. Our medical personnel feared that our medical studies would be invalid if we used these men because of their extraordinary consumption of alcohol.

After a few months, it was clear that the researchers were not undercover narcotics agents, for no police harassment ever followed our observations of trafficking and use. It became evident that the team members would not turn in those breaking the law. Thus, rapport was established with many of these men, and, although none of them were selected for the study for medical reasons, they were invaluable to the success of the study. The network concentrated in the bar included some of the city's best known traffickers who had extensive networks throughout the metropolitan area. They helped our research by introducing men to us and by legitimizing our presence.

For example, in subsequent encounters with users throughout the city, we would drop the names of these men. A standard pattern was that the user would be hesitant to talk, the conversation would end, and we would not see the person for several days. In the meantime, he would talk to one of our references from the bar, and our next conversation would be open and productive. Men at this point would often volunteer to go through the initial medical screen for the project.

By working in other meeting places, we were able to identify additional networks from which we could recruit subjects. We followed contacts throughout the city. The Central Park was especially important, for men who met there were brokers of information for contacts throughout the metropolitan area. The Central Park was the heart of the city, and the men working there as shoeshine boys were communication brokerages for various networks.

These shoeshine boys were very effective in directing the recruitment of the sample. They were a stable occupational group who had cultivated regular clients and established regular work hours. Several of the men had been shining shoes at the same corner of the park for 25 years. Many of them had participated in underworld activities in the past and had extensive networks stemming from these associations as well as other links. One of the men, for example, used to be a major trafficker, with his territory a rather large barrio in the northern part of the city; he maintained ties with the users in this barrio. Similarly, his links with men whom he had met while he spent time in the penitentiary were active; so too were his ties with fellows with whom he had worked in the coastal banana zone during his youth.

Through the contacts of the shoeshine boys and other key informants met in such places as athletic fields and shoeshops, we discovered that the social world of these working class men was elaborate and extensive throughout the working class. Our drives to "run an errand" for a contact often turned into hours-long treks over the metropolitan area as business was conducted. In such tours, it became obvious to us that the men had wide-ranging and often esoteric social networks which were not restricted to geographical or residential boundaries.

By following the networks of contacts and by remaining at centers of interaction, we met a wide range of potential subjects. We conservatively estimate that in the time that field research was conducted we encountered at least 1,500 persons.

We came to view the city as a series of interdependent relational subsystems. It was seen as a field upon which a complicated web of social networks was projected. This perspective enabled us to obtain a working class sample representing a wide range of barrios and occupational categories characteristic of that class. Subjects were contacted through their participation in social networks into which we gained entry, thereby providing us with a socially connected, geographically dispersed, economically active sample.[3]

Certain key individuals who were "regulars" in central working class meeting places such as bars, street corners, stores, shoeshops, and the Central Park became our links to various working class networks throughout the metropolitan area. These central figures were brokers for street news and points of reference for others in their circle of acquaintances. Once we had established rapport with these key individuals, they facilitated our research by introducing us to many men who were finally selected for our sample. Eight of these men were especially instrumental in the search for subjects. These men acted as our anchors in dealing with the men in their relational groups, and most of the study's participants came from their respective groups.

Table 1 summarizes the ethnographer's interaction with the key men and with members of their informal relational system during the period of sample recruitment and selection. It outlines the relationship of each key individual, or anchor, to potential subjects in his network, the ethnographer's encounter with the individual, and the ethnographer's subsequent interaction with him and his cohorts in order to build rapport and enlist their cooperation for the study.

Our incorporation into these relational systems was largely due to the establishment of a reciprocal relationship with the men.

Table 1. EIGHT KEY NETWORKS

Anchor's Relational Ties	Researcher's Encounter with Anchor	Researcher's Interaction with Relational System
Anchor: Manuel Manuel was a user and small-time seller of marijuana. He was the center of a street corner group including working class users and nonusers. His quick wit and forceful personality earned him leader status.	The researcher was introduced to Manuel by a resident of Manuel's barrio whom the researcher had met in a bar known as a center of drug traffic.	−Spent hours talking with men on street corner. −Visited men in their homes. −Provided personal assistance (loans, transportation, medical help, etc.).
Anchor: Ricardo Ricardo was a user of marijuana whose home was the center of a vegetable shipping business cooperatively run by him and friends. Business, family, friendship, and recreational ties bound this group of users.	The researcher was introduced to Ricardo by the researcher's housekeeper, who was related to him.	−Visited Ricardo's home and participated in social activities. −Accompanied men on recreational outings. −Provided men with legal assistance.
Anchor: Jorge Jorge was a nonuser residing in a squatter settlement where he passed time with young men linked by kinship, recreational, and economic ties. His prominence in the group was due to his skill in soccer and his father's status as a community leader in the settlement.	A friend of Jorge whom the researcher had met in a bar introduced the researcher to Jorge.	−Visited the men in their homes and joined in family activities. −Provided medical assistance to the men. −Participated in community activities (e.g., attending community meetings and soccer games, providing team with transportation).
Anchor: Antonio Antonio was a user of marijuana who was a shoeshine boy in the Central Park. Friendship, recreation, and work linked him to other shoeshine boys in the park, constituting a group characterized by street culture learned in youth.	Having heard that the Central Park was a site of marijuana traffic, the researcher went there and had his shoes shined, thereby meeting Antonio.	−Accompanied the men on recreational outings. −Visited the men in their homes. −Provided legal assistance. −Provided transportation to run errands.

Table 1 (continued)

Anchor's Relational Ties	Researcher's Encounter with Anchor	Researcher's Interaction with Relational System
Anchor: Hernando Hernando, a user, owned a shoeshop which was frequented by working class men who came to exchange street news and smoke marijuana. Besides supervising the shop, Hernando granted loans, resold stolen goods, and sold marijuana. An effective entrepreneur, he was respected by his cohorts in the shoeshop circle.	Having heard that marijuana was smoked by shoemakers, the researcher visited many shoeshops in working class barrios, thereby coming across Hernando and his group.	—Visited Hernando's shop often to talk with Hernando and his friends.
Anchor: Jaime Jaime was a young user who, like his close friends, continued adolescent patterns of street culture into adulthood. His prominence in his group stemmed from his accessibility and affability. Maintaining a social base in their working class barrio, the men move about it, quitting a job when they want, finding another when they need one, but spending most of their time relaxing with the group.	The researcher met Jaime on a street corner in his barrio, where he is often found passing time.	—Joined the men on recreational outings, often providing the transportation. —Provided legal assistance. —Met with the men in various places to talk. —Became godparent of one man's child.
Anchor: Carlos Carlos, a nonuser, was a free-lance junk merchant who drove a battered auto around the city. Economic and recreational ties linked him to a group of nonusers who respected him for his leadership in the barrio and for his success in business.	The researcher was introduced to Carlos by a bartender near Carlo's home.	—Spent hours with Carlos and friends in bars and cafes. —Visited the men in their homes.

Table 1 (continued)

Anchor's Relational Ties	Researcher's Encounter with Anchor	Researcher's Interaction with Relational System
Anchor: Eduardo Eduardo, a user, continued in adulthood the street hustling behavior learned in youth. He and his cohorts engaged in various part-time work to support themselves. Their social world centered on the group of peers. Because of his accessibility, Eduardo was a central communication link; his home was often the center of informal gatherings of the men.	A friend of Carlos (described above) introduced the researcher to Eduardo.	−Passed time with Eduardo and friends in a local bar. −Joined the men on recreational outings, often providing transportation. −Provided legal assistance. −Visited the men in their homes.

Renewing contacts with them day after day and frequenting their centers of interaction, we came to participate in their social life. We became privy to news of their difficulty with the law, their health problems, and their financial crises. As members of their social networks, we often used our resources to assist them in such times of need.

We became active brokers for the men with institutions, particularly the Ministry of Health and the Ministry of Security. With the latter, we entered into early negotiations to protect our study's participants, culminating in permission to issue to the participants a card guaranteeing immunity from arrest for personal marijuana use. The card, issued to a few men, caused confusion, especially since the police regarded it as a direct challenge to their authority. In due course, we discontinued the use of the card and resorted to our personal networks to help participants who were arrested for use of the drug. The project's Costa Rican medical coordinator was helpful in this regard, for he was also a colonel in the civil guard and had social and professional ties with officials in the Ministry of Security. When participants were arrested, we were usually able to obtain their release in a week to 10 days.

Similarly we helped the participants when they encountered financial problems. Periodic crises (e.g., overdue rent, food bills) were brought to our attention. We tried to help whenever it was feasible by extending personal loans, purchasing food, providing needed transportation, or paying rent.

Further, we provided the participants with access to health services. The medical screen of the initial base sample of 240 men detected many infirmities, and, through our quasi-official status in the Ministry of Health, we were able to handle referrals to medical services for the participants, many of whom had never received attention in the country's health care system before. Eyeglasses were also provided by the project team for those needing them.

For their part, the men reciprocated by granting informed consent to participate in extensive medical, neuropsychological, and socio-cultural studies. Particularly fruitful for the sociocultural component were the many hours spent in interviews. Extensive life histories were obtained from all the men in the final sample, and all the users were also given in-depth interviews exploring all aspects of their drug history and experience.

Because the interviews were conducted in the last nine months of the study, rapport had been well established, and material gathered was detailed and candid. The researchers conducted the interviews in an open-ended fashion, using the Rogerian reflective technique to encourage the respondents to elaborate on ideas as much as they desired.

The interviews were conducted in several sittings, generally taking four to eight hours to cover the numerous topics on the interview guide. Although the same guide was used for all the men, the information to be collected was not confined to the limit of a page space or closed questions. An accurate recording of the richness and depth of the interviews was made possible through the use of a tape recorder.

The use of the tape recorder during the interviews was not disconcerting to the informants, for rapport had already been established with them. The informants understood the ethnographer's desire for accuracy in transcription and knew that the information recorded would be kept confidential and that his anonymity would be protected. The resulting transcripts were thus precise, maintaining the informants' detail, progression of thought, and exact expression. Further, the participants were not distracted by note-taking behavior of the interviewer (e.g., wondering why the researcher noted some comments and not others).

The communication characterizing these interviews was open and honest. Our incorporation into the men's social networks was central to this dialogue. Moreover, participation in their social world enabled us to validate data through the reports of the men's colleagues and family. Further, our involvement with them on a regular basis minimized the attrition of participants, for over the two-year period only one man dropped out of the study. (This individual was arrested for possession of four pounds of marijuana, and the police wanted to prosecute him for trafficking.)

The intimate relationship with the participants engaged in an illegal activity carried with it heavy responsibilities for protecting them. Association with the project by any participant could not result in his suffering gratuitous and involuntary punishments. This problem was alleviated to some degree by using a research strategy which was not confined to a single area. Had a particular zone been selected for study, the research would have become too visible to outsiders, especially drug enforcement officers, thereby diminishing the anonymity of the participants. As it developed, our research appeared quite random from an outsider's point of view, making it difficult for an outsider to identify the participants. This helped us protect the anonymity of the men, an important consideration given the illegal nature of marijuana use and other activities of the participants.

To protect the men, we devised a number code system for the field notes and medical tests. Names were never used. Moreover, to maintain confidentiality of material, numbers were used in the notes, and the notes were locked in a file. Every effort was made to maintain the anonymity of the participants and the confidentiality of the information that they provided. Our friendship with the men as well as our research interest made us especially concerned for their welfare.

The greatest challenge to this effort came from the wife of a high

Costa Rican government official. She took an active role in matters related to social problems and was particularly alarmed about the use of marijuana in the country. In negotiations with the Ministry of Security, she acted as intermediary. A sensitive point in the negotiation concerned her desire to obtain a list of the participants. Obviously we could not oblige her, and, due to the diplomatic intervention of an official of the Ministry of Public Health, the woman did not persist.

A delicate balance had to be maintained not only with formal institutions such as the Ministry of Security but also with the participants who contended with these institutions' policies. The participants, for example, alleged that they had to pay bribes to the police to avoid harassment and claimed to have suffered injuries during police interrogations. These allegations were difficult to confirm, however, and the participants did not expect us to defend them against such alleged abuses, feeling that we were not in a position to help. We did not discourage this assessment of our role since we knew that the project could not continue if we did battle with the Ministry of Security.

It was critical that the ethnographers maintain this delicate balance in network participation. This was often difficult, for the researchers were part of many networks, those extending into the highest echelons of the government establishment as well as into the bars and street corners of some of the least reputable parts of the city. Several times in the research, a day began with the ethnographer in coat and tie at a minister's office and ended in a haze of marijuana smoke in a raunchy bar.

The size and complexity of the project required that it have a significant official presence in Costa Rica. Formal relationships were negotiated with the Ministry of Health, Ministry of Security, the University of Costa Rica, the Social Security Administration, and the Hospital México, the main institution in the social security system.

The emotional and political impact of the marijuana controversy in Costa Rica meant that each of the different institutions viewed their own role with regard to the drug crisis differently. Law enforcement officials felt that the study would justify repressive policies. Medical personnel were concerned about uncovering deleterious physiological effects, and the Ministry of Health seemed concerned with formulating national policy recommendations. The ethnographers found that, because the project had a different identity for each of the many participating institutions, it became necessary to describe in detail those areas of the research operations comprehensible to the staffs involved. For example, the Ministry of Security was kept abreast of project developments, but we did not elaborate the total implications of the "participant-observation" approach, such as the necessity of being with drug vendors at the time of drug sales or the importance of being with users while they smoked marijuana. Meanwhile, although we were open with our informants, we did not elaborate with them the need for us to spend time with the narcotics police, who were reassured about the scientific merits of the study. The success of the research rested upon being an active member of various networks and balancing the expectations of those networks' members with the needs of the research itself.

NOTES

1. Contract no. NO1-MH3-0233 (ND). The project's principal investigators were William E. Carter, Wilmer J. Coggins, and Paul L. Doughty of the University of Florida. The senior author, William R. True, was field office director and field research coordinator. Throughout the paper the term "ethnographers" is used to refer to the research activities of John Bryan Page, Claudine Frenkel, Dina Krauskopf, and William R. True. All shared data-gathering responsibilities for the sociocultural research. The project, extending from June 1973 to December 1975, involved the work of a team of 50 persons from the United States and Costa Rica.

2. Matching was performed as follows:

Sex: all participants were male.

Age: within four years (mean was 29.4 years).

Marital Status: free union or married were contrasted with being single.

Education: within a "step" of their match (steps were defined as none, primary incomplete, primary complete, secondary incomplete, secondary complete).

Occupation: artisan jobs were equated as men alternated among blue-collar positions according to demand; white-collar jobs were not matched with trades and crafts.

Alcohol Consumption: within four points on a 0-17 point scale adopted from the local Alcoholism Study Commission instrument. Low scores indicated abstemious behavior, high scores alcoholism. Participant observation revealed that a bracket of four points indicated roughly equivalent consumption behavior.

Tobacco Consumption: matching was achieved using a formula devised by pulmonary physiologists which converts individual smoking histories into the number of years that the individual has smoked an equivalent of one pack per day. Thus two packs a day for five years equals 10 pack years. Matching was within two pack years.

3. Proportions between users and nonusers in the base sample of 240 were approximately equal in all occupational categories. Although there were no professionals, two office workers were recruited. Twenty-four worked in comerce, selling various products or working in diverse cottage industries. Only three subjects were in agriculture and lived on small farms near San José. Thirty-two subjects worked in the transportation industry, either driving taxis, trucks, or buses or working in maintenance of these vehicles; several in this group worked in a lucrative produce-transportation business using their own trucks. The artisans comprised over half of the base sample (129); most of these men were skilled in more than one type of work, adapting quickly to changing market demands for different skills. The trade skills included shoemaking, tailoring, baking, carpentry, roofing, plastering, watch repair, machine repair, jewelry making, and electrical repair. The semiskilled laborers in the sample included gardeners, hod carriers, and carpenter's helpers. Twenty-nine subjects worked in services as shoeshine boys, guards, caretakers, and the like. There were eight whose occupations were not regular enough to be classifiable, and seven whose occupations were unique within the base sample. The participants in the base sample were recruited from 45 of the city's barrios representing all types of neighborhoods except for the most prosperous and the most impoverished. These were clearly working class areas.

REFERENCES

Academia de Geografía y Historia de Costa Rica (1952). Procedimientos (Año IV, 11:3-12). San José: Editorial Universidad de Costa Rica.

FURST, P.T. (ed., 1972). Flesh of the gods. New York: Praeger.

GOODE, E. (1969). "Multiple drug use among marihuana smokers." Social Problems, 17:50-56.

HARNER, M.J. (ed., 1973). Hallucinogens and shamanism. London: Oxford University Press.

Ministerio de Obras Públicas y Transportes, República de Costa Rica (1973). Características Socio-Económicas del Area de Estudio en 1973 (Informe Técnico de Trabajo no. 11). San José: República de Costa Rica.

RODRIGUEZ, C., and TERAN, E. (1967). Aspectos Históricos y Urbanos del Area Metropolitana de San José de Costa Rica: Tesis para Grado de Licenciatura en Geografía. San José: Editorial Universidad de Costa Rica.

RUBIN, V., and COMITAS, L. (1975). Ganja in Jamaica. The Hague: Mouton.

6

ETHNOGRAPHY IN THE STREETS AND IN THE JOINT

A Comparison

MICHAEL H. AGAR

In the drug field, anthropology is a recent entrant in the inter-disciplinary competition to understand American heroin addiction. Until recently, anthropology focused on the study of non-Western societies, usually comparatively isolated small groups with non-industrial technologies. American heroin addicts usually fell into disciplines concerned with social deviance or psychopathology. By applying an ethnographic perspective, though, anthropologists working in the late 1960s argued a then unique position. When allowed to characterize themselves and their daily activities in their own terms, the resultant description did not agree with the a priori assumptions of researchers with a background in pathology or deviance. This contradiction is reviewed in detail elsewhere (Agar, 1973a) and referred to below.

At any rate, among anthropologists who work in this area, an argument often occurs over the relative importance of institutional versus street fieldwork. Some researchers work only in the "joint" (institutional setting) while others work in the "streets" (community setting). Still others work in some style intermediate between the two, such as in a community-based treatment center. With a bias toward the study of human behavior in natural contexts rather than in isolated interviews or experimental settings, anthropologists tend to accept as given that truth can be found only in the streets. To some extent, the argument is valid. To a greater extent, life, at least ethnographic life, is more complicated than this. In the land of binary oppositions, street work is good, and work in the joint is bad. In reality, as everyone would agree, there are degrees of understanding of any different human group available in any setting. Since much ethnographic fieldwork has been based on out-of-context reports anyway, why not counterargue that most important aspects of junkie street culture can be learned without ever setting foot in the streets?

I would like to consider this argument from two different approaches. I do this from a background that includes work in an isolated institutional setting in Lexington, Kentucky, work in community-based treatment centers in Honolulu, San Francisco, and New York, and street work in New York. In the first section, I hope to show that both the street and the joint have yielded remarkably similar descriptions in terms of the major contributions of an ethnographic perspective to the study of heroin addicts. A major reason for this lies in the type of relationship established between the ethnographer and the group studied. In the second section, a comparison of data in the two settings will show that there are differences in the information obtained in the two settings. However, the argument will be that the differences are not specific to addict ethnography per se, but rather reflect the general ethnographic problem of human limitations in out-of-context reporting of actual behavior.

ETHNOGRAPHIC APPROACHES

Although it has been hased and rehashed in other discussions, it is useful here to recapitulate the general role of ethnography in the late 1960s in the drug field. At that time, the general description of the addict was that of a social-psychological failure. Explanations of the addict's situation ranged across most of the psychosocial variables that one could imagine. However, a few articles, based on an ethnographic mode of data collection, began to appear which contradicted the generally accepted picture of the addict. In these few studies, the addict was described as an active, intelligent, dynamic member of the street scene—anything but a social-psychological failure.

The point is embodied in three of the earliest articles using an ethnographic perspective. Indeed, one need look no further than the titles to get the message: Preble and Casey's "Taking Care of Business: The Heroin User's Life in the Streets" (1967), Feldman's "Ideological Supports to Becoming and Remaining a Heroin Addict" (1968), and Sutter's "The World of the Righteous Dope Fiend" (1966). Such work was far from the usual description of the junkie retreating from his legitimate or illegitimate failures or soothing his undeveloped superego with an analgesic balm.

The description of the social success aspect of the addict life-style, now well accepted in the drug field, is perhaps the major contribution of ethnographic type studies in this area. Yet, if we examine the articles and monographs that make this point, there are some notable variations among the ethnographers who produced them. Certainly they vary in age, life-style, and personal styles of adaptation to junkie fieldwork. More importantly for our purposes here, they also vary in the settings in which the studies were conducted. Put most simply, some were done in the streets, and some were done in the joint.

As far as this major finding goes, then, it really did not seem to matter where the study was done. Why, then, did ethnographers independently come up with a similar result whatever the setting they worked in? I would like to argue that traditional ethnographic biases have led us to stress *natural context* as a key feature of our approach. In fact, the key feature is not the research setting, but the *type of relationship* that is established between social scientist and informant.

All empirical social research rests on the bedrock of human communication.[1] Whatever the training of the social scientist, at some point he relies on the human contact between two persons.

One person—who may be the social scientist himself, a hired interviewer, or an unknown person who makes an entry in a record—wants to learn something from a second person. A human relationship is established, for however brief a period of time. Despite the fact that this relationship exists, insufficient consideration has been given to it and its implications for the kind of information obtained.

Research in the study of human communication indicates that different relationships can dramatically alter both the form and the substance of the interaction that takes place. As one general frame of reference to discussing this issue, consider Bateson's work. Bateson (1972) suggested that human relationships are of two basic types —symmetrical and asymmetrical. In a symmetrical relationship no one member has more control than the other, whereas in the asymmetrical relationship one member is "one up."

Clearly the form and substance of interaction can differ, depending on the type of relationship within which that interaction occurs. In the asymmetrical relationship, for example, it is the "one up" member who can initiate and terminate the interaction; it is he who chooses the relevant topics for discussion; the interaction occurs in a physical setting and communicational style of his selection.

In a symmetrical relationship, on the other hand, no one member has the right to control such matters. Either one can begin, end, or guide the interaction; if there is disagreement, no one member in particular can resolve it by fiat; rather, the solution to the disagreement is negotiated. Both participate in the selection of topics and the choice of setting and communicational styles. The relationship is more one of equality rather than one of dominance-submission.

Most social research in the drug field is based on asymmetrical relationships in which the drug user is the subordinate member. The interaction usually occurs in a linguistic style which encodes the dominant status of the social scientist. The social scientist initiates and terminates the interaction. He decides what topical areas are to be covered and what questions to ask to elicit information. He has the right to ask questions, and the drug user has the obligation to respond.

If a drug user attempts to alter the relationship, the social scientist will probably not allow this to happen. For one thing, his control in the relationship is defended as insuring a "scientific" procedure. For another, surrender of control makes him much more vulnerable, since conflicts must now be negotiated rather than resolved by his fiat. Under these circumstances, the drug user must concede the asymmetical relationship. His only alternative, if he does not want this to happen, is to refuse to participate.

The preceeding discussion can be summarized in the notion of scientific control. According to a widely held version of the scientific method, the social scientist defines the variables of interest and the hypothesized relations that hold amongst them. He operationalizes the variables, translating them into a series of questions designed to elicit information in a specific way from some carefully defined sample. When he communicates with the group, members must respond in the frame of reference of his design to insure that responses can be compared and fitted to his framework of variables and hypotheses.

In contrast, ethnographic research begins with a loose set of guiding notions that, more often than not, become altered or abandoned as the research progresses. Rather than beginning with a systematic deductive framework, the researcher first sets out to learn the framework of a group. Rather than entering into communication with group members with a list of variables and hypothetical relationships, he enters to learn what the group members themselves define as significant "variables" and "relationships" among those variables.

Note the emphasis on the world "learn" in the paragraph above. He has surrendered "control"—with himself as one up—in favor of "learning"—with himself one down. Eventually, though, the ethnographer also begins to pose questions. He may want more detail in some topical area discussed by asking questions whose answers he already anticipates. Eventually, he may develop more systematic eliciting procedures to question a larger population in a more controlled way. In fact, his work at this point resembles that of the social scientist who began in the one-up position initially. Note the difference, though.

The ethnographer moves from a learning, one-down position into a symmetrical relationship as he begins to pose questions. First of all, note that the move to symmetry is at the discretion of the group member. This can obviously create sampling problems, since much of the questioning is done with those who do allow this symmetrical relation, and, of course, not everyone will. Second, the symmetrical relationship allows the group member to criticize the question as inappropriate, suggest modifications, or generally negotiate the framework, rather than take it or leave it.

To give an example of this process, let me use my experience at the National Institute of Mental Health's Clinical Research Center at Lexington, Kentucky. As a newly commissioned officer in the U.S. Public Health Service, I was shown my office in the research section and told to "do anthropology." I began spending time in patient areas of the institution, advertising myself as one who wanted to learn what it was like to be a junkie. I hung around patient rooms and day rooms, played basketball, ate meals in the dining area, went to parties—all those things that make it difficult to convince nonanthropologists that one is working.

Mostly I listened. I learned a new way of talking and a new way of viewing and interpreting and acting on the social world. I was tested several times by being told of violations of institutional rules to see if I would report them. I was invited to spend two weeks living in the joint. Eventually, I was accepted by a variety of different cliques.

After about nine months, I began developing more systematic methods in collaboration with the junkie-patients. The idea for "simulations" of street events, for example, was suggested by several junkies. When I designed frame elicitation sentences, they were checked with junkies before they were used. For example, a frame developed with white patients was criticized by blacks. To para-phrase, they would usually say that they knew the scene, but used a different script. With their help, the frame was redesigned and subsequently was received better by other blacks. Even in its most systematic phase, then, the format of the study was negotiable between researcher and subjects.[2]

Hopefully, this brief sketch illustrates the more abstract discussion of relationships. A similar sketch could be given by an ethnographer who has done fieldwork anywhere. While this relationship business is not all there is to doing ethnography, it is certainly a key feature. It also helps explain why ethnographers, working in both institutional and community settings, came up with similar descriptions of street addict life. So why go into the streets at all?

STREET DIFFERENCES

Although I had done limited street research in Honolulu and San Francisco, my first extensive street work took place in New York between 1973 and 1975. It ranged from methadone clinics and neighboring street scenes in the Lower East Side to a variety of settings in other neighborhoods. My first reaction was that my earlier institutional work in Lexington held up fairly well. The understanding that I had gained about street life enabled me to interpret behavior appropriately and engage in street conversations in a knowledgeable way. Although I tried to define my role openly, as often as possible, I later learned that several rumors had circulated. I was an ex-junkie who had gone back to school; I was a Synanon representative. Both of these examples were attempts to categorize me as one whose knowledge was a bit out of date but who nevertheless knew more than a straight person should.

In spite of this general congruence, though, there were some striking differences. Most impressive, at least at first, was that street life did not appear nearly so glamorous as institutional reports would have it. Things did not look so good on the street corner. In retrospect, this difference should have been expected. When a particular event is performed, it can obviously vary in its performance. It can be done well or poorly. It may be interrupted or run smoothly. It may be more or less successful in outcome. When an event is described out of context, which type of performance is described? In my work in Lexington, I apparently was usually given descriptions of the well-done, smooth-running, successful end of the spectrum. In the streets, I was personally exposed to the whole range of possibilities. Although the basic framework for interpreting events still held, the number of unsuccessful or mediocre performances was an instructive lesson in variability.

Other differences were also apparent, though perhaps not quite as important as this first one. For example, in institutional work, discussions of the event called "hanging out" were elicited. The general impression received was that hanging out was kind of a nonevent, a time filler with minimal constraints on behavior while an individual waited for more important events to occur.

In the streets, I learned that, though hanging out placed minimal constraints on behavior, it was far from insignificant. In fact, while hanging out, I usually witnessed critical information exchange among members of a group. Who was on the streets and who had been busted? What was the man doing these days, and were there any new faces that might be narcs? Who had the good stuff? Hanging out was a context usually filled in with trading of current news from the scene, news that was critical to one's operation as a street junkie.

Clearly, then, some important differences did exist between the institutional and street research. While the first section argued that setting did not make a difference, I now want to argue that it does. The problem is related to the general one of our-of-context reporting. For any number of reasons, including human memory limitations, clinical defense mechanisms, cognitive dissonance, and others, out-of-context reports are bound to be less than completely accurate descriptions of events.

In this particular case, the major differences seemed to be in the area of negative behavior—unsuccessful events, street hassles, and so on. In short, there was a bias in the institutional data toward presenting street life in its best possible light. This is not surprising, since the Lexington junkies were talking to a sympathetic square. Usually when a square deals with junkies, he is doing something to them—arresting them, treating them, condemning them, etc. With the usual ethnographic attitude, my orientation was "I don't care what you are doing; just let me hang around and watch." My position made me receptive to a favorable description of street life, and that is what I got.

We have now come full circle, back to the unique features of the relationship that the ethnographer establishes during his fieldwork. In this section of the paper, though, the conclusion is quite different. The moral here is that the nature of the relationship can yield a somewhat distorted description in out-of-context discussions if direct observation of behavior in natural contexts is not available to validate such discussions. Of course, this is true of any out-of-context reporting, including survey interviews or psychological experiments.

TOWARD CONFUSING THE DISTINCTION

Now that the differences between the street and the joint are perfectly clear, let us confuse them. Until now, we have seen that the ethnographic relationship seems to yield an understanding of the major themes of junkie subculture whatever the research setting. Yet the street setting was critical in tempering the institutional descriptions with a dose of street hassles. From this, though, it does not follow that the only way to learn of hassles is in the streets.

In Lexington, a group of addicts suggested that they "role-play" some street events to give me a better feel for "the life." This began a series of tape-recorded "simulations" together with elicitation based on them. This strategy, discussed in detail elsewhere (Agar, 1973b), was an attempt to better approximate the streets. After the previous section, it is interesting that one major result of these approximations was an understanding of some of the street hassles.

Using these data, I obtained information on such undesirable events as the "bust," the "burn," and the "rip off." Also the importance of the amount of sickness felt by the junkie was highlighted. So critical was this hassle that it could reverse preferences in such crucial areas as picking a dealer, finding a place to use heroin, risking arrest, and so on. The point here is simply that an understanding that better approximated street life was available in the joint. In fact, had I stayed longer and learned to ask better questions, I might have learned right in the joint almost everything that I eventually learned in the streets.

Still, though, street work was important, though I am not sure whether my motives for saying that are personal or professional. Or perhaps I am simply anxious about spouting ethnographic heresy. Hopefully, it is clear that assigning a study a higher validity score simply because it was done in a street setting is a questionable practice at best.

METHODOLOGICAL DIFFERENCES

There are some other differences between the two settings as well, particularly in the area of methodology. In the institution, the ethnographer literally has a captive audience. Further, he represents something of a novelty to break the tedium of institutional life. In the streets, he is more likely to be an interruption in an active daily routine.

Partly for this reason the work I did in Lexington and the work I did in New York differed dramatically in the systematization of methods. In Lexington I had the time and the continuous uninterrupted contacts to develop formal ethnographic methods out of preliminary informal fieldwork. A large pool of informants was always available for such tasks as formal eliciting and card sorting.

In New York, on the other hand, a brief informal encounter might be the only time I would see a particular individual. Further, since I did not operate out of a storefront or other neighborhood base, my contacts with addicts were usually in public settings. Although a particular individual might trust me, he still had to be sensitive to peer pressure from those around him in talking with an outsider.

In this kind of situation, in a coffee shop with a couple of people nodding out at the counter, the pay phone continually busy, and a flow of traffic in and out, it would have been difficult to lay out a stack of index cards and ask a person to sort them into piles according to similarity of meaning. Besides, such contacts were often interrupted as someone came in to talk or as an addict discovered that he had to leave for a real or imagined appointment.

As a result, the work in New York relied primarily on anecdotal data. Such data are challenging to deal with, trying to find the patterns underlying bits of conversation here and snatches of observation there. However, while it was a creative exercise, it also was more anxiety-provoking. How could one know how much he had hammered data to fit emergent patterns? How generalizable was it? What sort of credibility could one expect without a more systematic public display of the reasoning process that led from empirical data to underlying pattern?

Fortunately, working with an urban population of interest to other researchers, including investigative reporters, some confirmation of results was available from triangulation, or multiples thereof. For example, one theme I pursued with anecdotal data was the integration of methadone into the street junkie subculture of the late 1960s. As I was writing up the data, articles began to appear in the New York press, City Council hearings were held and a report published, and another ethnographer, Irving Soloway, operating independently in Philadelphia, began to disseminate his results. These, plus a survey done among youthful offenders in the city, all were consistent with the conclusions that I had reached.

Such outside sources would have been available, systematic study or not. But in the absence of systematic data it was invaluable to have such other sources as a check on my own conclusions. However, the moral of the story remains. In my own experience, you cannot beat the institution for repeated contact, controlled interviewing, and systematic data collection. On the other hand, as the previous section argued, the streets are where it all happens, and direct observation adds breadth and depth and also fills in some rather crucial details.

A STRATEGY FOR ETHNOGRAPHY

All of this suggests a general procedure for doing ethnographic work with urban American heroin addicts, or perhaps with any group involved in illegal activities. First, consider some of the strengths of the institutional setting:

(1) The ethnographer has a reason for being there as another "straight" staff member. He is located at an acceptable point of contact between the street world and the straight world.

(2) The addicts have to be there anyway and are either in residence or appear repeatedly.

(3) There is time to allow rapport to slowly develop, as well as time to test the ethnographer's motives.

(4) Uninterrupted one-to-one or panel interviews can be more easily scheduled and conducted.

For at least these reasons, an institutional setting would appear to be a natural starting point for ethnographic work. Now, assuming that the setting serves a local population—and most of them do—eventually the ethnographer will find himself with invitations from addicts to move out into the streets. I do not know why such invitations always occur, but they do. Perhaps it is simply friendliness or a desire to show rather than tell, or perhaps it is an interest in exploiting the ethnographer for some purpose, or again it might be an interest in testing him in real rather than hypothetical situations.

For whatever reason, though, eventually an invitation will be offered. A transfer from the institutional setting to the street with a trusted "native" has several advantages, assuming that the native's credibility in the local scene is good. This is a rather important judgment to make, and I am not sure how to explicitly define its parameters. One observes the addict in the clinic, the way other patients relate to him, his record, staff opinions (sometimes the worse the staff say he is, the better an introducer he is), and so on.

At any rate, there are several advantages to following up on such invitations:

(1) You have a guide to the territory. You quickly learn the social spaces in the neighborhood and the kinds of persons and activities that occupy each.

(2) You have an introduction into at least some groups on the scene. The importance of this cannot be overemphasized. A straight outsider is often a "mark" just waiting for a disaster to occur. An introduction from a trusted insider immediately establishes an openness together with certain rights and obligations as so-and-so's friend.

Not everyone will respond to you positively, of course, but many will. The importance of an introduction was first demonstrated to me in San Francisco during some short fieldwork that I did for the Haight-Ashbury clinic. An addict whom I had met in the clinic was walking with me through the Mission District. Passing a fast-food franchise, he told me to wait on the corner. In a few minutes, he emerged with a young couple, obviously strung out, and after introductions we went to drink coffee. They taught me a great deal in the subsequent half-hour conversation. Similar experiences occurred in New York as well.

In short, contacts in the clinic eventually lead to street work. With a variety of contacts, different street scenes can be sampled with ample opportunity for direct observation. If one wished, one could eventually establish oneself on a permanent basis in a particular neighborhood. I never did I preferred to free-float rather than establish a fixed location.

I chose this alternative for several reasons. First, avoiding a fixed location meant that I was less likely to become known as a neighborhood fixture by law enforcement officials. Second, it was easier to hide. Fieldwork with heroin addicts can be exhausting. Before moving to New York, I had decided that, on the basis of my Lexington experience, I wanted to guarantee that I could disappear from the field when I needed to. Finally, as part of a large interdisciplinary research agency, I was being viewed as a source of pretest and noninstitutional samples for sociological and psychological research projects. Rather than deal with this demand of bureaucratic politics and collegial public relations, it was simpler to avoid a fixed base, a single population study.

In short, while street versus joint is a worthwhile dichotomy for discussions of methodological and substantive differences, it is perhaps more obscuring than helpful when developing a field strategy. Each setting has something unique to offer the researcher. A productive ethnographic strategy would try to use the strengths of each setting in the overall design of research.

NOTES

1. Much of the material in this section is taken from Agar (1976).

2. Although I am unfamiliar with the details of their argument, there is a similarity to the grounded theory approach of Glaser and Strauss (1967). Ethnographic fieldwork predates their work by several decades, though.

REFERENCES

AGAR, M.H. (1973a). "Ethnography and the addict." In L. Nader and T. Maretzki (eds.), Cultural illness and health. Washington, D.C.: American Anthropological Association.

——— (1973b). Ripping and running. New York: Academic Press.

——— (forthcoming). "One-up, one-down, even up: Some features of an ethnographic approach."

BATESON, G. (1972). Steps to an ecology of mind. New York: Chandler.

FELDMAN, H. (1968). "Ideological supports to becoming and remaining a heroin addict." Journal of Health and Social Behavior, 9(2):131-139.

GLASER, B., and STRAUSS, A. (1967). The discovery of grounded theory. Chicago: Aldine.

PREBLE, E., and CASEY, J.J., Jr. (1967). "Taking care of business: The heroin user's life on the street." International Journal of Addictions, 4(1):1-24.

SUTTER, A. (1966). "The world of the righteous dope fiend." Issues in Criminology, 2(2):177-222.

PART II

ETHICAL CONSIDERATIONS

7

WORKIN' THE CORNER
The Ethics and Legality of Ethnographic Fieldwork Among Active Heroin Addicts

IRVING SOLOWAY and JAMES WALTERS

The great bulk of the social science literature of the study of addictive diseases has fallen within the purview of sociology and psychology.

Although the literature of these disciplines has been noteworthy in increasing our understanding of the psychochemical effects and the epidemiological configurations, as well as the psychodynamics, of drug-abusing populations, the contribution of these disciplines to an understanding of the etiological and cultural factors in the addictive diseases has, in our opinion, been somewhat less than satisfactory.

Much of the modern sociological and psychological literature attempting to study drug addiction has revolved around an a priori concept of drugs providing an escape, a retreat, from life stresses to which the addicted person has been subject and with which he cannot cope without the aid of an intervening chemical. This basic tenet of drugs as escape—this assumption of pathology—weaves its way through the literature of addiction. Among its best-known proponents are Cohen (1955), Cloward and Ohlin (1961), Merton (1957), Yablonsky (1962, 1965a), and Chein et al., (1964).

In the last half dozen years anthropologists have begun to address their efforts toward the study of drug abuse and addiction in modern American culture. In 1969 Preble and Casey published a critical paper entitled "Taking Care of Business: The Heroin User's Life on the Street." This article addressed itself to the stereotyped image of urban heroin addicts held in popular and scientific literature. Preble and Casey attempted to show that the junkie is an individual who has a culture, who is actively involved in the life of the total community, who uses rather sophisticated entrepreneurial skills in operating his particular "hustle," and who has a role, an identity, a status within his wider community. In 1971, Robert S. Weppner called on anthropologists in particular and social scientists and drug treatment program planners in general to begin exploring, appreciating, and considering the "functionally adaptive aspects of addiction," since the world of the urban heroin addict possesses a "cohesive set of values, norms, and behaviors which differentiate it as a cultural entity." His statement represented a watershed in the social sciences' study of addiction.

The ethnographer schooled and socialized in an academic tradition and in a tested field method which originally studied geographically isolated, "exotic," and primitive peoples now approaches the study of modern American culture in the same basic way that his predecessors approached the study of hunters and gatherers in the Australian desert. The anthropologist attempts to view his subject culture as a cohesive, internally consistent social and cultural unit, the members of which share a system of cognitive and symbolic orientations and a system of culturally relevant rules which order the behavior of the members of the culture. Every culture has a world view, an orientation, which defines and orders reality, and the ethnographer seeks to present a description of human behavior which reflects the universe of the "native." He seeks to describe and explicate the value system of the group under study. Ideally, the anthropologist makes no assumptions of pathology, no reference to dysfunction, once the cultural unit to be studied is entered and fieldwork has begun. The anthropologist suspends judgment until the ethnography has been written. Then a comparison can, and perhaps should, be attempted; then an effort can be made to explore differences and similarities of diverse cultural units; then questions can be formulated which seek to understand cross-cultural regularities of human behavior.

Essentially, the methodological factors which seem to separate, to polarize at times, the anthropological from the sociological approaches revolve around the pivotal concepts of *relativism* and *participant observation.*

The justification—indeed, the necessity—for participant observation was formally enunciated by Bronislaw Malinowski in 1926 when he admonished his fellow anthropologist to

> relinquish his comfortable position . . . on the verandah . . . where . . . armed with pencil and notebook . . . he has been accustomed to collect statements from informants. . . . He must go out into the villages. . . . Information must come to him full-flavored from his own observations of native life, and not be squeezed out of informants as a trickle of talk. [pp. 146-147]

This prescription—this code of participant observation—is certainly easier to accept and execute when the culture that one is studying is radically different from the cultural roots of the fieldworker. No matter what the bizarre practices of a group may be, no matter that they practice cannibalism or infanticide, the ethnographer is emotionally and methodologically insulated, since these people are "exotic" and not of the anthropologist's culture and are, therefore, seen as somehow amenable to objectification. But, when an anthropologist sets out to study a group of people who share his own macroculture and when that group of people are defined and define their own existence as criminal, when one decides to attempt to enter their world and to study it, the fieldworker arrives at a true moral, ethical, and legal existential crisis. The failure of urban anthropological studies of modern American culture is that this critical phenomenological juncture has not been substantively dealt with by urban anthropologists in any meaningful way.

> The basic reason for this lack of self-reference lies in the widely held assumption that there is, and should be, a discontinuity between the investigator and the object investigated. If we accept this assumption . . .

the scientist can afford to remain largely indifferent to his own existential, sociological, historical, and philosophical environment. [Scholte, 1974:435]

In this regard, Weppner's "as-if-a-culture" model may be a valuable heuristic and methodological tool, for it does enable the fieldworker to suspend a priori judgments and *postpone* this existential conflict. Thus, the participant observer can enter a "presumed cultural" group and generate a valid portrait. However, the published record of such attempts has been grounded not in field studies, but rather in retrospective studies of institutionalized subjects.

For example, the most methodologically and epistomologically ambitious work by an anthropologist studying addicts is Agar's *Ripping and Running: A Formal Ethnography of Urban Heroin Addicts* (1973). Agar attempted a cognitive analysis of heroin addicts who were incarcerated at a federal hospital in Lexington, Kentucky. His work centered on semantic analysis and decision theory and was grounded in a psychodrama-type simulation of street behavior. This technique, first suggested by Agar (1969) in his article "The Simulated Situation: A Methodological Note," seems rooted in the theoretical rationale of the natural controlled experiment (Goodman, 1970).

Control, however, is a two-edged sword from which an experimental mode can also suffer. There has not been a truly effective rebuttal of the phenomenological objection that the intrusion of experimental control so distorts reality that the resulting relationships are not products of the tested variables of subjects as they naturally exist but rather functions of the experiment itself. Probability statements, experimental replication, psychodramas, and efforts to make the experiment seem as natural as possible only confound the issue. For, philosophically, *in vitro* and *in vivo* assuredly are antipodes.

Moreover, Agar and Weppner published materials on addicts who were prisoners at a federal institution mandated to treat convicted drug addicts. Writing on the economics and interactional aspects of procuring heroin in South Philadelphia, Walters (1973, 1975) interacted with his informants not as an ethnographer but as a policeman (Walters was a member of the Philadelphia Police Department when he collected his field data).

All of these authors' works present serious methodological difficulties regarding the reliability of self-reported retrospective data and regarding the phenomenological perspective of the ethnographers' relationships with the informants. Both of these issues are critical intervening variables. In commenting on his own work, Agar recognized the conceptual and methodological pitfalls of studying such a complex social and cultural phenomenon as heroin addiction in a closed institutional setting:

> The addict is physically clean, participating in a treatment program where his street behavior is defined as symptomatic of a psychological disorder. There is some evidence that the addict can present quite a different "self" under these conditions. [1973:10]

For the anthropologist who wants to study drug addicts *qua* drug addicts, who wishes to look at the process of people *being* addicts, it is necessary to move out of the institutional setting and onto the street. This move involves enormous ethical and legal issues, as well as very real emotional and physical hazards. However, it is necessary that anthropologists confront and resolve those complications if meaningful urban anthropology in modern American culture is to be done. If addicts are studied at Lexington, then the result is a study of patients. If addicts are studied in jail, the result is a study of prisoners. If the ethnographer's goal is to understand addiction, he must resolve himself to entering the natural habitat of the addict —the streets, the back alleys, the shooting galleries.

For the past five and a half years this had been precisely the goal and experience of one of the authors. The remainder of this paper is a reflective narrative of that experience, focusing particularly on the ethical and legal issues which the ethnographer faced daily.

A FIELDWORKER'S NARRATIVE

The author's professional involvement with urban heroin addicts began in 1970 when he completed a follow-up study of heroin addicts who had been treated at a methadone outpatient facility (Moffett, Soloway, and Glick, 1972). In 1971 he completed a master's thesis (Soloway, 1971) which examined the communicational and interactive behavior of heroin addicts in group therapy. During the course of gathering material for these two projects the author realized that the overwhelming majority of the studies of heroin addicts had been conducted within institutional settings and that it would be methodologically necessary to attempt a traditional participant observation ethnography of active, urban heroin addicts. He had a personal network of friends who were addicts and dealers. He engaged in full-scale participant observation in South and West Philadelphia from July 1970 until May 1972.

In the earliest stages of fieldwork, his entry was greatly facilitated by his being a recognized and trusted neighborhood member of that tightly knit "urban village" because of his own childhood there and, now, by reason of his new affiliation with a methadone treatment program. Seen by the general community as a resident who had "made it," the ethnographer was assumed by the junkies to be a quasi-advocate, one "sort-of-their-own" who had shared enough of their world view and values to be their trusted "inside track" in the treatment program.

Formal entry into the field was begun in a rather serendipitous way. Fridays at methadone treatment centers were very special days, since weekend dosages of methadone were distributed. It was one day of the week which no client dared miss. This presented the ethnographer with an excellent opportunity to observe and interact with large numbers of junkies. The lobby of the program clinic would be filled with 200 or more addicts at any one time throughout these afternoons. On one such Friday in July of 1970, the ethnographer was taking in the sights when he was approached by Mario, an old neighborhood friend and patient at the program. Mario complained of some family difficulties and asked if he could discuss them with the ethnographer at lunch. The anthropologist was asked to visit with Mario's family and act as an arbiter in his difficulty with his wife and his mother. This initial instrumental episode evolved into an attached relationship between Mario and the ethnographer. Mario enjoyed the assumed status of this affiliation and particularly his access to the anthropologist's office and time at the treatment center. He saw the ethnographer as his "special friend" and often publicly affirmed his assumed status by loud greetings in the hallways of the clinic and by purposeful introduction of other patients to the anthropologist. By these behaviors and outright verbal assertions Mario proclaimed that he had status not only within the program, but also "on the street," and that not only did *he* have status because of his relationship with the anthropologist, but also that the latter deserved status because of his relationship with Mario.

It was not unusual for Mario and the others to rest in the comfort of this assumed relationship and not seek to test the "real." Dramatically, Mario once did, however. High on dope one day, he came to the treatment center for his daily dose of methadone. Seeing that he was high, the nurse refused to dispense it, whereupon Mario threw a tantrum and spat out a stream of invective at her. As he began to calm down, however, Mario began protesting his friendship with the anthropologist—still a staff member—who was subsequently summoned. With great self-assurance Mario reminded him of their friendship, assured him that he was not high, and expectantly asked the anthropologist to authorize his dosage (which the latter was unauthorized to do even if he wished). The anthropologist not only refused to intercede but also told Mario, "I'm no lame social worker from the suburbs; you're high and everybody knows it. Now, stop being such a cunt!" Visibly stung by this rebuke, Mario ended the conversation and skulked away. The precarious researcher-informant relationship having been risked, it should be noted that Mario was back in the author's office the following day apologizing and reasserting his friendship.

Loudly and often Mario bragged that he could take the ethnographer anywhere to see anything, that Mario was his "ticket in." One day the anthropologist said to him, "Mario, you're full of shit! Show me a shooting gallery." His game read, Mario was on the spot to "put up or shut up." In order to maintain status—"face"—not only with the ethnographer but also with his peers, Mario had to produce. He took the ethnographer to another of the latter's old acquaintances, Tommy, a small-time dealer and addict, though not a methadone program client. With no questions asked and with all the nonchalance of a trio of old friends, they went down into the "gallery," Tommy's basement. There, Mario purchased four bags of heroin at $5 per bag and "shot" (injected) two bags. He laughingly offered the ethnographer "a taste," which the latter laughingly declined. But the three stayed talking for two hours as a stream of addicts constantly drifted through, buying, shooting, "nodding," and leaving. So began the anthropologist's *intimate* involvement with the active life of junkies on the street, and, after almost a year of building rapport and confidence, he began to move into the impossibly clandestine culture of the urban heroin addict. He entered the natural habitat of the junkie, and he began to realize that "junkie" is only one segment of the heroin addict's social identity. He began to see that heroin addicts live in communities in which most of the members are *not* addicted, that the interaction between addicts and nonaddicts in the community does not revolve around drugs, that junkies have other, perhaps equally significant roles that they fulfill. They are husbands and fathers and sons and neighbors and laborers and students and friends. In short, he found that, while the role and status of drug addicts are a critical and central part of their identity and that they maintain their universe around their chemical dependency, they must also be studied as members of a larger, more differentiated sociocultural unit.

ISSUES IN ANTHROPOLOGICAL FIELDWORK

The root problem in such anthropological fieldwork, as J.C. Jarvie (1969:505) has pointed out, is that participant observation demands that a researcher be both stranger and friend to his subjects—yet, the two roles are mutually exclusive. The bind on the ethnographer's personal ethic is, of course, that his total integrity cannot be maintained in either role. Moreover, the cutting edge of that dichotomy is very sharp, and not even the preexisting attached relationships of the author avoided this conflict. Such tension was doubly compounded in our case by the instrumental nature of his occupation in the community. Indeed, so absolute is this division of roles that Jarvie goes on to boldly assert that "The success of the method of participant observation *derives* from exploiting the situations created by the role clashes: insider/outsider, stranger/ friend, pupil/teacher" (1969:505).

We agree; and, if Jarvie was the first to enunciate this principle, a history of anthropological tradition operationally bears it out. Merely to say, however, that the exploitation is "the way it is" does nothing to answer the self-flagellating issue that Jerry Hyman (1968), for example, raised. An ethnographer competent and sensitive enough to have learned what behaviors would put his hosts, a Tlingit family, in an indebted position, Hyman maneuvered to have himself invited to attend a potlatch. In the cited article he bemoaned such ability and willingness to exploit! Could not the same be said of us, for Mario was placed in an extremely "face-threatening" position by the ethnographer? If, at the very least, the goal of our discipline is to discover and document the world and world view of our host cultures, then implicit is the expectation that we will seek to discern their rule system, the way they "perceive and structure their world" (James, 1972:130). If ethnomethodology itself is new, the need for validating hypotheses is not, and in that sense Hyman's understanding of what behaviors would obligate his host was a hypothesis looking for validation. Whether or not to exercise that option is the crucial question. But, if a host-informant welcomes an anthropologist into his home as an honored member of his family—as Hyman was—then the latter's prerogatives of action have been *granted.* In a similar fashion, by his boasting Mario was inviting challenge. It seems, then, that an anthropologist who rises to such ethnomethodological challenge does not violate any of the ethics of our discipline at all. What he must look to ensure is that the challenge be delivered in a culturally decorous fashion and that it not violate his own stance. In short, he must seek to maintain *relativism,* and this, more than questions of ethics, may be the pitfall of many.

Being neither the moral nihilism nor the absolutism that Jarvie (1969:507) seemed to suggest, relativism is a principle that does not absolve the ethnographer from following his *own* culturally formed conscience, but it does demand that he not *project* those values onto his subject population. If this issue is indeed crucial in the history of fieldwork, then it bears some further discussion.

Relativism operationally guards against two dangers, the ethnographer's own ethnocentrism and an equally dangerous inverted ethnocentrism—i.e., going native and personally identifying with the studied value system. This neat epistomological dichotomy has presented few problems in the past, when the bulk of our research focused on obviously different, exotic cultures, especially in simple microcultures. Among such peoples, whose behavior was so often visibly strange, we could safely assume that we were dealing with a different culture. But is observed behavior, in and of itself, the totality of culture? We think not. Culture is that set of underlying values which prompts behavior. Much controversy has focused on the issue of whether values are homogeneous and class-undifferentiated (Merton, 1957) or the contrary (Hyman, 1953; Davis, 1946; Miller, 1958). Hyman, for example, showed that varying class levels had varying levels of aspiration in their quest for education, affluence, and occupational success. Thus, he argued, we exhibit a class-differentiated value system. It seems to us that the focus of this differentiation is not values operative at different levels; Hyman did not suggest that education, affluence, and occupational success were not universally valued. Rather, he, and the class differentialists, speak about *levels of aspiration*—that is, goals. We suggest that the whole argument can be more fruitfully discussed in terms of values, goals, and norms and that it is within this framework that the study of behavior is most productive.

Values exist at a high level of abstraction and are ascribed to all levels of that society which we call *American*. Indeed, these may be functions of a global psychobiological need. At any rate, all Americans *value* strength, status, affluence, self-worth, individuality, and control over their own destinies. These values, however, are *operationally defined* by a vast network of goals—value symbols—whose attainment is prescribed by norms of appropriate behavior. Goals, then, translate abstraction into reality and must, then, represent group statements of perceived probability of success. It is at this level, then, that class and subcultural differentiation *must* be observed. Seeking to refer more to value-symbols than values, Hyman Rodman (1963) implicitly accepted this framework when he wrote:

The lower class person, without abandoning the general values of the society, develops an alternative set of values. Without abandoning the values placed upon success, such as high income and high educational and occupational attainment, he stretches the values so that lesser degrees of success also become desirable.... The result is that the members of the lower class ... have a wider range of values than others within the society. [p. 201]

Furthermore, few would argue with Cloward and Ohlin's (1961) tenet that the avenues of successful goal attainment may be *either* appropriate (legitimate) or inappropriate (illegitimate)—the latter *operationally* defining *deviancy*. We think it important, however, to stress that patterns of deviance are not a priori indicators of either value or goal differentiation. Rather, they are *behaviors* defined as inappropriate by the wider culture. Thus, the behavioral diversity seen in such complex societies as America does not necessarily demonstrate a mosaic of discrete cultures. It may be, and we believe that it is so, that ours is culturally a relatively homogeneous society whose diversity represents an *expected* variance of goals and goal attainment. In American urban ethnography, then, both the field-worker and the studied population share the same value set.

If this is true, then modern American urban anthropology represents a challenge to the traditional assumptions of relativism and participant observation. If it is true that both the observer and the observed share the same basic value system, then what a priori assumptions can the ethnographer suspend? What a priori value judgments ought the ethnographer to suspend, especially when the focus of investigation is a deviancy labeled criminal? Are we to bring to the study of American junkies the same dispassionate eye with which we observe and record suicide among the Gond? Or infanticide among the Cashinaua? If, indeed, we can, how long would it be before we did violence to our very selves?

If such questions as these are of a moral-ethical nature, are they not compounded by issues of legal culpability when an ethnographer conducts participant observation among criminal deviants in their *natural settings*? As Polsky noted (1969:133-134):

If one is effectively to study adult criminals in their natural settings, he must make the moral decision that in some ways he will break the law himself. He need not be a "participant observer" and commit the criminal acts under study, yet he has to witness such acts or be taken into confidence about them and not blow the whistle. That is, the investigator has to decide that when necessary he will "obstruct justice" or have "guilty knowledge" or be an "accessory" before or after the fact, in the full legal sense of those terms.

Refusing to be intimidated by the reality of the issues he raised, Polsky proclaimed that such research is surely important enough to warrant his cavalier approach to fieldwork. Such "hipness" stands in polar opposition to Lewis Yablonsky's responsible righteousness. Yablonsky asserted that one ought not conduct participant observation among the criminally deviant, because such vicarious research interest acts to justify and reinforce their criminality (1965b). Both of these positions, of course, are rooted in the same assumption of unavoidable illegality.

The following account serves as a crystallization of all these moral-ethical-legal questions.

A FURTHER NARRATIVE

The anthropologist had been doing active fieldwork for about 15 months and had been participating in the daily round of activities of several junkies. Ralphie was one of his key informants. In the course of his study, the anthropologist had witnessed several heroin and methadone sales, had lived for three weeks with Ralphie and his (nonjunkie) wife, had been a part of the junkie's everyday world. Tonight was nothing new.

The anthropologist had been "hanging out" in a corner candy store with Ralphie and Sam for about three hours. The three men had spent the day looking for a particular dealer in southwest Philadelphia who was rumored to have just received a quantity of heroin from Los Angeles. Ralphie and Sam wanted some of the reportedly superior "brown dope."[1] They could not connect with the dealer, however. On the way back to South Philadelphia, the three men had stopped at the methadone clinic to pick up their weekend supply of methadone. The trio then drove to Germantown and sold two bottles of the methadone-Tang mixture to some high school kids for $30. Ralphie, Sam, and the anthropologist went to West Philadelphia and purchased a "six pack" (six bags of heroin). Ralphie and Sam each injected three bags and, having earlier spit out the methadone which they had taken at the clinic, were able to get high.

About 9 p.m., three hours later, Ralphie and Sam were beginning to say that they needed more heroin. Another addict, Angelo, joined the trio, and the four men drove through the rain to a side street in a black neighborhood in South Philadelphia. The car stopped about four car-lengths from the corner. Ralphie and Sam left the car saying they'd be "right back." By the glow of a penlight, the anthropologist began to make a few notes on three-by-five cards while keeping up a desultory stream of chatter with Angelo, who had moved to the driver's seat.

After about four or five minutes, the anthropologist heard running feet slapping the wet sidewalk. The right side doors of the car opened, and Ralphie and Sam jumped in. Angelo moved the car out of the street onto a major thoroughfare and began driving north at a high rate of speed.

Laughing and joking about buying a bundle of dope, Ralphie turned to the anthropologist and said, "Here's a present for you." The anthropologist felt Ralphie drop a heavy object into his raincoat pocket. It was a loaded snub-nosed revolver.

"What the fuck is this for? What did you jerk-offs do?" the anthropologist asked.

"We took off a store."

"Ralphie, you cocksucker, let me the fuck out of this car!"

Sam turned in his seat, laughing. "You gonna put this in the book?"

"What's wrong with you bananas? Look, Angelo, slow the fuck down, you're gonna draw attention to us."

Ralphie told Angelo to go to North Philadelphia, and the anthropologist said that he wanted to be dropped off at a bar there. Ralphie took the revolver from the anthropologist and asked whether he wanted any money from the stick-up, or whether he wanted a bag or two of heroin.

"Go fuck yourself," said the anthropologist.

"Don't think I haven't tried," said Ralphie.

Both Sam and the anthropologist were dropped off at the bar, where Sam bought his dope and shot it in the washroom. Sam and the anthropologist then went to an all-night diner where Sam gave a detailed account of the armed robbery. Three days later Ralphie completely substantiated that account.

SOME LEGAL ISSUES

Having been witness to numerous narcotics offenses (sales, possession, use, and sales to minors), the anthropologist was now privy to an armed robbery and a weapons offense. Indeed, at one point he even seemed an accessory to criminal flight. He was certain that he was breaking invaluable ethnographic ground, that he was in fact living out Polsky's prescription that criminals must be studied in their natural habitat. But, as delighted as he was by the worth of his data, he was just as terrified at his assumption of complicity and ultimate prosecution. Unquestionably, concern about criminal liability is well grounded. But is the assumption of liability for "guilty knowledge" a correct one? Perhaps not.

In our case, three legal issues seem to pertain, for each of which the ethnographer presumed himself to be liable: accessory after the fact, present at the time of the offense, and hindering apprehension. An examination of the Pennsylvania Penal Code—the relevant jurisdiction—proved to be surprisingly informative. Moreover, because each point is a virtual transcription of the relevant issue as stated in the Model Penal Code, we shall quote at length:[2]

A. *The nature of "accessory after the fact"*
Pennsylvania Penal Code 306-8; Model Penal Code 2.06.

An accessory after the fact is "one who, knowing that someone has committed a felony, receives, relieves, comforts, or assists felon, or in any manner aids him to escape arrest of punishment."

Commonwealth of Pennsylvania v. Clark: 189, A2d 321, 200 Pa. Super. 316, 1963.

Commonwealth of Pennsylvania v. Finkelstein: 156, A2d 888, 191 Pa. Super. 328, 1960.

But "mere knowledge of perpetration of a crime does not involve responsibility for its commission, nor does silence following such knowledge make one an 'accomplice' or an 'accessory after the fact.' "

Commonwealth of Pennsylvania v. Giacoble: 19, A2d 71, 341 Pa. 187, 1941.

Commonwealth of Pennsylvania v. Tunstall: 72 Montg. 452, 70 York 125, 1957.

Thus, "For one to be an accessory after the fact: (1) a felony must have been completed, (2) person charged must have assisted the felony personally, and (3) he must have then known that the party had committed a felony."

Commonwealth of Pennsylvania v. Darnell: 54 Lanc. Rev. 115, 1954; affirmed 116 A2d 310, 179 Pa. Super. 461.

B. *Presence at time of offense*

Pennsylvania Penal Code 306-9; Model Penal Code 2.07.

"The mere presence at a homicide and knowledge of its commission does not make a person guilty unless he aids, assists, and abets."

Commonwealth of Pennsylvania v. Giovanetti: 19, A2d 119, 341, Pa. 345, 1961.

Moreover, "If one is only a 'terrified onlooker,' neither his presence at a homicide nor his failure to report it would make him an 'accomplice.' "

Ibid.

C. *Hindering apprehension or prosecution*

Pennsylvania Penal Code 5105; Model Penal Code 242.3.

"A person commits an offense if, with purpose to hinder the apprehension, prosecution, conviction, or punishment of another for crime, he:

"(1) harbors or conceals the other; or

"(2) provides or aids in providing a weapon, transportation, disguise, or other means of avoiding apprehension, or effecting escape; or

"(3) conceals or destroys evidence of the crime, or tampers with a witness, informant, document, or other source of information regardless of its admissibility in evidence; or

"(4) warns the other of impending discovery or apprehension, except that this clause does not apply to a warning given in connection with an effort to bring another into compliance with the law; or

"(5) volunteers false information to a law enforcement officer."

But again, "Mere silence, even in felonies, after knowledge of the crime's having been committed, did not make the party failing to report the offense an 'accomplice' or 'accessory after the fact.' "

Possibly the single disqualifier in this issue would be the "reason to know" clause of the criminal conspiracy statutes. This law places a burden of complicity on one who knew, or had reason to know—should have known—of a crime *prior to its commission.* It relates, however, to specific acts and not just a general tenor of acting. For example, mere knowledge, indeed certainty, that an addict-informant, because of his criminal past, will burglarize in the unspecified future would not make a researcher liable under this law. If, on the other hand, one were party to his plan to burglarize "Mr. X" specifically, and especially if one knew when that was to occur, then the researcher possibly would share in a criminal conspiracy by virtue of his failure to forewarn.

The relevance of these Pennsylvania laws is clear: becoming privy to information about criminal deviance does not necessarily carry with it an onus of complicity or legal responsibility. Indeed, even the anthropologist's admonition to "slow down" was not in violation of the law, since it served to "bring another into compliance with the law," specifically, a traffic law (Pennsylvania Penal Code 5105; Model Penal Code 242.3).

In addition, the laws relieve the investigator of any alleged "responsible citizen's" burden of reporting crimes once discovered or witnessed. Moreover, because at least 23 other jurisdictions have revised their criminal codes to greater or lesser degrees in relation to the Model Penal Code, similar situations may obtain in other states.[3] Ethnographers and other investigators embarking on American fieldwork would be advised, therefore, to suspend not their value judgments, but rather their facile assumptions, and familiarize themselves with the law.

Let us not bask too very long in this unaccustomed legal comfort, for, while such laws seem to relieve us of responsibility prior to a governmental investigation, they pertain very little after such an investigation has begun. Once a criminal investigation and/or prosecution has commenced, we are still absolved of a legal responsibility to come forward, of our own accord, with our information. Once summoned to so testify, however, we have no legal recourse but to divulge our information and its source under the threat and consequence of a contempt citation. This was made amply clear in the U.S. Supreme Court's landmark decision in 1972 against Paul Branzburg, a journalist investigating junkies in Kentucky, and Earl Caldwell, a journalist investigating the Black Panthers and other militant black organizations.

Summoned by the grand juries of two separate jurisdictions—the former in Kentucky, the latter in California—each was asked to testify regarding what he had learned and observed and whom he had observed making statements and committing other overt acts which he had witnessed. The two men built their respective defenses around several familiar assertions: a state privilege statute which protects a newsman's sources (Kentucky Revised Statutes, sec. 421.100) and, of course, the First Amendment to the U.S. Constitution. Specifically, Branzburg and Caldwell held that the principle of the First Amendment is seriously threatened by the secrecy of grand jury proceedings which serve to "drive a wedge of distrust and silence between the media and militants" (U.S. Supreme Court Reports 33 L. Ed 2d/408US665) and that such a step ought not to be taken in the absence of compelling governmental need and unless other sources of information have proved futile.

In response, the Kentucky Court of Appeals denied the applicability of statute 421.100, holding that it does not pertain when the events in question were *personally* witnessed by the investigator. And in a much more sweeping and pointed decision, Justice Byron White, expressing the views of five members of the U.S. Supreme Court (a sixth was also in agreement but issued his own opinion), held that the First Amendment accords a journalist-investigator no privilege against appearing before a grand jury and answering questions as to either the identity of his sources or the information which he has received in confidence. Indeed, to the specific points asserted by the appellants, the Court held that the press is not free with impunity to publish everything and anything it desires, for the right to speak and publish does not carry with it the unrestrained right to gather information. Moreover, a journalist has no privilege to refuse to testify until the state demonstrates "compelling need" or demonstrates that the relevant information is unavailable from other sources. How these rulings will operationalize regarding scientific investigations is open to testing. Jennifer James (1972:139), for example, reported having once been subpoenaed to testify to a county prosecutor, but the subpoena was dropped when she publicly disclosed a signed agreement to safeguard the identity of her sources. Had she not been spared the confrontation, however, the crisis would certainly have been upon her, for the code of ethics of the American Anthropological Association places its highest priority on protecting informant identity and confidentiality.

Urban American fieldwork, then, may confront the researcher with moral, ethical, and legal crises on an almost daily basis. It is neither within the scope of this paper nor proper for us to discuss morality, for that is, and must always be, a researcher's private affair. The legal and ethical issues are clear and confronting, however, and all too often misunderstood. Our purpose has been merely to shed some light on such misconceptions. It seems clear to us, however, that if participant observation is to continue, then clearer operational guidelines for the fieldworker must be formulated. Approaches must be found to avoid the dilemmas and pitfalls of a facile and unconstructive "hipness" on one hand and stagnating righteousness on the other.

NOTES

1. Brown dope is a form of heroin obtained from Mexico. Middle Eastern heroin refined in France is white.
2. The authors wish to thank John D. Egnal, Graduate Fellow in Clinical Law at Temple University Law School, for assistance in reviewing the legal literature.
3. The American Law Institute has compared the revised criminal codes of 24 jurisdictions in light of its proposed Model Penal Code. Eight jurisdictions have closely paralleled their model: Delaware, Hawaii, Kentucky, North Dakota, Oregon, Pennsylvania, Texas, and Utah. Four have relied little on the model: Georgia, Kansas, Minnesota, and New Mexico. Seven states fall somewhere in between: Colorado, Connecticut, Illinois, Montana, New Hampshire, New York, and Ohio. Five are currently being compared: Arkansas, Florida, Maine, Virginia, and Washington.

REFERENCES

AGAR, M.H. (1969). "The simulated situation: A methodological note." Human Organization, 28(4):322-329.
――― (1973). Ripping and running: A formal ethnography of urban heroin addicts. New York: Seminar Press.
American Law Institute (1962). Model penal code. Philadelphia: Author.
CHEIN, I., et al. (1964). The road to H: Narcotics, delinquency, and social policy. New York: Basic Books.
CLOWARD, R., and OHLIN, I. (1961). Delinquency and opportunity. Glencoe, Ill.: Free Press.
COHEN, A. (1955). Delinquent boys. Glencoe, Ill.: Free Press.
DAVIS, A. (1946). "The motivation of the underprivileged worker." In. W.F. Whyte (ed.), Industry and society. New York: McGraw-Hill.
GOODMAN, P. (1970). "The natural controlled experiment in organizational research." Human Organization, 29(3):197-203.
HYMAN, H. (1953). "The value systems of different classes." In R. Bendix (ed.), Class, status, and power. Glencoe, Ill.: Free Press.
HYMAN, J. (1972). "The potlatch." In M. Glaser (ed.) The research adventure. New York: Random House.
JAMES, J. (1972). " 'On the block': Urban research perspectives." Urban Anthropology, 1(2):125-140.
JARVIE, I.C. (1969). "The problem of ethical integrity in participant observation." Current Anthropology, 10(5):505-508.
MALINOWSKI, B. (1926). "Myth in primitive psychology." In Magic, science, and religion. New York: Doubleday.
MERTON, R. (1957). Social theory and social structure. Glencoe, Ill.: Free Press.
MILLER, W. (1958). "Lower class culture as a generating milieu of gang delinquency." Journal of Social Issues, 14(3).

MOFFETT, A., SOLOWAY, I., and GLICK, M. (1972). "Post-treatment behavior following ambulatory detoxification." In C. Chambers and L. Brill (eds.), Methadone: Experiences and issues. New York: Behavioral Publications.

POLSKY, N. (1969). Hustlers, beats, and others. New York: Anchor.

PREBLE, E., and CASEY, J.J., Jr. (1969). "Taking care of business: The heroin user's life on the street." International Journal of the Addictions, 4(1):1-24.

Purdon's Consolidated Pennsylvania Statutes Annotated (1973). Philadelphia: G.T. Bissel.

RODMAN, H. (1963). "The lower class value stretch." Social Forces, 42(7):205-215.

SCHOLTE, B. (1974). "Toward a reflexive and critical anthropology." Pp. 430-457 in D. Hymes (ed.), Reinventing anthropology. New York: Vintage.

SOLOWAY, I. (1971). "Videotape recording of narcotic addicts in group therapy: The analysis of communicational and interactive behavior." Unpublished M.A. thesis, Department of Anthropology, Temple University.

WALTERS, J. (1973). "A heroin copping community: Economics of residency." Quarterly Journal of Probation, Parole, and Correction, 30(4).

——— (1975). "Copping: A functional analysis of drug abuse." Unpublished manuscript.

WEPPNER, R. (1971). "The application of anthropological techniques to understanding the subculture of addiction." Paper presented at the meetings of the Society for Applied Anthropology, Miami.

YABLONSKY, L. (1962). The violent gang. Baltimore: Penguin.

——— (1965a). Synanon: The tunnel back. Baltimore: Penguin.

——— (1965b). "Experiences with the criminal community." In A.W. Gouldner and S.M. Miller (eds.), Applied Sociology. New York: Free Press.

8

ETHNOGRAPHY AND SOCIAL PROBLEMS

JENNIFER JAMES

Crime in the United States can easily be considered as one of the more serious social problems facing our society. Explanations for the existence and increase of criminal behavior are diverse, and current solutions show unpredictable results. The field of traditional criminology, as it has been represented by psychology and sociology, has begun to circle back on itself. Punishment or rehabilitation, indeterminate sentencing or strict minimums have been alternating over the last two decades of research efforts and recommendations. The basic pattern of information remains similar: hindsight demography (Packer, 1968; Wilson, 1975).

The application of the research principles of anthropology, specifically ethnography, is a recent phenomena in criminology. In the late 1960s, Henry (1965), Liebow (1967), Edgerton (1967), Keiser (1969), Spradley (1970), and Humphreys (1970) began research efforts that have resulted in an increased American urban anthropology with an emphasis on the ethnography of social problems. Since that time, Agar (1973), Blum (1969), James (1973, 1974), Ianni (1972), Weppner (1973), and others have added to the literature and addressed the question of understanding cultural values in order to develop realistic solutions to social problems. Their research has demonstrated the unique contributions of ethnography to understanding some areas of criminal behavior, and it has also pointed out the importance of interdisciplinary approaches. This paper will examine (1) the possible contributions of ethnography, (2) the necessity of approaching sociocultural problems through an interdisciplinary methodology, and (3) the advocacy that is growing out of these approaches to understanding criminal subcultures.

ETHNOGRAPHY

Ethnography is the study of culture from within, the attempt through field observation to record how individuals perceive, construct, and interact within their social and economic environment. In this sense, ethnography provides a unique perspective that is more likely to be devoid of the labels applied by sociology and psychology. The anthropological perspective embraces the subjective reality and accepts the value system in the culture in question. There is in this perspective no overarching concept of deviance and norm applied from without but rather a concept of norm as supported by the informant's social context. Thus the addict, the prostitute, or the alcoholic is described in terms of his own subcultural value system and his interaction with the conflicting value system of the larger society. He is not viewed in the context of deviance.

Ethnography provides a contrast to the perspectives of other disciplines traditionally utilized to study social problem groups. Weppner (1973) pointed this out in his review of anthropology in contrast to medicine, psychology, law, and sociology. The medical perspective views addiction as a physiological disorder. The psychologist writes of the individual—the passive, inadequate addict personality. The jurist deals with concepts in immorality, and the sociologist with labeling, societal failure, and deviance. Weppner presented the anthropological perspective as the acceptance of the drug addict's concept of drug abuse and life-style. The methodology basic to this research perspective requires closer examination. It is important to further delineate the separate contributions of ethnography and the importance of combining it with the methods of other disciplines.

Kerri (1974) has divided the anthropological research perspective into six subcategories, which are useful here as explanatory tools. Kerri's concern is with precision in applied anthropology. Precision translates into a concern for accuracy. In an attempt to evaluate the "science" in anthropology, he examined different types and levels of anthropological statements and their practical implications, and he divided anthropological statements into descriptive, contextual, coassociational, covariate, causal, and predictive. Each of these statement types can be illustrated with examples from our addiction and prostitution research.

Descriptive statements provide specific and detailed information on whatever elements are under observation (1974:361). Through participant observation the ethnographer describes his perceptions and uses methods, such as ethnoscience, to describe the subject's perceptions. The ethnographer can extend the precision of his description through the use of statistics, network analysis, and direct quotation. A group of female prostitute-addicts can be described by age, education, class, appearance, language, observed behavior, and environment.

In a recent paper I evaluated some aspects of the relationship between prostitution and heroin addiction (James, 1976). A prostitute-addict was described by length of heroin usage and symptoms of withdrawal, by demographic variables, by age mean (25 years), by race (74% white; 26% black), and by educational mean (12 years). Participant observation provided evidence of their actual appearance and behavior on the street (p. 18). Language analysis expanded the description through the definition of such terms as "junkie chick" (p. 21). Quotations from observers on the street, both addicts and nonaddicts, added another descriptive dimension (p. 14). The use of the techniques of description available to anthropologists and sociologists provides at least an outline picture of the female addict. Any discipline separation between the sociologist as descriptive ethnographer and the anthropologist is unnecessary.

Contextual statements are seen by Kerri as further refinements of descriptive statements. Under what circumstances have we observed the behavior of prostitute-addicts? Essentially the data of participant observations reveal the context in which the addict comes into contact with prostitution as a support system. A contextual statement is an extension of the descriptive statement. It places the described phenomena as part of a larger whole—in this case, the subcultures of both prostitution and addiction. It clarifies the utilization of prostitution as a female addict support system if the existence of and interaction between the two subcultures is understood. In our research the environment and behavior of the addict prostitute and the nonaddict prostitute were significant.

> In the city is an area where (primarily) addicts and addict-prostitutes hang out. There are also a number of areas for prostitutes. The patterns of work are very different in these two areas. In the first (addict-prostitute area), there are many times when the sidewalks are deserted; then, in a few minutes, a couple, rather than a single woman, will appear. The man leans against the building waiting to see if his woman can catch a customer. The woman uses little caution. She will walk over to cars at the traffic light or wave them over to the curb, oblivious to the danger of the constantly patrolling police cars. In contrast, in the straight-prostitute streetwalking areas, some women, in pairs or singly, are always on the street after 8:00 p.m.; never are they in the company of "their man," and they appear constantly on the alert for police.

> The styles of the addict-prostitute and nonaddicted prostitute are very different. The addict cares little about clothing, her man is often on the street with her, she rarely works with another woman, she is careless about whom she chooses as customers and from whom she tries to steal, and frequently she gets arrested as a result. She usually works the same areas regardless of the threat of arrest once she has become "known" to the police. This style of work clearly differentiates her from "professional prostitutes" who are careful about clothes, who consider having their man anywhere in the working vicinity as being low class, who usually work with another woman, and who are careful with customer choice, stealing, and the police. These women are much less likely to be arrested than the addicts and always move to another town or area of the city if they feel that they are "known" to the police. The addict-prostitute is afraid to move because of the importance of her drug connection. [James, 1976]

The importance of this observed differentiation between the two categories is its significance to the women themselves. The prostitutes, through direct comment and observation, constantly draw a line between themselves and the addict-prostitutes. Shifting between the two groups is primarily a one-way process with clear labeling by the prostitutes once a woman begins to use narcotics.

Coassociational and *covariate statements* describe the association between a particular unit—e.g., the addict—and the context of addiction and prostitution. These statements also describe the degree of association, e.g., between prostitution and addiction. An example from our research is the association between entrance into prostitution and addiction. The association indicates the following equation:

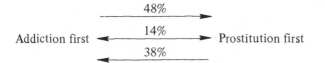

Prostitution follows addiction in 48% of the subjects, precedes it in 38%, and is simultaneous in 14% (James, 1976:17). This sample consists only of women who were both addicted and involved in prostitution at the time of the interview.

Causal statements are also functional statements. These statements indicate the degree and strength of a relationship as well as the nature and direction of the relationship (Kerri, 1974:363). In the previous example, the hypothesis that addiction is a direct result of involvement in prostitution cannot be proven. Forty-eight percent of the sample became addicted to heroin and then sought prostitution as a means to support their habits. The causal relationship has a duality in the 38% of the sample who were first involved in prostitution and then sought heroin as a release or recreational aspect of the life-style. The 14% demonstrating simultaneous involvement reaffirm the relationship between prostitution and addiction. Causal analysis requires the explanation inherent in descriptive and contextual statements.

Predictive statements are the highest and most important level of this type of analysis. The possibility of predicting behavior and explaining it is the goal of most social science research. The variables of an event are used to preduct its occurrence. The explanation analyzes the causes of the event (Kerri, 1974:364). The combination of all the previous categories of data statements creates the possibility of prediction and explanation. In the case of involvement in prostitution and addiction the relationship between the two activities is strongly supported by the descriptive, contextual, coassociational, and causal data. We can predict that women involved in heroin addiction are very likely to become involved in prostitution as a support system. This involvement will most likely occur after addiction but may also occur beforehand or simultaneously.

Anthropological methodology can move from the descriptive to the predictive level in its provision of a holistic view of the life-style and value system of a culture or subculture. This holistic view is essential to the development of realistic solutions to such social problems as prostitution and addiction. The foundation of the methodology is the description that explains the data and enhances the possibility of behavior prediction. Further use of the data gathered in our research supports these points when the analysis of the relationship between prostitution and addiction is extended.

PROSTITUTION AND ADDICTION

Ethnographic field interviews and observation, for example, are most useful in filling out the spaces left by statistical measures and formal interviewing. The existence of a subculture of addiction has been well documented, and the presence of women in that subculture is obvious but rarely reported in depth (Weppner, 1973). The concept of life-style presented by Weppner (1973), Agar (1973), Preble and Casey (1969), and others is equally applicable to the female addict. Ethnography reveals this side of the prostitute and addict-prostitute subcultures. At least two alternative cultural systems are present, with separate goals, values, and rules of appropriate behavior.

Group interviews with prostitutes, during field observation, emphasized the separation that they make between themselves and women who are addicted. Their desire for money is one example. Heroin addiction, they maintain, would defeat their reason for working for a better life-style; it would use up all their income.

> Okay, the way I see it, when you're into prostitution, heroin doesn't contribute to what you're into [i.e., making money]. But a woman who's into heroin addiction—well, prostitution could contribute to that by giving her other means of financing her habit.

The issue is also one of status. Prostitutes will not socialize with addicts and report strong negative feelings toward narcotics.

> I'm very prejudiced when it comes to that [narcotics addiction] because I hate that. The connection that prostitution leads to narcotics, it's not true. There's people that get into prostitution to support their habit and nothing else, you know, and there are people that have been into prostitution for years who have never touched heroin whatsoever.

And

> It's a matter of professionalism. You just don't mess with it. The really big-time women, they don't have time for that, for the addiction problem.

Their language structure, as well as the content of their conversation, also emphasizes separation. Linguistic analysis, primarily the development of drug and prostitute taxonomies, produced definite dimensions of contrast between the two subcultures of addict and prostitute. All the prostitutes who were interviewed avoided including addicts as a "kind of prostitute." They defined them instead as a separate group who were not professional and had no place in the "fast life" business or social scene. There are no terms in the basic prostitute taxonomy that refer specifically to addicts, but there are many terms for nonprofessional women who might be "chippying" around with narcotics. "Jive-ass," "flaky broad," and "fleabag" are used to refer to both incompetent women who try to prostitute and narcotic drug users. Addicts are referred to as "hypes," "junkie chicks," "dope fiends," and "junkie broads." The terms are applied to all female addicts regardless of whether they prostitute themselves or not.

In the addict taxonomy there do not seem to be any positive terms for the female addict within the subcultural argot. "Junkie broads" are on the lowest level of the social ladder. Positive terms such as "stand-up cat" and "righteous dope fiend" are never applied to women (Sutter, 1966; Feldman, 1968). There are also no terms to delineate their use of prostitution as an economic support system other than those used by the professionals, i.e., nonaddicted prostitutes. One unique term, "bag bride," was used by addicts to refer to women who were not prostitutes but granted sexual favors in order to get heroin.

This combination of field observation and linguistic analysis points out that two separate subcultures exist: one for prostitutes and a second for addicts and addict-prostitutes. Prostitutes prefer to describe an addict-prostitute as having never been a "professional" and as being low-class—a woman who has never been really committed to prostitution as a defining factor in their taxonomies. The existence of separate subcultures accommodates these women but does not provide a very complete explanation for women who shift from prostitution to addiction other than their lack of commitment to the original goals of their involvement in prostitution.

The importance of the above ethnographic data in explaining the relationship between prostitutes and addicts is most clear when it is reviewed in the context of all the other available data. At this point, anthropology and its various levels of analysis merge with the disciplines of sociology, psychology, and psychiatry. Complete information is essential to broaden the perspective for change. It is also essential to the provision of the accuracy, internal consistency, clarity, and built-in evaluation necessary for successful change.

INTERDISCIPLINARY APPROACHES

The complexity of the dynamics involved in female addiction and prostitution obviously requires the use of an interdisciplinary framework. The results from any one methodology are insufficient to clarify the relationship between the two states of prostitute and addict. Our examination of this problem in a recent paper, "Prostitution and Addiction: An Interdisciplinary Approach," points this out (James, 1976). The examination of one question, the dynamics of entrance into the state of addict-prostitute, provides a clear example of the insufficiency of analysis on the basis of a single methodology. In the area of social problems and solutions this insufficiency is crucial to accuracy.

Accuracy is a key consideration in the utilization of an inter-disciplinary approach. In past ethnographic research we have encountered this problem which, although it is not unique to anthropology, can be illustrated by the experience of that discipline. Traditionally, ethnographic differences of opinion regarding research results, as when Robert Redfield and Oscar Lewis wrote conflicting descriptions of Tepoztlan, had their main impact on the scientific progress of the discipline. By contrast, contemporary urban research has consequences beyond the social science disciplines, and, consequently, the price of inaccurate research may be higher. This price is paid in terms of the reactions of the agencies, institutions, and cultural groups that permit research within their populations. If the work of the anthropologist is found, or even perceived, to be inaccurate, his presence will soon be resented and blocked by groups who regard themselves as victims. The difficulties presently being experienced by anthropologists seeking to conduct research in some foreign countries or in certain communities in the United States provide examples.

The price may also be paid in misguided use of research findings by legal, social, and political agencies. Judgments made on the basis of inaccurate research will rarely provide successful solutions to human and social problems. Such failures can further widen the gap between academic research and its application in the community. The basic point here—accuracy and objectivity in data collection and reporting—seems deceptively simple, but the total situation is complex. Some of the implications of this discussion may be clarified by an example involving the semantic techniques of ethnoscience.

The main purpose of ethnoscience as a method is to discover and describe through semantic analysis the ways in which the members of the study population perceive and structure their world (Goodenough, 1957:167; Frake, 1964:112; Wallace, 1962:1). If this is carefully stated in publications, the researcher may feel relieved of any responsibility for considering the accuracy of the view of the world thus described. Unfortunately, data published both in and outside professional journals are utilized by many who do not understand the distinctions assumed by the researcher between "cultural reality" and "objective reality." To present only the "cultural reality" of one group among several opposing groups can be irresponsible. Although it is too time consuming to conduct a study of all possible groups and domains (i.e., conceptual partitions into which the perceived world is divided), some attempt to check areas of controversy must be a part of this kind of research. If it is not, publications of research results may contain assertions that are "true" and "accurate" to the informants, but both inaccurate and offensive to other involved groups.

An example of this situation would be the view of the jail possessed by many of my informants, as opposed to other views of the jail held by the police and city administration. Many of my informants had been prisoners in more than one jail and often gave generalized replies in response to my questions regarding the jail in which they were currently incarcerated. Thus, a statement regarding the physical layout of a jail may be accurate in terms of the informants' perceptions and conceptualizations of "jails," but not in terms of the jail in respect to jail personnel, incidents that occur (e.g., theft of personal property), or adequacy of medical care. Publications of this generalized "cultural reality" of the informant may be perceived as irresponsible by agencies who think in terms of their own "cultural reality," which is confined to a single jail. The misunderstanding and charges of inaccuracy which can result are obvious.

Also relevant to the issue of different "cultural realities" clouding the assessment of accuracy is the problem of the pluralistic nature of the urban situation (Spradley, 1968:1-2), especially when one is dealing with activities defined by the groups in power as illegal. While it is impossible to describe a situation as viewed by all possible participants, some attempt must be made to at least acknowledge the differing perspectives. For example, the perspective of the prostitute and addict conflicts at many points with that of the vice squad officer. An example of such conflict is the question of "police brutality" versus "self-defense." Vice squad officers maintain that they are kicked, knifed, and abused by prostitutes and that any seeming brutality on their part is self-defense. Few women when specifically questioned said that they had been roughly handled by police, yet most stated on a general level that police beat up other girls or forced them to make sexual payoffs. Detailed research revealed that very few of the informants had been physically abused by the vice squad. Other groups in the population, for example, those who had read sketchy accounts in newspapers, will have their own views of whether a given incident is a case of "brutality" or "self-defense." Conflicts such as this are ubiquitous in pluralistic urban environments, and such conflicts must be carefully researched and described for the qualifications of research results and made clear to potential users of the data. Unless such efforts at methodological rigor are maintained, research will contribute little to understanding or to effecting change.

There are other unique problems in street ethnography which must also be evaluated if the cornerstone of accuracy is to remain fixed. (I discuss only street research here because of its relevance to both addiction and criminal ethnography.) The acceptance of the subjective dimension within ethnography introduces the problems inherent in methodologies that step outside objective controls. Four examples of these areas of concern are value impositions, translation competence, social unit boundaries, and internal consistency.

Value imposition is a key problem for the anthropologist when conducting research in his own society. With the addict subculture the issue has two extremes. One is the cultural belief of the larger society that addicts are morally deviant and maladjusted. This moral bias and narrow concept of life-style choices has permeated much of the literature on addicts, and the researcher, regardless of his identity as an anthropologist, is also a product of his society. At the other extreme is the rejection of the majority norm, the attitude of those who have been called "bleeding heart liberals," whose value imposition takes the form of wholehearted acceptance of the addict and his life-style. The assumptions of the "moralist" produce biased research, and so does the approach of the "liberal." Both attitudes represent evaluations made prior to field observation and seriously decrease the potential utility of the research.

Translation competence is a similar, yet distinctive communication problem also encountered when working with a group within one's own culture (Spradley, 1968:5). The informants know the researcher's world and deal with questions accordingly. With prostitutes and addicts this problem is compounded by the nature of the "hustling" business. For example, a prostitute depends for her success and survival on her ability to judge people and handle them, to give the customer what he wants while not doing more than she wants, thus selling her ability to make the man feel that he is satisfied. "Conning" is an art of the profession, and the researcher is as likely a victim as the customer.

Another aspect of translation competence in this type of urban research is the researcher's tendency to think that he is getting better data than he is because of the seeming cooperation of his informants. This cooperation has many dimensions and must not dissuade the researcher from cross-checking information obtained in personal interviews. In addition, he is involved in his own problem of translation competence because he can easily misuse his ability to supply missing information from his knowledge of the system.

Maruyama has pointed out the existence of this problem in prison research (1974:319):

> There is no relevance resonance between the inmates and the usual interviewers. The inmates feel exploited by the interviewers. In order to keep the intrusion of the exploiters to a minimum, inmates use sophisticated phony answers which make the interviewers happy.

Solutions to the problems of translation competence include extensive interviewing in various contexts, such as group discussions, free conversations, and individual interviewing in depth, and utilizing semantic techniques such as card sorting (Kelly, 1955:222-223) to eliminate the normal structure of an interviewing situation, thus enabling the researcher to discover and validate certain data. Other possible solutions include the cross-checking of informant responses through such available sources as institutional files, arrest records, and the comments of friends, relatives, and others in the business. But the most reliable solution is time and the use of combined methods. In general, the more time spent with informants under varying circumstances, the more reliable are the data gathered. The use of multiple convergent measures further ensures an accurate resolution of conflicting information.

Another problem which has emerged as one of general concern to anthropology in urban research procedure is the definition of social unit boundaries (e.g., Spradley, 1968:3-4; Cohen, 1969). It arose in this study of prostitutes and addicts because of the crosscutting networks that are a part of the "fast life." The prostitutes who do not utilize "hard" drugs maintain, as has been previously noted, that the addicts represent a distinct subculture. They point out that drug addicts turn to prostitution as a way of supporting their habits but are not otherwise a part of the prostitute subculture. Prostitutes who consider themselves professionals point out that the "hypes" dress sloppily, treat their customers poorly, and are more inclined to pull "rip-offs" (i.e., steal). Many prostitutes refuse to let addicts become a part of their "stable" (i.e., an arrangement of one male and more than one woman doing buisness together), and they state that a "good" pimp will kick a girl out if she uses drugs, or he will try to break her habit; otherwise, the drug becomes the controller, rather than the pimp. The overlapping activities of prostitution and drug addiction make it difficult to separate these components of the hustling situation.

Another aspect of the problem of defining social unit boundaries is the crosscutting of cultures or subcultures. Research within subcultures (e.g., those of prostitutes) that are by definition a part of another culture (e.g., the larger "American culture"), as well as other subcultures (e.g., "black subculture"), presents problems of over-lapping forms which obscure important cultural differences. This is obvious in research with prostitutes who are members of different racial groups. In attempting to understand the prostitute life-style, one finds that racial differences form a crucial set of variables. Although the women live and operate in similar environments, sharing the same customers and pimps, they are different in many ways. Black prostitutes must be considered in terms of the black community and subculture which accepts, *in varying degrees,* hustling as legitimate, just as white prostitutes must be considered in terms of the larger white culture which views overt hustling, *in varying degrees,* as deviant. Any discussion of deviance in prostitution must take cognizance of these differences in cultural backgrounds. The researcher is faced with differences of race within the subculture of prostitutes, even though such differences may be minimized by the prostitutes themselves.

Accuracy as objective logic is also tempered by the problem of internal consistency. The use of multiple measures in coordination with basic ethnography makes an important contribution to its resolution. Questionnaires can provide built-in tests of consistency through the repetitive inclusion of questions that are important measures. A drug history, for example, can be approached through more than one structure within a single questionnaire. Taped interviews can provide further checks, as can arrest records and other available formal files. The final explanatory check of complex issues can rest with the perspective gained from the field methods of ethnography, including participant observation, network analysis, and ethnoscience.

The above issues of values, translation, social units, and consistency are important to basic accuracy in social problem research. Careful and combined measurement, realistic description, and a check-and-balance system provide a data foundation upon which workable solutions can be built. The clear presentation of this data for full utilization then becomes the final issue in the area of accuracy—an issue that is partially resolved by balancing ethnography with the other social science disciplines.

Clarity is often the quality least sought after by research authors, yet most important to the productive utilization of results. Social scientists are forced by the academic structure to write for each other rather than for those who are directly responsible for seeking solutions to social problems. Accurate interpretation is often sacrificed, not enhanced by the jargon of the statistician, the clinical tester, or the ethnoscientist. It usually precludes any understanding of the utility of the data in direct application. Here ethnography provides perspective, insight, and understandable description. The life-style of the addict is described, for example, in the context of a daily routine parallel to our own in meaning if not in content. Holistic descriptions can be understood more easily than fragmented data analysis. Preble and Casey (1969) described the life of the addict as an economic career. Sutter (1966), Blumer (1967), Finestone (1957), Feldman (1968), and Agar (1973) also provided descriptions of the addict life-style in contrast to demographic or psychological analysis of the individual. These writers have created a picture that is the meat on the bones of more formal measures.

Ethnography in its descriptive strength provides the perspectives within which to evaluate and analyze other sources of information. Alone it runs the risks mentioned before of value imposition and translation competence. In combination with other social science measures it becomes the vehicle of understanding, based on solid data, for those who implement social programs. The reverse is true for any of the other available measures. Demography or clinical analysis alone is out of context and provides a reduced perspective for the reader. The issues of accuracy and clarity in research publications or presentations of any kind are central to their implementation and the third area of concern of this paper: advocacy.

ADVOCACY

Ethnography offers another area of support for change in social problems in the form of advocacy. The process of "learning a culture" and understanding its differing world view provides great impetus for support of the individuals whose life-styles may be under attack. The philosophy of tolerance inherent in anthropology and the clarification of diverse value systems catch the researcher in a professional commitment and occasionally a personal one. Protection of informants often demands an advocative stand. This in turn involves the anthropologist in careful definition of his goals and responsibility. The nature of ethnography, the very character of description, forces consideration of these research parameters.

The involvement in advocacy should be anticipated and therefore begins with the initial research proposal. The design of a research project determines the nature of the results. The research structure can also determine the possible ways in which the results might be used to resolve social problems. Since the design of a research project precedes field experience, many problems—both ethical and methodological—should be considered beforehand, but often are not, and thus become difficult to resolve post hoc. Research goals must be considered first. They may be divided into two major types: the *scientific goals* (the researcher's hope that he will contribute to a body of theory whose purpose is that of scientific explanation) and the *social goals* (the researcher's hope that his findings will result in the resolution of social problems).

There is now a substantial body of literature and tradition regarding research which is explicitly intended to apply the procedures of this science to the solution of social as well as scientific problems. This kind of research often goes by the name of applied anthropology or applied sociology. However, anthropological and sociological research may have social consequences whether or not it is conducted with explicit social goals in mind. When the researcher has not anticipated the social consequences and is thus compelled to consider them only after the fact and after the results are published, problems may occur when his results are used for purposes that he did not intend. This is especially true in areas of illegal behavior.

The problem just described has always been with us. But because of the tradition of conducting anthropological research in non-Western, relatively isolated societies to which one seldom returned, it has often been an invisible problem. Anthropologists have rarely been around to witness the social consequences of their research; but, with the accelerating trend toward urban research in Western societies, the anthropologist is now more frequently witness to these consequences. They occur around him and directly affect and involve him. Scientific goals have traditionally been regarded as sufficient to justify research efforts. Experience now leads us to realize that social goals must likewise be articulated, at least by the researcher himself and, ideally, prior to the research, whether incorporated in the research or not.

Closely related to research goals is the question of *responsibility* for research results—that is, the responsibility for consequences for the informant group, rather than the broader question of responsibility to "science," a university, the nation, or mankind. Social scientists have sometimes been accused of prostituting themselves and their informants to the institutions and agencies that provide research funds. This problem has generated considerable discussion, but little agreement. Responsibility for research findings is complicated because the researchers are divided on the basic issue of the "moral scientist" (and his possible subjective conflict) and the "pure scientist." Although it cannot be resolved here, this issue must be noted as increasingly crucial in urban research.

The basic questions facing the researcher concern how his data can be used and by whom, what he can do about it, if anything, and who is to be in control. Initially these issues raise the question of sponsorship of research because the first problem is that of finding financial support for the intended project. The issue of research goals articulates most clearly here with that of responsibility. Many problems have arisen when researchers have not been aware of conditions inherent in the acceptance of research funds from certain agencies. If the social goals have not been articulated, the researcher is in no position to consider conditions attached to grants or reject as potential sources those agencies whose conditions conflict with his sense of responsibility. If, for example, one of the conditions of financial support involves making recommendations regarding future interaction between the funding agency and/or other groups and the study population, then careful comparison of the goals of the researcher and those of the concerned agencies is crucial. Careful selection of sources of financial support can be an important initial means of controlling the uses of one's research results.

The issue of responsibility obviously extends to publications. Once research is published, depending on how freely available the publications are, all effective control over interpretation and utilization is lost. This fact has important implications when publishing in professional journals, but the implications are multiplied when publishing in journals or books in which "science" is not the only consideration, as in the popular press. Safeguards that do not affect the scientific usefulness of the data should be built into the reporting structure regardless of the publication medium.

The problems of research goals and the use of published research can be further resolved through the use of evaluation and complementary research. Evaluation refers to the continuation of research into areas in which social problem solutions have been structured from a researcher's information. Complementary research is the examination of the other parts of the system within which the examined subculture functions.

Evaluation is rarely considered as an advocacy mechanism, yet it provides a powerful check on the application and the utility of research findings. Too often the researcher is free to provide the original scientific analysis of a social problem and then abandon the resulting social service projects to questionable interpretation and application. While recognizing the separation between science as knowledge and science in practical application, the social problem researcher must be aware of this responsibility. This responsibility must involve at least the design of an evaluation measure to support or discount the solutions developed from his research.

Complementary research is as important as evaluation. It is difficult, for example, to understand the addict subculture without parallel investigation of the criminal justice system, the rehabilitative social agency system, and the legal and social policy makers. The perspective stemming from an isolated analysis of prostitution or addiction neglects the environment within which they must respond. Nader, in her article "Up the Anthropologist: Perspectives Gained from Studying Up" (1969), documents the importance of a broader selection of groups to study. Studies of policy-making elites would reveal a considerable amount about the pressures applied to addicts and the construction of solutions to the problem of addiction. It is easy to predict that each group is striving to maintain its own sense of values—frequently regardless of relevant data or harm to other units within the system.

Direct advocacy carries all of the above areas of responsibility one step further into community action. There are many articles discussing the potential areas of action for the researcher willing to take an advocate position. The options are numerous and varied. The anthropologist can function as a consultant or adviser for the group that he has studied or the policy makers who affect that group (Barnett, 1956; Peterson, 1974). The role may be limited to the provision of information or include an active role in the development and execution of change. Community involvement is another advocate role with many facets. The anthropologist can participate in the development of services—health, education, legal, etc.—to improve the environment of the group to which he is relating (Jacobs, 1974). Legal advocacy is another important role for the researcher. He can function as an expert witness in court cases and in the legislative review of legal codes (James, 1974; Aswad, 1974). Testimony at public hearings provides a route for the exertion of some control over the presentation, interpretation, and utilization of research results. The anthropologist can also function as a trainer for any personnel who will be involved in providing services for or controls on the group that he has studied. The researcher can also fulfill an educational role that expands far beyond the university. Depending on factors of time, energy, and commitment, he can inform the nonacademic community of his research and its potential for productive social change. The problem in all these forms of advocacy is one of balancing accurate information with informant protection. The main issue is the recognition that knowledge is power and neutrality is in effect support of the status quo. Research and advocacy in the area of social problem resolution must be carefully balanced.

The problems of advocacy in any of its forms are, of course, important to consider. Aside from time and energy there is the question of maintaining "scientific objectivity." Can the rules of logic and method combine with advocacy and objectively resolve value conflicts? There is also the question of the effect on the research environment. Legal action, for example, may alienate agencies that can provide or deny access to informants. An identifiable position as advocate may lead funding agencies to deny support because of documented researcher bias. The individual researcher is left to decide these issues for himself. He must maintain a balance between responsibility to informants and his desire to further the scientific aims of his discipline. In research with prostitutes and addicts, the problems of maintaining balance involve largely the judgment as to whether the publication of research findings increases understanding and possible assistance to the informant population or whether it contributes to their further degradation and incarceration. This judgment can be made only by the individual researcher who has faced and come to terms with the philosophical questions implicit in anthropology and advocacy. His chances for accurate judgment will be greatly enhanced through the understanding of the strengths and weaknesses of ethnography and the safeguards of an interdisciplinary methodology.

CONCLUSION

The most important issues in the use of ethnography as a source of information for the solution of social problems are perspective and accuracy. Ethnography provides an enhanced possibility for a value-free description of a particular life-style. When combined with the perspectives of other social science disciplines, this perspective can be safely grounded in objective methodologies. There is a possibility of productively combining a description of the subjective realities of an illegal subculture with logical measurements and analysis. Accurate information on social problem groups and the larger system within which they interact is crucial to realistic change. Advocacy on behalf of social change is the final and perhaps most important step in the use of ethnography. It is also the only reasonable justification for probing the life-styles of these human beings.

REFERENCES

AGAR, M.H. (1973). Ripping and running: A formal ethnography of urban heroin addicts. New York: Seminar Press.
ASWAD, B.C. (1974). "Comments." Human Organization, 33:322-323.
BARNETT, H.G. (1956). Anthropology in administration. Evanston, Ill.: Row, Peterson.
BLUM, R.H. (1969). "A cross-cultural study." Society and drugs (R.H. Blum and Associates, eds.). San Francisco: Jossey-Bass.
BLUMER, H. (1967). The world of youthful drug use. Berkeley: School of Criminology, University of California.

COHEN, Y.A. (1969). "Social boundary systems." Current Anthropology, 10:103-116.
EDGERTON, R.B. (1967). The cloak of competence. Berkeley: University of California Press.
FELDMAN, W. (1968). "Ideological support to becoming and remaining a heroin addict." Journal of Health and Social Behavior, 9:131-139.
FINESTONE, H. (1957). "Cats, kicks, and color." In H. Becker (ed.), The other side. New York: Free Press.
FRAKE, C.O. (1964). "A structural description of Subanun religious behavior." Pp. 111-129 in W.H. Goodenough (ed.), Explorations in cultural anthropology: Essays in honor of George Murdock. New York: McGraw-Hill.
GOODENOUGH, W.H. (1957). "Cultural anthropology and linguistics." Pp. 167-177 in P.L. Garvin (ed.), Report of the seventh annual Round Table Meeting on Linguistics and Language Study. Washington, D.C.: Georgetown University.
HENRY, J. (1965). Pathways to madness. New York: Vintage.
HUMPHREYS, L. (1970). Tearoom trade. Chicago: Aldine.
IANNI, F.A.J. (1972). A family business. New York: Russell Sage Foundation.
JACOBS, S.-E. (1974). "Action and advocacy anthropology." Human Organization: Journal of the Society for Applied Anthropology, 33:209-215.
JAMES, J. (1972). "On the block: Urban perspectives." Urban Anthropology, 1:125-140.
––– (1973). "The prostitute-pimp relationship." Medical Aspects of Human Sexuality, (November):147-160.
––– (1974). "The law and commercialized sex." Proceedings of the 10th annual meeting of SIECUS (Sex Information, Education, and Counseling for the United States), New York.
––– (1976). "Prostitution and addiction: An interdisciplinary approach." Unpublished manuscript.
KEISER, R.L. (1969). The Vice Lords: Warriors of the streets. New York: Holt, Rinehart and Winston.
KELLY, G.A. (1955). The psychology of personal constructs (vol. 1). New York: W.W. Norton.
KERRI, J.N. (1974). " 'Sciencing' in anthropology: Toward precision in the science of applied anthropology." Human Organization: Journal of the Society of Applied Anthropology, 33:359-365.
LIEBOW, E. (1967). Tally's corner. Boston: Little, Brown.
MARUYAMA, M. (1974). "Endogenous research vs. delusions of relevance and expertise among exogenous academics." Human Organization: Journal of the Society of Applied Anthropology, 33:318-322.
NADER, L. (1969). "Up the anthropologist: Perspectives gained from studying up." In D. Hymes (ed.), Reinventing anthropology. New York: Vintage.
PACKER, H.L. (1968). The limits of the criminal sanction. Stanford, Calif.: Stanford University Press.
PETERSON, J.H. (1974). "The anthropologist as advocate." Human Organization: Journal of the Society for Applied Anthropology, 33:311-318.
PREBLE, E., and CASEY, J.J., Jr. (1969). "Taking care of business: The heroin user's life on the street." International Journal of the Addictions, 4:1-24.
SPRADLEY, J.P. (1968). "Urban anthropology: An ethnographic approach." Unpublished manuscript.
––– (1970). You owe yourself a drunk: Ethnography of urban nomads. Boston: Little, Brown.

SUTTER, A.G. (1966). "The world of the righteous dope fiend." Issues in Criminology, 2:177-222.
WALLACE, A.F.C. (1962). "Culture and cognition." Science, 351:1-7.
WEPPNER, R.S. (1973). "Anthropological view of the street addict's world." Human Organization: Journal of the Society for Applied Anthropology, 22:111-121.
WILSON, J.Q. (1975). Thinking about crime. New York: Basic Books.

9

FIELD ETHICS FOR THE LIFE HISTORY

CARL B. KLOCKARS

It has become almost commonplace to observe that the social
sciences, envious of the power, prestige, and respectability of their
natural science sisters, have sought to imitate their models, methods,
and morals. The imitation has never been completely happy, but for
no small part of the history of sociology the Comtean prophesy of a
social science reconstructed in the idealized image of the natural
sciences was taken as gospel. Heretics like Popper (1959) were long
considered to be carping critics of the details of this vision rather
than its substance; and, with the aid of rapidly developing statistical
and instrumental technologies, the epiphany of what Nietzsche once
called "the dogma of the immaculate perception" appeared immi-
nent.

The revelation never came, of course, but exactly where we went
wrong is still unclear. We know that, while George Lundberg (1955,
1956) was preaching his best, even his choir boys (to say nothing of
the congregation of the faithful) were reading *The Professional Thief*
(Sutherland, 1937), *Street Corner Society* (Whyte, 1955), *The Jack
Roller* (Shaw, 1930), and a lot of other materials that the High Priest
of Hard Social Science had placed on his Index. We began to find out

UNIVERSITY COLLEGE LIBRARY CARDIFF

that all types of things that were never mentioned in public were going on behind the lab doors of our natural science sisters. And the Scientific Method—explained Kaplan (1964), Kuhn (1962), and Feyerabend (1975), as they joined Popper in capturing the center stage of the philosophy of science, natural and social—was a stork story for big children, beginning students, and outsiders.

I have said this much about the history of the imitative relationship between the natural and social sciences because the twin products of that history have been a healthy suspicion by social scientists about imports from the natural sciences and a realization that many social science problems, methods, and theories require approaches which take special recognition of their specifically social nature. But exactly how the social sciences ought to proceed now that they can no longer consider the idealized model of the natural sciences as a strong or steady guide is perhaps the central theoretical and methodological question of our discipline. One answer to this question (though it is actually more of a strategy for answers than an answer itself) is that social scientists turn to the history of their own works and the works of others to examine what in fact were the real contexts of discovery and verification. By examining these contexts rather than reporting edited accounts that conformed to acceptable and idealized reconstructions of what opinion determined real scientific work to be, social scientists would truly learn what social scientists did when they were doing well as social scientists.[1]

Working within the mandate of this suggestion, I should like to examine a problem which I believe proceeds from the historically imitative relationship between the social sciences and natural sciences, namely, the ability of research ethics cultivated in the light of laboratory practice to survive the rigors of exposure to the natural environments of field research. In particular, I should like to examine application of such ethics to the life history method when the subject is an active criminal; and I should like to draw upon some of my experiences of the past few years with the research, publication, and promotion of a life history of a dealer in stolen property, *The Professional Fence* (Klockars, 1974).

THE ETHICAL MODEL FROM THE NATURAL SCIENCES

The single most influential document on the ethics of research in the United States is the Department of Health, Education, and Welfare's *Institutional Guide to DHEW Policy on Protection of Human Subjects* (1971). It is influential not because it is particularly profound but because researchers cannot get research support from DHEW or any of its divisions (e.g., Food and Drug Administration, National Institute of Health) without satisfying the requirements outlined in it. Because DHEW supports both natural science (biomedical, biological, pharmacological) and social science research with human subjects, its policy document is a particularly good example of an attempt to build a guide to ethical research on principles which bridge both natural and social science problems.

My reading of the *DHEW Guide* finds that it works with three ethical guides. The guides are DHEW policy and, as such, specify the responsibilities of researchers receiving DHEW grants and of institutional review committees charged with examining both social and natural science research projects involving human subjects. The three guides are:

(1) "The rights and welfare of the subjects are [to be] adequately protected."

(2) "The risks to subjects are [to be] outweighed by potential benefits."

(3) "Informed consent of subjects will be obtained by methods that are adequate and appropriate."

Although it might be possible to interpret these statements of DHEW policy in various ways, I suggest that they collapse into a single ethical principle upon a careful reading of the sections of the *DHEW Guide* which elaborate on them. That principle is the risk-benefit principle referred to in statement 2 above, and to demonstrate this we need to turn to the Guide's elaboration of statements 1 and 3.

Statement 1, which provides that the rights and welfare of human subjects be adequately protected, has a "deontological" ring about it. That is, it would seem to be an ethical statement which depends upon some first premises about human rights and welfare. However, in the *DHEW Guide*'s elaboration, the institutional review committee is instructed to meet this policy requirement by evaluating the risks of the project and seeing to it that adequate safeguards (encoding of names, storing data securely, destroying depleted data, etc.) are introduced and unnecessary risks are not taken. With one exception, the entire theme of the *DHEW Guide*'s elaboration of this statement of policy is the economy and control of risk taking in the image that, by entering the smallest risks necessary in the risk-benefit equation, not only will the subject be best served but the equation will be most likely to balance in favor of the researcher.[2]

Statement 3 requires that informed consent be obtained by methods that are adequate and appropriate. It goes even further to identify the "elements of informed consent," of which there are six:

(1) "A fair explanation of the procedures to be followed, including an identification of those which are experimental."

(2) "A description of the attendant discomforts and risks."

(3) "A description of the benefits to be expected."

(4) "A disclosure of appropriate alternative procedures that would be advantageous for the subject."

(5) "An offer to answer any inquiries concerning the procedures."

(6) "An instruction that the subject is free to withdraw his consent and to discontinue participation in the project or activity at any time."

Clearly, the six elements of informed consent are simply what a subject who lacked the technical sophistication of an institutional review committee would need to act like one. In the informed consent specification and the elaboration which follows it, the subject emerges as a mini-institutional review committee not only in his relationship to the researcher but also in the risk-benefit way in which he is expected to evaluate the proposal from the researcher. The only difference is that the institutional review committee can veto the entire project and needs no elementary explanation to do so. The subject, however, can only veto or otherwise call a halt to his own participation and must rely on the fair but simple explanation of the researcher in reaching his decision.[3]

Thus, I think it is accurate to characterize DHEW policy as predicated on a risk-benefit ethics. In raising in the next section of this essay a series of ethically challenging events from the biography of *The Professional Fence*, I intend to return to the questions of (1) whether or not such an ethics bears any relationship to the way in which a social scientist working as a life historian of a criminal subject meets those challenges in the natural setting of his work and (2) whether or not a risk-benefit ethics is a fruitful and appropriate way of talking about the ethical challenges of such work.

FIELD ETHICS FOR A LIFE HISTORY
December 1971 to March 1976

I first met the man who was to be the central character of *The Professional Fence*, a man whom I was later to name Vincent Swaggi, in the first week of January in 1972. I had managed to identify Vincent as a major dealer in stolen property by interviewing thieves at Graterford Prison, a state institution near Philadelphia. Although in the introduction to my interviews with the thieves whom I interviewed I explained that I was not interested in the identify of any particular fences, I found that many thieves were quite willing to identify their fences, and others would yield to an interviewing gimmick I describe in *The Professional Fence:*

> I soon found that names would come up naturally and that trying to avoid real names often involved an awkward substitution of a fictitious name for the real one. Furthermore, after interviewing nine or ten experienced thieves, I found that I could often tell what fence they were talking about by the descriptions they gave or the locations they mentioned. When I thought I knew the fence an inmate was describing, I would say something like, "Hmm, that sounds like Swaggi," or Jones or Big Leo or whoever I thought it was. If I was right, the thief was always impressed. It showed him I knew what I was talking about. If I was wrong the thief would usually correct me with, "No, it ain't him, it's ———." Once I had established who the fence was that the inmate was talking about, I could ask more detailed questions about that particular fence's business. [p. 212]

I had developed a "book" on a number of Philadelphia area fences from interviews conducted in this way; but, largely on the advice of a thief who knew Vincent very well, I wrote him the following letter, which might be considered a request for "informed consent":

30 December 1971

Dear Mr. Swoggi [sic] :

We have never met. Since I know something about you, I ought to tell you something about me. I'm first of all a professor of sociology and criminology at Beaver College. I teach criminology, theory, research, etc. . . . I've published some articles, and for the past two years I have been writing and researching a major book. The topic of the book is the professional receiver of stolen goods. It can and will be an important and interesting book.

I have read everything ever written about the "fence." Most of it is junk. Fencing is an old occupation. The first time the word fence was used in print was 1610. Since then there have been some very famous fences both real and fictional. I wouldn't suppose you had ever heard of Jonathan Wild, Moll Cutpurse, or Isaac Solomons, but they were all major fences in the 18th and 19th centuries in England. Many real fences throughout history have been men with amazing abilities and almost giant characters. Such men, though, are few and far between.

There is surely an art to being a fence, and there are but a very few great artists left. I have some suspicion that the art and character of fencing is dying or changing. There are certainly a lot of nickel-and-dime hustlers and pushers who will pick up swag for peanuts, but they are not true professionals or artists of the caliber that the occupation of fencing has known.

During the past two years I have talked with close to a hundred thieves. The majority of them have been at the state prison. To date, I have almost 50 hours of tape-recorded interviews, stories, and anecdotes about fences and fencing.

I am not a cop. I can keep things confidential, and there are quite a few guys who can give me "references." (Tommy Blue was the man who suggested I write to you before I try to see you. Eyeball sends his regards.) Eyeball didn't give me any information that might be harmful to you. For one thing, I'm not interested in anything of that sort anyway.

Let me tell you what I am trying to write about. *First,* I want to try to describe the style and quality of the professional fence. How does he live?

What does he do? Who are his friends? What kinds of people does he deal with? How does he handle them? *Second,* what kind of man must a fence be? Actor, businessman, artist, or hustler? What skills must he have? Why does he choose and stick with his business? *Third,* I'd like to know how the business has changed, both in the past ten or twenty years and since it began in the 17th century. Is amateur competition greater today than ten years ago? Is the old time fence a thing of the past? Do unprofessional thieves make for unprofessional fences? And, *fourth,* I'd like to write about the fence as a "criminal without victims," a man whom thieves, the neighborhood, and his customers are glad to have around, a man with no direct victims.

I am not interested in any details which could get anyone in trouble. Names, dates, specific crimes, specific places, specific people are of no interest to me. If I were a cop, I'd have to warn you of your rights before talking to me. Since I tell you that I'm not a cop and will not make any such warning, nothing that you say to me could be used against you. Also, as you are aware, there is a statute of limitations on receiving. It would be just as helpful to talk about things the way they were three years ago as they are today.

To be honest wtih you, I'd like to write your biography. It could become a classic book. I'll call you during the first week of January. Please don't turn me down without letting me take you to lunch and tell you more.

Sincerely yours,

[Signed]

Carl Klockars

Professor

Sociology and Criminology

There are a number of errors in the letter to Vincent. Some are intentional and others are not. First, I misspelled Vincent's last name. That was unintentional. Second, I claimed to be a "professor of sociology and criminology"; I am an assistant professor of sociology. I misrepresented myself in this way because I assumed that Vincent would not be familiar with customary academic rankings or disciplinary divisions. Third, I had not read everything about fencing, and a lot of it is not "junk." Fourth, I had talked to many thieves, but 60 might have been a better estimate than 100. I thought the puffing might impress Vincent with my seriousness.

Fifth, the statement that, because I did not warn Vincent of his rights, nothing he said to me could be used against him is totally false. I honestly have no idea where I got that idea from, and I do not know why I thought it was true at the time that I wrote the letter. I included it of course because, if it were true, it would certainly have eliminated some serious risks in doing the life history of Vincent. Vincent never mentioned the error to me, although, as I shall explain, we did consider the risks of our work most realistically at later stages of the project. Finally, the whole letter is slanted in ways that distort the true intent of my work. I did want to look at fencing as a "crime without victims," but not because I believed it was one but because I believed it was not, though people often behaved as if it was.

I enclosed with the letter a copy of Sutherland's *The Professional Thief,* attached to which was a handwritten note which read, "This is what I want to do with you." I did so not only because I thought it would set a precedent for what I wanted Vincent to do but also because, if Vincent was not receptive to my letter, getting my book back would give me an excuse to see him and try to convince him in person.

As it turned out, however, most of these little gambits, gimmicks, and deceptions were probably unnecessary. For when I did call Vincent as I said I would in the letter, he said he was interested and willing to talk to me. When I went to the store which was the front for his fencing business, I was asked by the man at the counter (who I later learned was Vincent's brother) whether I was the college professor who was going to write the book about Vincent. When Vincent finally arrived, he introduced himself and suggested that we go into the back room of the store where we could "talk private." Once there, Vincent asked me but a single question: Did I plan to use real names in the book? I said no and added that I would change names, dates, places, and descriptions so that no one would know it was about him. Vincent responded to my assurance with a sentence that began, "Well, I was born in New York City in . . . " and he did not stop talking for the next 15 months. About an hour after I first met Vincent he started letting me watch his transactions with thieves.

For the next 15 months Vincent and I met once and sometimes twice a week. I would arrive at his store late in the afternoon, watch him wheel and deal for an hour or so, and then he would take me to dinner where we would discuss what Vincent had been up to since our last meeting. Not once in 15 months would Vincent let me pay for dinner. After dinner we would go to Vincent's home, where we would sit and talk about his life and business in ways more formal and directed than at dinner.

The Evolution of Informed Consent

In planning the interview strategy, I had decided to begin with what I considered to be the most benign areas of Vincent's life: his childhood, family, schooling, adolescence, and other activities whose historical distance or noncriminal nature would render less sensitive. But this too was less necessary than I had thought originally. Vincent was quite willing to discuss his criminal activities, even those which were ongoing—and we did so always over dinner. Moreover, from the very first day we met, Vincent demonstrated his willingness not only to talk about his criminal ventures but to let me watch him at them. What the three months that Vincent and I did spend on these less sensitive subjects did do was to let Vincent know, at a time before a special kind of commitment would be necessary from him, exactly how my definition of our project differed from his. Vincent learned very soon, for example, that I had a downright annoying need for verification of details. We wrote and telephoned the convent where Vincent had spent his early years in an orphanage. We tried, but failed, to get his school records, He ordered his birth certificate to settle a dispute that we had over the exact year of his birth. Reconstructing one's early years is not by any means easy work. My demands for documentation and my critical scrutiny of the way in which experiences and periods fitted with one another called for an effort on Vincent's part that I know he had not anticipated.

In these first few months, but realizing it only tacitly at the time, Vincent was learning what a life history was. His definition of our project changed during those early months, and it assumed a meaning to him which replaced the one with which he had begun. I think that originally Vincent wanted a book which would have let him dazzle people with the type of stories he was so splendid at telling. As our project evolved, Vincent saw *The Professional Fence* not only as testament for him (which is how he saw it from the beginning) but as a document that would have to withstand the most careful scrutiny if it were to survive.

This sense of our project as a document that would establish Vincent's anonymous immortality in criminological circles gave me what I consider to be one of the strongest controls over the reliability and validity of Vincent's accounts. Many times I reminded Vincent that the book was going to be read by very sharp people and that, if they detected a single misrepresentation or error, the whole book could end up being discredited. Vincent understood this, often responded with threats and descriptions of what he would do to such potential critics, and, I believe, controlled excesses in his accounts to limits that life historians can tolerate.

There were real risks to our project and to Vincent's security and safety which we discussed. Some, but not all, of these risks can now be discussed more openly than they could when Vincent was alive.

Tape-recorded Interviews. The first was the issue of whether or not I should use a tape recorder during our interviews. Vincent balked at the idea when I broached it at our second interview meeting not only because he did not have sufficient reason to trust me that early in the project but also because he did not understand that so much of the book would be in his own words. Nor could he understand why my notes would not suffice in that I was the writer and would surely be able to make his stories even more exciting than he had told them. I say in *The Professional Fence* that we did not tape the interviews for reasons of security, but that is true only in part. The security problem was the real problem only in the sense that, at the time that the taping question came up, Vincent's relationship neither to me nor to our project was strong enough to overcome it. In fact, about three years later Vincent and I did make a tape which the publisher used in promoting the book.

The Greatest Undercover Agent in the Country. The second issue over which Vincent and I wrestled was how to deal with his relationship with the police—both Philadephia city police and the FBI. Although the historical literature on fencing is full of references to fences' informant relationships to police, it must have been six months before I felt comfortable enough to approach the topic with Vincent and well more than a year before I felt I could ask questions which would open up areas that Vincent had not voluntarily opened for me in advance. In fact, only after the book had been published and I had known Vincent for more than three years could we discuss the topic of informing without resorting to a fascinating, and for Vincent a face-saving, semantic fiction.

In part, Vincent was as successful as he was (more than a quarter of a century of dealing in stolen goods and less than six months in jail) because the police gave him a limited license to operate as a fence as long as he continued to supply them with high quality information that they could use in securing arrests and convictions and in recovering stolen property. Vincent used this relationship to control troublesome thieves when necessary, but Vincent's character and interpersonal skills were such that such extreme measures were seldom necessary. His "license" covered trading only in stolen property in limited quantities. It did not cover, as it was issued by detectives or higher ups in the major theft division of the city police department, trade in narcotics of any kind. For the same reason, information about narcotics was less sought after by those who licensed Vincent than was information about stolen property and theft. When Vincent had narcotics information, he supplied it to people either in the U.S. Customs (when it involved smuggling), in the FBI (when it involved interstate dealing), or so high up in the Philadelphia police organization that divisional interests did not matter. Vincent had a particular flair for attracting businessmen contemplating fraudulent bankruptcy, and he was no stranger to offers of counterfeit money.

The problem for us was that, while we both knew that the professional fence was also a professional informant, the terms "informants," "squealers," "finks," "rats," "snitches," or whatever other derogatory title one uses makes the subject difficult to talk about, even among friends. At those times when the subject came up because it followed a particular anecdote or "fit" because we would be discussing *other* informants and how Vincent handled them, Vincent would sometimes tell stories about "helping the police" (which is good) by doing some "undercover work" (for which face repair work is also not necessary). As enough of these stories accumulated so that Vincent knew that I knew, I was given access, if I were careful to preserve the semantic fiction, to the activities of, as Vincent liked to call himself, "the greatest undercover agent in the country."

This problem squarely pitted my obligation to protect Vincent against the need to present an accurate account of the realities of the fencing business. On the one hand, to quote Vincent, "You tell about that an' I'll have every gang in the country gunnin' for me." On the other, I believe that no fence can operate for very long without becoming an informant. To solve this problem, I worked out a series of compromises, which, though I told Vincent about them, I do not think he ever really understood. First of all, I used historical material on Jonathan Wild to demonstrate the close, if not perfect, association between fencing and informing. Wild was not only the greatest fence in history, but the father of the modern police system as well. Here is how I conclude the chapter on Wild, which I describe as a necessary introduction to Vincent because it includes things about Vincent that he would not permit me to say:

> But our age is certainly different from Wild's. Our laws are more complex; our police are better trained. We are, in fact and image far more subtle. The portrait of his modern counterpart that follows requires closer strokes and more detail. They are not necessary to describe the elements of Vincent's system, which, with almost inconsequential substitutions, are identical to Wild's. They are needed only to capture the modern meanings and impressions that continue to make Wild's ancient system work. [p. 28]

In addition, I heavily footnoted those sections of *The Professional Fence* which dealt with informing or the possibility of it with references to many works (thieves' autobiographies, etc.) which do describe the fence-informant connection. Also I decided to include one or two anecdotes from Vincent which were examples of informing but which had special features that I suspect would not set most gangs gunnin' after him:

I had two guys, black guys, drive up one day. They had rifles. I could tell just by lookin' at 'em they were army rifles. So I told 'em I'd take all they could get, an' I got on the phone to a guy I knew from the FBI. I told him I didn't want the guys arrested, but I didn't want all these guns gettin' into the hands of Black Power, either. So I get the OK to buy. They found out they were comin' out of a boxcar an' stopped it. I figure I done a good thing there, don't you? [p. 195]

While patriotism can usually be counted on to hide even very serious sins, I was not willing to rest Vincent's safety on its possible transparency. I felt obliged to make the truth opaque to all but the most vigorous readers, who I assumed would have little relationship with the gangs that might worry Vincent. I did so in the final prose passages of the summary chapter, "The Sociology of Vincent's Place." I say there that Vincent meets his obligations to the state by returning stolen property rather than (as Wild did) apprehending thieves. However, in the final line of that paragraph I describe what I said about what Vincent does in this area as "ingenious," a word whose noun form earlier in the chapter was defined in its 18th century sense and developed when applied to people like Vincent, to mean the capacity to make things seem like something they are not.

Our Little Secret

Although such elaborate deception about Vincent's undercover-informant activities may seem a bit excessive, the question of how deeply the disguise needed to be driven was a function of the possibility that Vincent's true identity would be discovered. I did all those things that the life historian can do to protect his subject's identity. I changed names, dates, places, event sequences, shaded certain things, and invented others. But all of that was more ritual than reality.

I pointed out to Vincent that being identified as the professional fence could lead to trouble. For one thing it would be an embarrassment to the Philadelphia police, and they would have to do something to save face with legitimate types who just did not understand the way things worked. There was also the possibility of tax problems, but Vincent insisted that he had always played it straight with Uncle Sam. I also told Vincent that I would not reveal his identity unless it meant that I was going to jail if I did not, and he told me that he really could not expect me to do more. These contingencies notwithstanding, Vincent just could not resist a little advance publicity.

He told everybody—judges, lawyers, politicians, prosecutors, thieves, hustlers, and most of his good customers. He started this word-of-mouth publicity campaign a full year before the book was released. By December of 1974, when a full-page review of the book appeared in the *New York Times Book Review,* any people who did not know who Vincent Swaggi really was simply confessed that they were outsiders to the Philadelphia crime scene. In fact, the *Times* reviewer, Tom Plate, an editor of *New York* magazine, began his review not only by identifying the city in which Vincent operated but also by adding details about the store that I had not included in *The Professional Fence.* Plate's review began:

> In downtown Philadelphia there is a cluttered little store where you can purchase just about anything at incredibly low prices. The store is perhaps 15 feet wide and 40 feet deep and stacked from floor to ceiling with goodies of every description. Outside, except when its raining, sits a lawn chair or two and, when the little store is empty of customers, the proprietor sits there too, sometimes in his Hanes undershirt, following the street action. Although to the casual observer he hardly looks the part, this small-business man sitting proudly in front of his modest general store in his sweaty Hanes undershirt is also an important East Coast underworld figure. He is a fence. [p. 3]

Vincent was outraged by this part of the review! He had never sat out in front of his store in his undershirt. That was the type of thing that certain crude people who worked in his store might do, but never Vincent. Vincent insisted that I call Plate about this. I did and he sent apologies to Vincent. Plate had been in Vincent's store on one occasion and mistook Vincent's brother for Vincent.[4]

The *Times* review was highly favorable and generated interest in Vincent from many directions. The *Today* and *Tomorrow* television talk shows, as well as the David Susskind Show, invited Vincent to appear. The *Tomorrow* staff was even willing to come to Philadelphia with all their video equipment and meet with Vincent at a place of his choosing. For many reasons (none of which I am yet prepared to speculate on openly) Vincent turned down these offers. He did, however, begin selling *The Professional Fence* in his store and gave away more autographed copies than he sold. The first 25 copies I ordered from the publisher on my author's account. The remaining copies came from the book departments of John Wanamakers and other fine Philadelphia bookstores.

The *Times* review also generated some interest on the part of the Philadelphia police. To be precise, they responded not to the *Times* review itself but to a letter to the police commissioner about it from an outraged, respectable citizen. The police sent two major-theft squad detectives to interview me about the book and Vincent. I sold one of the detectives an autographed (by me) copy at wholesale.

There were also local newspaper articles. A three page story about the book and me appeared in the *Philadelphia Bulletin* of December 15, 1974. The author of the article detected that Vincent must be from Boston because of a few things that I had let slip during my interview with him. For much the same reason a reporter from the *Philadelphia Daily News* categorically declared that Vincent was a New York City fence, for, if he had been from Philadelphia, the reporter would know about it. The *Pennsylvania Gazette* of February 1975 devoted almost the entire issue to "Vincent the Fence," including a cover featuring Vincent being interviewed by me. Although the artist who did the cover worked from pictures of me and had never seen Vincent, his rendition of Vincent looked more like Vincent than his of me did of me. Much to his amazement the editor of the *Pennsylvania Gazette* got a phone call from Vincent shortly after the issue appeared. Vincent identified himself as Vincent Swaggi, gave the editor his true name and address, and asked to be given some extra copies. I had both the *Times* review and the *Gazette* cover framed for Vincent, but for reasons of security he hung them in his home rather than his store.

Those first six months of 1975 were very exciting times for Vincent and me. Every couple of weeks I would bring Vincent another stack of reviews to savor, and occasionally he would have a couple that I had not seen. But by June the excitement had died down. The prospect of a movie, which looked so good when producer Jule Styne called early in January, now looked very distant. Vincent, who knew he had cancer but thought he had it licked, started to get worse. He began losing weight in August, was bedridden by September, and died on November 28, 1975.

Literally hundreds of people attended his wake—doctors, lawyers, judges, city officials, dozens of police, and a few good thieves. Less than one in 10 signed the guest register. The funeral was much smaller—family, two girlfriends, two good customers, and me.

In January I received a call from an investigative reporter of the *Philadelphia Bulletin*. He said that he had been assigned to do a story on *The Professional Fence* and asked if it might be possible to meet Vincent. I told him that Vincent had died, and he said that he wanted to do the story anyway. I told him no again, explaining that, like him, I had a responsibility to keep my sources confidential and that the family would not appreciate such a story. He said that such a story would help sell more books, and I told him to go fuck himself and hung up. I then called Vincent's daughter, who was now running the store, to tip her off to the fact that the reporter was nosing around. Two days later the reporter called me back. He had talked to the police, had Vincent's criminal record, his obituary, and half a dozen stories that his police source had given him. I asked him how much a suit against the *Bulletin* would bring if he had the wrong person, gave him the same advice that I gave him on his first call, and phoned Vincent's daughter again. The following day he arrived at the store with a photographer, and Vincent's brother gladly showed them around. He took pictures of the store, Vincent's office, and some of the decorations there—the picture of Mayor Frank Rizzo, the award from the American Legion as the local post's man of the year, Vincent's green fedora that the family had decided to leave exactly where Vincent had left it. These photos and a three-page story appeared in the *Bulletin* on Sunday, February 29, 1976, a little more than five years after I first met Vincent. The story was romantic, a glorification of Vincent's criminal career. The family was not offended. Two letters to the editor appeared in the following Sunday's *Bulletin*. One complained about the article's glorification of a criminal; the other praised *The Professional Fence* as the kind of research that criminologists ought to be doing.

THE DHEW MODEL AND
THE BIOGRAPHY OF THE PROFESSIONAL FENCE

In examining the biography of *The Professional Fence* with an eye toward developing an ethical perspective appropriate to life history work with criminal subjects, I do not hold up either Vincent or myself as ethical exemplars (though Vincent, who always insisted that St. Peter was looking for a bargain like everybody else, might well have wished me to speak for myself on this matter). We are certainly, though, able to qualify as examples, if not exemplars—as the raw materials with which an ethical system must work even if it finds that we deserve to be made examples of. But however Vincent and I in the biography of *The Professional Fence* are rated, the research model itself must pass two elementary tests to prove that it is equipped to serve as an example. First, it must be shown that the classes or categories of events with which the model works correspond to classes or categories of events in the experience that the model seeks to judge or guide. Second, it must be demonstrated that the model is in fact a guide, that is, that at important points it says something about what a researcher ought or ought not to do. One can surely ask more than this of research ethics, but I fail to see how one could settle for anything less. For the sake of convenience in evaluating the DHEW model, I will call the first test "The True Category Test" and the second "The True Guide Test."

The True Category Test

The DHEW model for ethical research with human subjects works with at least five categories of acts or actors in its risk-benefit equation: "subjects," "researchers," "risks," "benefits," and a six-element image of "informed consent." If we should find, for example, that life history research has no "subjects," the DHEW model would be in deep trouble.

Anthropological research does not have subjects. We work with informants in an atmosphere of mutual trust and respect. [Mead, 1969]

Such were the opening lines of Margaret Mead's response to a request from the National Institute of Health for a statement of procedures in research on human subjects. Though patently false when stated so baldly, the statement invites a dramatic and radical critique of the DHEW model. Such a critique plays on the fact that anthropological research, like life history research, is never conducted within the boundaries of a single role relationship. Vincent was not only my subject but also my teacher, student, fence, friend, and guide. Likewise, to Vincent I was not only researcher but biographer, confidant, customer, friend, and student. These roles, most of which involve multiple obligations and responsibilities and expectations, are potentially in conflict not only in the researcher-subject dimension but in other dimensions as well. To speak of the working relationship between the life historian and his subject as a researcher-subject relationship simply misconstrues what happens in the context of life history work. The researcher who treats his friends as subjects will soon find that he has neither.

Such problems rarely arise in tightly defined researcher-subject relationships which characterize most biomedical and pharmacological research. The problem of conflicting role obligations in biomedical experimentation, where researcher-subject and physician-patient dilemmas arise, has been highly troublesome to attempts to develop ethics for biomedical research. However, such problems do not begin to approach the complexity of conflicts and reciprocal obligations and expectations characteristic of anthropological or life history fieldwork.

Multiple Roles and Informed Consent. There are at least two cases of consequence which proceed from the multiple role relationships common to life history research. The less radical, but by no means unimportant, case against the DHEW model is that it is simply inadequate in its elaboration of the ethical responsibilities of life history research. For example, the failure to fulfill certain friend-friend obligations might be just as abusive of the subject person as the failure to fulfill certain DHEW "protected" researcher-subject obligations. This case against the DHEW model is weak, though, not only because one cannot specify what the range of obligations may be, but also one cannot anticipate what roles might grow up. Hence, the DHEW model embraces the fiction of a single role relationship and perhaps does so because DHEW, while maybe recognizing that other relationships are potentially abusive and equally inevitable, may recognize that such relationships are impossible to police.

The more radical case against the DHEW model is that roles other than subject-researcher do not merely add to the obligations of the anthropologist or life historian; such roles also *contradict* the special requirements that the DHEW model specifies for the subject-researcher relationship, in particular the specific requirements of informed consent.

This case, I think, can be made against the DHEW model by pointing to ways in which joint obligations to the project evolve in life history work. For example, as Vincent became actively employed in and committed to the work of *The Professional Fence,* our relationship became more collegial than subject-researcher. In this process of becoming a coworker on his own life history, he gave up not only his right to the privacy of that history but also the right to refuse challenges to the authenticity of his own account of it. He could be told of some of the procedures that would be employed in challenging his accounts and even participate in the procedures—for example, by obtaining birth certificates and school records. But other procedures could not be disclosed to him. For instance, one of the ways in which the reliability of his accounts could be tested was a test-retest interview strategy. After I had spent nine months with Vincent and had interviewed him about every aspect of his life and work that I considered important, I began the entire interview process over again from the beginning. This assures that every anecdote reported in *The Professional Fence* is separated by an account of it that was taken six months later. Though I have great respect for Vincent's capacity to fabricate, separating the first account from the second by six months or more *and* not telling Vincent that he would be asked to repeat his accounts satisfied me.

In a similar fashion, the strength of this collegial relationship and the development of a concept of *The Professional Fence* as a scientific document in which both Vincent and I shared an equal responsibility for accuracy (an attitude that I feel is essential to the life history of an individual subject), forced Vincent into a compromising position with respect to disclosing his informant activities, just as it forced me into a compromise of the informed consent requirement of disclosure of risks. Vincent did not want a discussion of his informant activities in the book. I told Vincent that some recognition of the role that informing played in fencing would be necessary and that I would do this by talking about *other* fences and finding references to fences as informants in the biographies and autobiographies of thieves. This would, I told Vincent, adequately supplement his account. Admitting to the need for an account that would satisfy expert scrutiny, Vincent agreed to my proposal. What Vincent was not told and did not realize was that this supplemental information would be placed in *The Professional Fence* as oblique evidence, accessible only to skilled readers, that he himself was an informant. In this case Vincent was exposed to a risk but not told about it, because he would not be able to understand the nature of the precautions that would be used to protect him.

A third case in which role obligations that develop in the course of life history work disfigure the reality of the DHEW model of informed consent involves the matter of respect. Life history work and, if Margaret Mead can be regarded as a steady guide, anthropological fieldwork as well require a relationship of respect between subject and researcher. In life history work with a single subject, an important but unspoken and unexamined assumption by the subject is that the atmosphere of respect that characterized the working relationship will be carried over into the life history document. Moreover, it has been my experience that this understanding which arises, develops, and is assumed by the subject quite outside any of the mechanics of informed consent is as important to the subject as any assurance guaranteed by that procedure.

Mead (1969) suggests that the anthropologist must satisfy this responsibility by portraying the events that he describes with "full justice" to "the cultural framework within which a given practice, however apparently abhorrent, occurs." She goes on to say,

A classic example is the way in which aged among the Eskimo asked to be walled up and left to die. Their voluntary sacrifice—which was all that they could do, under such primitive conditions, for the wellbeing of their children and grandchildren—can either be portrayed as the dignified and voluntary act they conceived it to be or it can be transformed into killing grandmothers by using the terminology of peoples who have both a superior technology and a different ethic about suicide.

There is some safety, though, in the cultural and social distance that the anthropologist enjoys that is not available to the life historian of criminal subjects. In cases of domestic deviance, the problem of preserving expected respect in a dignified presentation of undignified conduct is far more severe. It is a problem which calls on both the literary and the social-scientific talents of the life historian in an atmosphere in which readers are acutely aware of subtle tones that might mark a life history either as "romantic," "sentimental," or "biased" on the one hand or "moralistic" or "judgmental" on the other. Few of us, I suspect, would question Mead's interpretation of the request of elderly Eskimos as a gesture in the interests of children and grandchildren. (Is it truly a rational gesture of a social nature, or is it obediance to a command of a wise and legitimate God?) But "rationales" for criminal behavior—*Honor Thy Father* (Talese, 1971) notwithstanding—are, and I think should be, received with suspicion.

I suspect that ways of satisfying this ethical and methodological problem will strongly depend upon the nature of the life history project and the characteristics of the particular deviant subjects. My own resolution of this problem took the form of giving Vincent a full and complete opportunity to array and explain all of his defenses and justifications and to do the same with what I understand to be the norms surrounding the prohibition of the trade in stolen property. But then I was lucky enough to be talking about dealing in stolen property rather than contract murder; and, then too, I had Vincent, who could sell a refrigerator to an aged Eskimo.

In attempting a "True Category" test of the DHEW model, I have attempted to show that not only is the single role relationship of subject-researcher inadequate to the ethical challenges of life history work, but, because it misunderstands the consequences and conflicts that multiple role relationships introduce to such work, it also imposes ethical requirements that are inappropriate. In the three examples that I have discussed, my claim is that informed consent should not be obtained in the first case (test-retest interviews), need not be obtained in the second (the informant question), and is not and cannot be obtained by any mechanism specified by the DHEW model in the third (the preservation of respect in the document at the same level that it was maintained in the fieldwork). Each of these three critical cases derives from the lack of correspondence between the DHEW model and the field realities of "researcher," "subject," and "informed consent."

The Risk-Benefit Equation. A similar lack of correspondence between the DHEW model's categories and the reality of fieldwork is to be found not in the categories of "risk" or "benefit," but in the mechanism that is supposed to bring them together to guide the researcher in resolving ethical questions. Risks are supposed to be "outweighed" by benefits, according to the DHEW model. And in fact such "weighing" of risks and benefits should be done not only by the researcher in designing his project but also by the institutional review committee in evaluating it and by the subject in considering his decision to give his informed consent. I am not aware of any such weighing of risks and benefits ever occurring in the history of *The Professional Fence.*

Certainly there were discussions of risks: what they were, where they might come from, how they might be avoided, and what I would do if "worse came to worse." Those discussions were held with everybody—with Vincent, with members of my institution's review committee, with colleagues experienced in criminological research, and even with an insider at the National Institute of Mental Health (which funded my research) who confidentially suggested that I keep my records in another state and confessed that he "loved this kind of clandestine shit." There were also discussions of benefits, but they were extremely rare and vague. In fact, the "Statement of Compliance" filed by my institution lists only "that the project has significant potential for contribution to criminological knowledge" as its potential benefit. Except for this document and statements that I made to obtain the grant, there was almost no other discussion of benefits. Counting your chickens before they hatch is bad form.

Vincent may have considered benefits in his decision to work with me, but I am no clearer today about what benefits he considered in reaching his decision than I was in 1974 when I wrote:

I still do not know why Vincent consented to my offer that first day. My letter was persuasive and, I think, established my credentials to Vincent's satisfaction. Perhaps Vincent simply wanted something new to talk about; perhaps he considered having a college professor write a book about him flattering; perhaps he was proud of his success and skill and wanted to talk about it. I have asked Vincent why he chose to work with me. He always says he wanted to help me out if he could. As time went on, both helping me and enjoying our meetings did apparently figure into his motives. I have no best hypothesis, and sometimes Vincent's explanations of his own motives are quite unsatisfactory. [p. 217]

The fact of the matter is that not only were the benefits of *The Professional Fence* project only vaguely discussed and remembered but they were never, to my knowledge, brought together with risks to manage the kind of weighing that the DHEW model describes. People simply do not reach decisions that way. Such a model is really notoriously unsuccessful as a theory of how people do in fact evaluate problems—as a risk-benefit discussion of cancer with any cigarette smoker will quickly demonstrate.

My own experience suggests that the operative model in life history research is more likely to be risk-risk than risk-benefit. By this I mean that all the discussions about risks in the biography of *The Professional Fence* dealt with how to reduce them, avoid them, anticipate them, and meet them. None ever involved the relationship that those risks bore to potential benefits. Even the case of disclosing Vincent's informant activities is best understood in terms of the *risk* that his life history would be discredited as opposed to the *risk* that every gang in the country would be "gunnin' for him."

It is not, however, a sufficient critique of the DHEW model's requirement that risks be outweighed by benefits to show that it is a poor psychological theory of decisions or that ethical questions were in fact dealt with in field situations under a risk-risk model. What must be shown is that it is also a bad model for the ethics of life history work with human subjects. I suppose that another way of saying the same thing is that, when you hear a life historian talking about the benefits of his research outweighing the risks to his subject, somebody either has been, or is about to be, had.

The True Guide Test

I can imagine but one occasion on which I might be tempted to use a risk-benefit evaluation of my research with Vincent. If, in spite of all the precautions that I took to preserve Vincent's anonymity, he were exposed and suffered injury from that exposure, I might offer a defense consistent with the DHEW risk-benefit model as follows:

> The risks were known to Vincent, and he accepted them freely. I considered those risks justifiable because of the potential benefits of my research:
>
> 1. Criminology, before *The Professional Fence*, knew very little about the trade in stolen property. My work promises to guide law enforcement and legislative efforts in the reduction of property theft and the prosecution of a type of criminal essential to it.
>
> 2. Moreover, I defend the risks that I took and the right of researchers like myself to take similar risks in the pursuit of knowledge which may benefit mankind, and I would claim this right even if *The Professional Fence*, as a single effort in the work of scientists, proved fruitless.

Defense number 1 places Vincent on one side of the ledger and the entire problem of property theft on the other. With any imagination at all, rhetorical weights can be added on the side of the researcher and his topic: the best estimate of the cost of stolen property handled by fences in the United States is $6.4 billion. In defense number 1 the research act and its risks are defended because of the contribution which that act can or does make to the common welfare. As if that were not enough, defense number 2 places alongside whatever impact *The Professional Fence* might have in reducing an important social problem the weight of the entire criminological research tradition and what, in the long run, it can contribute to the general welfare. In either case—"act utilitarian" or "rule utilitarian," as they are known in philosophical circles—Vincent does not stand a chance.

One way to attack such arguments would be to claim that neither *The Professional Fence* nor criminology (actually the "role" of criminologist) will ever produce enough benefits to outweigh the costs that they incur, but surely that cannot be true. The more telling attack on both defenses is not that they are weak but that they are far too strong. So strong in fact that they sustain such a Machiavellian attitude toward research subjects' injury or risk that they cannot possibly be used to guide any decision about whether a researcher should risk injury to his subjects or should be judged guilty of their abuse. This attitude relieves the researcher of his responsibility too soon and absolves him of his guilt far too easily, for the true test of any ethics of research with human beings is whether or not it forces the researcher to suffer with his subjects.

NOTES

1. The strategy is recommended by Kaplan (1964).

2. The single exception from the "teleological" theme of the elaboration of policy statement 1 is the "deontological" directive that the committee and researcher see to it that the project not abrogate, supersede, or moderate the legal rights of the subject. Deontologically speaking, the law is the law.

3. Of course, here too the law remains the law: DHEW policy on informed consent also provides that the informed consent agreement, "written or oral, entered into by the subject, should include no exculpatory language through which the subject is made to waive, or appear to waive, any of his legal rights, or to release the institution or its agents from liability for negligence."

4. Tom Plate is the author of *Crime Pays!* In his chapter on the business of fencing, he featured a character from Philadelphia to whom he gave the pseudonym "Spider." Spider was Vincent.

REFERENCES

FEYERABEND, P. (1975). Against method: Outline of an anarchistic theory of knowledge. London: NLB.

KAPLAN, A. (1964). The conduct of inquiry. San Francisco: Chandler.

KLOCKARS, C.B. (1974). The professional fence. New York: Free Press.

KUHN, T.S. (1962). The structure of scientific revolutions. Chicago: University of Chicago Press.

LUNDBERG, G. (1955). "The natural science trend in sociology." American Journal of Sociology, 61(November):191-202.

――― (1956). "Quantitative methods in sociology." Social Forces, 39(October):19-24.

MEAD, M. (1969). "Research with human beings: A model derived from anthropological field practice." Pp. 152-177 in P. Freund (ed.), Experimentation with human subjects. New York: Russell Sage Foundation.

PLATE, T. (1974). Review of The professional fence. New York Times Book Review, December 8.

POPPER, K. (1959). The logic of scientific discovery. New York: Basic Books.
SHAW, C.R. (1930). The jack roller. Chicago: University of Chicago Press.
SUTHERLAND, E.H. (1937). The professional thief. Chicago: University of Chicago Press.
TALESE, G. (1971). Honor thy father. New York: World.
U.S. Department of Health, Education, and Welfare (1971). Institutional guide to DHEW policy on protection of human subjects. Washington, D.C.: U.S. Government Printing Office.
WHYTE, W.F. (1955). Street corner society (2nd ed.). Chicago: University of Chicago Press.

PART III

DESCRIPTIVE STUDIES

10

METHADONE, WINE, AND WELFARE

EDWARD PREBLE and THOMAS MILLER

In a study based on observations from just before 1965, the senior writer reported on the street life of New York City heroin users from four representative lower-class communities (Preble and Casey, 1969). It was a coincidence that the year 1965 marked the beginning of methadone maintenance as a large-scale treatment program for heroin users—a program which has significantly changed the street life of drug users reported on in that early study, though not in the way that was anticipated and hoped for by the advocates of the program. Now, 10 years later, the use of methadone—legally and illegally—dominates the street drug culture in New York City, and its ramifications constitute a much more varied and complex pattern than was the case 10 years ago and before.

In the post-World War II period to 1965, the use of heroin spread at an increasing rate among the members of lower-class communities, especially, but not exclusively, among minority ethnic group members—blacks and Puerto Ricans. At that time they constituted,

AUTHORS' NOTE: The research upon which this paper is based is being supported by U.S. Public Health Service grant R01-DA-01051 from the National Institute of Drug Addiction.

together, about 70% of the heroin-use population. The other 30% were to be found mostly among lower-class Irish-American and Italian-American ethnic groups. The major conclusion of the Preble and Casey study was a departure from the then widely accepted view—based on medical models—that heroin use provides an escape from the worries and problems of life and has its greatest appeal for passive, dependent, generally inadequate persons. Direct observations in the community of the daily activities of heroin users, as well as data from over 200 recorded, individual life history interviews, revealed a picture just about the opposite of the one based on medical models. It was found that

> Their behavior is anything but an escape from life. They are actively engaged in meaningful activities and relationships seven days a week. The brief moments of euphoria after each administration of a small amount of heroin constitute a small fraction of their daily lives. The rest of the time they are aggressively pursuing a career that is exciting, challenging, adventurous and rewarding. . . . [The heroin user] is hustling (robbing or stealing), trying to sell stolen goods, avoiding the police, looking for a heroin dealer with a good bag, coming back from copping, looking for a safe place to take the drug, or looking for someone who beat (cheated) him—among other things. [Preble and Casey, 1969:2]

It was concluded in that study that "the quest for heroin is the quest for a meaningful life, not an escape from life," and that "for the slum inhabitant it enables him to escape, not from purposeful activity, but from the monotony of an existence severely limited by social constraints, and at the same time it provides a way for him to gain revenge on society for the injustices and deprivations he has experienced."

In 1975, 10 years after these observations were made, the present writers had the opportunity to begin a study of the street drug culture in two white ethnic, lower-class communities in New York City, both of which were in the Preble and Casey study—Yorkville and East Harlem. The methods and techniques are similar to those used in that earlier study—participant observation, life history interviews, local history, demography, and anecdotal record. The only significant difference in the two studies is that the research subjects in the present study are exclusively from white ethnic groups—predominately Irish-American and Italian-American. They are, however, from urban slum communities and share most of the values and behavior patterns of their minority group counterparts.

Since May 1975, the writers and another fieldworker associate—an ex-heroin addict who used heroin for 15 years—have lived and worked in one of the study communities (Irish-American). The senior writer had worked in the community off and on for 20 years; the two fieldworkers have lived there all their lives. The study headquarters is a storefront located in a block which has the highest rate of drug use and drug selling in this community of a 44,000 population.

Because the project has been in progress for only one year, including a two-month administrative and exploratory period, any definite conclusions at this point would appear premature. However, the evidence regarding major shifts within the street drug culture over the past 10 years is so dramatic and consistent that some preliminary observations and conclusions seemed warranted even at this early stage of the study. The data so far on which this report is based include participant observation in the community, a block-by-block head count of drug users in the community, and one-hour life history interviews with 50 subjects, all of whom were interviewed three or more times, for a total of 200 interviews.

The participant observation is centered around participation in and observations of the social life of the community on the streets and in social and recreational facilities, social clubs, bars, candy stores, lunchrooms, and the homes of community residents. The already established relationships of the writer with many residents of the study area and the established relationships of the indigenous workers facilitated a natural entry into the social life of the community. In instances where there had been no previous contacts and relationships with community members, the study personnel relied upon the simple approach of honesty and directness regarding the nature of their work.

The head count of drug users was conducted by all three workers in the specific blocks that each knew best. This was accomplished by direct questioning of key informants who provided information about others in a given block. Data were solicited regarding the total number of drug users who used any kind of commonly used drugs—heroin, methadone, other analgesics, cocaine, pills (barbiturates and amphetamines). Marijuana and alcohol use are so common and hallucinogenic use so rare in the community that they were not considered in the count, except when used in combination with other drugs. Breakdowns of the overall number were made according to age, sex, and forms of drug use.

The life history interviews were conducted privately at the study headquarters on an individual basis. It was anticipated that five interviews with each subject would be an optimum number, considering the limitations of time, personnel, and funds. A $10 fee is paid to each subject for his participation. The interviews are designed to get information about the nature and extent of drug use in the community and to elicit developmental and environmental data about individual subjects.

The street drug culture in New York City today revolves largely around the distribution and use of methadone—legal and illegal. Between 1965 and 1975 about 600 articles have been published on methadone maintenance treatment (*International Journal of the Addictions,* 1971; *Biological Abstracts,* 1971-1976; *Psychological Abstracts,* 1971-1976), so it is not necessary to recount here the history and development of methadone maintenance as the primary treatment modality in use today for heroin addicts. Suffice it to say that the rationale for its use was that it would reduce the crime associated with heroin use and permit former heroin users to lead socially productive lives. It had been demonstrated many times that methadone dependence by itself is not significantly debilitating, physically or psychologically. Thus the interest of society would be served at little, if any, harm to the methadone maintenance participant.

Based on the pioneering research of Dole and Nyswander starting in 1963, a modest start was made in 1965 to experiment with a methadone maintenance program for voluntary participants (Dole and Nyswander, 1965). In 1968 and the following years, objective evaluations of the New York programs have been made by Gearing and her associates at the Columbia University School of Public

Health (Gearing, 1970a, 1970b, 1971, 1973; Gearing and Schweitzer, 1974). These very favorable reports have been influential in the proliferation of methadone maintenance treatment programs, until today there are approximately 32,000 patients in New York City programs, public and private. The Gearing reports from 1968 to 1974 showed, among other things, a positive social productivity rate for members of the study groups ranging from 50% to 85%, the improvement being correlated with the length of time in a program (from one to six years). The criteria for positive social productivity were (1) being employed full or part time, (2) attending school or another training program, (3) being a homemaker. The criteria for negative social productivity included being unemployed, receiving welfare assistance, or being supported by illicit activities. Another measure of social productivity used by Gearing was the decline in city welfare cases involving methadone maintenance patients over a six-year period. Here the percentage went from about 50% down to 14%—again, the improvement being correlated with length of time in a program. Although the senior writer was somewhat skeptical about these favorable evaluations from the beginning (basing his skepticism on participant observation and verbal reports in heavy drug use communities where he was engaged in activities not directly connected with drug use research), he was not prepared for the contrary revelations which emerged from the current intensive study of the street drug culture.

The 50 persons whom we have interviewed have each been routinely asked about their own social productivity and about their estimate of the social productivity of other methadone patients they know (using the criteria of productivity noted above). The estimates have ranged from none to 20% productive, with a mean being about 12%. Almost all the subjects were on welfare or Social Security disability, as were the other methadone patients they knew. Because we were working at this point with a small number (50), we attempted to secure some reliable, official count of the percentage of methadone patients receiving benefits from either welfare or Social Security. The only official information that we could get was from the New York City Department of Health (Hurdle, 1975), which told us that 69% of the city's methadone patients were receiving medicaid benefits, which is a good, if indirect, measure of the percentage who are receiving support from either welfare or Social Security and thus not socially productive. This figure was more in line with our interview data and street observations.

In order to try to account for this wide discrepancy in our data and the data from the formal evaluation reports, we inquired at the Columbia University School of Public Health about the methods used to determine whether or not a patient was employed, going to school, or acting as a homemaker. The answer was that the information came from the agencies administering methadone maintenance programs, and their information, in turn, came from the patients. At an earlier time it had been required that the patients exhibit paycheck stubs as proof of employment, but this requirement had been dropped (Gearing, 1975). Thus the data regarding social productivity came exclusively from the patients, without any documentation. Given the vested interest of treatment agencies and their methadone patients in making a good record, this source of information must be suspect, and it might explain the discrepancy between what we directly observe on the streets and what is reported in formal statistical evaluations.

The most typical drug scene on the streets today is two or more methadone users sitting on a stoop or standing on a street corner with pints of wine in paper bags panhandling for change to get more wine. Forty-proof fortified wine can be bought for about 85 cents a pint; thus it is possible to support a methadone-wine habit with a little honest effort. One research subject summed up the scene this way: "They pick up their methadone, get their welfare check and pay their rent, and drink booze." This is the simplest and most common pattern which is found among those who are the least capable and enterprising.

One step up from this pattern involves those who add pills to the methadone and wine—usually barbiturates (such as Seconal and Tuinal) or tranquilizers (such as Valium and Elavil). The street price for barbiturates is $2 and the price for tranquilizers is $1, although there is some fluctuation in price. The average drug user with this pattern will use three to five pills a day. It is possible to support this three-way habit with welfare funds and panhandling, but such resources are marginal. A common practice is to sell part of one's methadone supply (usually about one-third) in order to finance the wine and pills. A 100 milligram dosage of methadone brings $10 to $15 on the street.

Up another step is the pattern which consists of methadone and cocaine on weekends and wine or pills, or both, for the rest of the week. This pattern, because of the high price of cocaine, requires a substantial supplementary income, usually from sales of methadone and hustling (robbing and stealing). In a variation of this pattern, heroin is used instead of, or along with, cocaine. In this case the methadone does not block the effects of the heroin, because, as they say on the street, the wine and pills together "eat up the methadone," that is, reduce its effect.

These are the main patterns of mixed drug use with methadone as the base, both physiologically and financially. According to our head-count survey and a consensus from the interview data, these combination patterns are to be found among approximately 80% of the drug users in our study area. Approximately 16% use heroin only, and 4% use methadone only.

Our head count revealed a total of 722 chronic hard drug users in the study area. The true figure is probably over 1,000 (out of a population of 44,000), because we have not yet been able to get a count of hard drug users who are white-collar and professional persons living in the area. They are discreet and circumspect and do not do business on the street. We know they exist, because they occasionally arrange to buy drugs through some of our regular street research informants, but we cannot safely estimate a number at this time.

According to our count, there are 264 adults and 458 adolescents (ages 14-20) who are using hard drugs in the study area. The breakdown with regard to types of drugs used is as follows:

Male adults: heroin (23.5%), methadone with other drugs, including alcohol (36%), methadone only (1.5%), poly-drug use (39%).

Male adolescents: heroin (11%), methadone with other drugs, including alcohol (5.2%), methadone only (10.4%), poly-drug use (74.3%).

Female adults: heroin (21.5%), methadone with other drugs, including alcohol (27.0%), methadone only (0.4%), poly-drug use (51.1%).

Female adolescents: heroin (8%), methadone with other drugs (28.4%), methadone only (0.2%), poly-drug use (63.4%).

The predominance of methadone, legal and illegal, has greatly affected the behavior and activities of drug users. In the Preble and Casey study (1969), when heroin was the primary drug of choice on the street, it was observed that heroin users were, of necessity, ambitious, enterprising persons who were actively engaged in a challenging career. It was stated there that they were actively engaged in meaningful activities and relationships seven days a week, all in the interest of acquiring the large sums of money required for the purchase of high-priced heroin. They were hustling (robbing and stealing), trying to sell stolen goods, avoiding the police, looking for a dealer with good heroin, coming back from buying heroin, looking for a safe place to inject the drug, or looking for someone who has cheated them—among other things. With the advent of methadone on a large scale (32,000 registered methadone users in New York City and a large, undetermined number of illegal methadone users), the street scene has changed. With free methadone, cheap wine, and welfare benefits, a drug user does not have to "hustle." As one research informant put it:

Like I say, once you get on methadone you lose your hustle, there is nothing to rob for anymore. Most of the time they did all the thieving just to get high, but once you get on the program [methadone] it makes you lazy. Now you go there every day and get your dose, and that's it.

One informant compared this with being a civil service employee. Another informant said:

They pick up their methadone, get their welfare check, pay their rent, buy pills, and drink booze. They don't go to work. They don't give a fuck about nothing. To me that's going from bad to worse [that is, from heroin to methadone].

We have many pages of excerpts from interviews which express the same opinion, although there are notable exceptions which will be given later on.

There is evidence from our interview data that if heroin becomes available again in large quantity and at a reasonable price, many methadone patients will drop methadone and go back to heroin. They know that methadone and barbiturates are narcotic, addicting drugs, but heroin is in a preferred category by itself, as is illustrated by the following quote:

> Well, I've been taking a lot of pills [barbiturates] lately and methadone regularly, but I haven't been fooling with no drugs [heroin].

If heroin does reappear in quantity and good quality on the street again—which has been widely predicted—the drug scene will change again, but as of today methadone use and the life-style that goes with it dominate the street drug culture.

The above data and observations raise certain questions and require some attempts at interpretation:

(1) What are the overall effects on the individual and social beahvior of drug users as a result of these changed conditions?

(2) What are the consequences for society at large, especially regarding crime and other social costs?

(3) Why has methadone become so popular with ex-heroin users?

(4) Why is there a large illegal methadone street market, with its high prices, when it can be obtained at no or little cost from legal sources?

(5) How important and what are the effects of welfare and Social Security support for methadone patients?

(6) What effects will the possible (and generally anticipated) return of heroin to the streets in good quality and price have on methadone programs?

We will attempt to answer each question in turn.

1. The Individual

The effects of individual and social behavior among drug addicts since the advent and eventual widespread use of methadone as a maintenance narcotic agent must be evaluated according to several categories of methadone users, as outline above.

(a) In our study population, only about 4% use methadone as it was ideally designed to be used, that is, without a significant amount of use of other drug substances, such as alcohol, barbiturates, amphetamines, and cocaine. In this category are those who are likely to be working or getting an education and who are leading a satisfactory home and social life, with little, if any, criminal activity.

(b) The methadone-alcohol user is somewhat comparable to a Bowery alcoholic. He survives on welfare and panhandling and leads a stuporous life in hallways (in bad weather) and on the stoops (in good weather). He has a high rate of physical and mental deterioration (due to the alcohol) but is no more than a minor nuisance to other community members. The following verbatim interview excerpts from persons in this category are typical:

> "There is no need to hustle. You beg for change, and your pride and desire go."

> "Like I say, once you get on methadone you lose your hustle, there's nothing to rob for anymore. Most of the time they did all their thieving just to get high, but once you get on methadone it makes you lazy. You get your dose everyday and that's it."

> *Question:* "Taking into consideration today the use of methadone and wine, is it true that the person is worse off, physically and mentally, than when he was on heroin, but society is better off?"

> *Answer:* "You hit it right. The guys now are dying from drinking. You never heard of a junkie going in for an alcoholic dry-out."

> "With methadone and wine, you just get lethargy [sic] ."

> "Guys get on methadone, start getting welfare checks, drink wine and get lazy. When I was on dope I was doing one supermarket a night. No more. They lose their heart on methadone."

(c) The next category includes those who combine methadone along with alcohol and/or pills (preferably barbiturates). This kind of habit requires an income beyond what one can get from welfare or Social Security and panhandling. The necessary supplementary income comes from small-time hustling. The most common source comes from selling part of one's methadone, at $10 to $15 a dose. Or, if one does not want to part with any of his methadone, he can, in some cases, "cop" (buy) methadone for someone else, usually a young person, who does not have the courage or connections to cop for himself. He may get from $2 to $5 for this service.

Another source of income related to methadone programs is the sale of "clean urine" (no presence of drugs) to those who are about to be subjected to a urine test as a condition for staying in a program. The seller of the urine is on the same program, but has not used drugs, except perhaps alcohol, for a few days, and his urine is clean. In the early days of methadone programs it was relatively easy to heat a bottle of clean, usually cold urine—obtained earlier from another person not on drugs—with hot water from the bathroom tap in order to fool the attendant who routinely checked to see if the urine was warm and thus fresh. Measures were taken to prevent this deception simply by turning off the hot water supply to the bathrooms. To counteract this move, patients heated the bottom of the bottle with matches, but the black smoke stains soon gave that away. Currently the patient is ahead in this contest by paying a fellow patient—clean at the time, as mentioned above—to precede him into the bathroom, hide one bottle of part of his fresh urine in a prearranged place and then return another bottle of his remainign urine to the attendant. Recently, however, some of the more strict and sophisticated programs insist on the return of a reasonably full bottle of urine from each patient. Thus the game continues, and a bookmaker will give you odds on the patient staying a step ahead. The odds he will give you on a female patient successfully cheating on the urine test are higher than on a male because of their convenient cavity. One of our female subjects reported:

> I place a balloon of clean urine, concealed and kept warm at the same time, in my vagina, so when I put the cup down there I simply release the balloon and the urine goes into the cup. It works perfectly.

Still another form of small-time hustling associated with metha-done programs is to sell pills (usually tranquilizers) which are legitimately prescribed for some patients. They may sell about six of these a day for one dollar each. Some of these hustlers also make a modest amount of money by selling wine on Sundays to the methadone winos. They may charge $1.50 a pint for bottles they bought earlier in the week for 85 cents and stored up for Sunday sales.

Other small-time, bread-and-butter hustles used by this type of person are the common ones: shoplifting, stealing batteries and tape decks out of automobiles, working small "con games," fencing "swag" (stolen goods and property), and committing relatively easy burglaries. These are all relatively safe criminal acts, and they provide the necessary extra income to support a methadone-pill habit, with perhaps some alcohol at times.

The individual and social behavior of this type of user is different from the "stoop and hallway" user described above. He is more active, alert, and ambitious, has not completely "lost his heart," and derives some satisfaction out of the hustling activity for its own sake, even though "getting a head" (high) is his main goal. He stands somewhat nearer to the old-time pure heroin user who had to "take care of business" all day long in order to support a $100-a-day heroin habit.

(d) The top status methadone-cocaine user is the one who prefers cocaine as a supplementary drug. Cocaine is expensive, not because a given unit of weight is more costly than a comparable weight of heroin, but because there is an almost insatiable psychological desire to administer it at very short intervals—15 to 30 minutes, as compared to three or four hours for heroin. The unit price is about the same. In order to support cocaine use, even along with methadone, the user has to make some big "scores" (lucrative criminal acts, such as burglaries and robberies) in order to have even a "cocaine weekend." For the balance of the week he is likely to use the less expensive alcohol and pills in order to achieve the desired "head." A confirmed cocaine user who has experimented extensively with almost all drugs will tell you that it is incomparable.

The following verbatim interview excerpt from a female subject who has used almost every kind of drug chronically for many years makes the point:

Question: How about cocaine?

Answer: Oh, I love cocaine; I'm getting it tomorrow. A friend of mine is bringing me a bottle of pure cocaine tomorrow. I love it, oh, I love it!

Question: How long have you used cocaine?

Answer: I have cocaine marks on my arm [from hypodermic injections]. I would walk around for hours with dope on me, and I wouldn't touch it. I could be sick as a dog until I would have that cocaine. I woke up one morning with nine abcesses on my arms. I even went so far as going to my feet. I was thinking about going in my neck, and then I knew I was bad.

Question: Is it true what they say about cocaine, that when you take a shot, within 15 or 20 minutes you are ready to go again?

Answer: Right. With cocaine I can't stop taking it till there's no more. If I know it's in the house, I have to get up from bed and get another shot. It's only a five-minute high because you get that rush. It's a beautiful feeling when you get that rush. The cocaine is really up; it's real up. Two weeks ago I spent $150 in one hour on cocaine.

The individual and social behavior of these methadone-cocaine users is close to that of the pure heroin user, who has to scheme and hustle all the time. The main difference is that his hustling activity is reduced somewhat by the relatively safe sales of his extra methadone and the welfare or Social Security benefits he receives as a result of being enrolled in a legitimate methadone program.

2. Societal Costs

The consequences for society at large of methadone programs are hard to measure. Along with the costs of welfare and Medicaid in the case of the first category of patients (methadone-wine users), there is the nuisance and minor expense dur to panhandling. An unscalable cost is the fear and anxiety experienced by some persons in observing and being approached by such persons.

In the second category (methadone-pill users) there are the welfare costs and a higher loss of goods and property due to criminal activity, even at a minimal level. Again, there is the fear and anxiety.

In the third category (methadone-cocaine users), there are the welfare costs and a much higher loss due to criminal activity. The fear and anxiety here is higher because of the greater potential for physical threat and violence against victims.

Only a careful and sophisticated economic analysis might be able to estimate these combined social costs. Only small, isolated studies along this line have appeared, with mixed conclusions. A considerable majority of them, which have been concerned only with the costs of criminal activities, have concluded that methadone maintenance programs have reduced the social costs of drug use, as compared to the times of almost exclusive heroin use. The research subjects in the present project are in agreement in about the same proportion. This has to remain an open question at this time.

3. Methadone Popularity

The question of why methadone has become popular with ex-heroin users can be answered simply, at least for about 85% of them: (a) the almost automatic welfare or Social Security payments which go to an enrollee, (b) the expensive and inferior nature of heroin on the street during the past few years, (c) the lesser risks of criminal charges. The remaining small percentage, approximately 15% in our estimate, are benefiting along the lines that the program was designed for; namely, they are drug free, except for methadone, are socially productive, and are not engaged in criminal activities.

4. Illicit Methadone

The illegal market is so large and open that one subject said: "It is easier to buy black market methadone on the street than it is to buy baby Enfamil in a store."

There are principally four kinds of ready customers for black market methadone: (1) teenagers who are experimenting with many kinds of drugs and have not made a commitment to any particular drug or combination of drugs, (2) persons who are enrolled in programs but whose prescribed dosage does not satisfy them, (3) persons, usually with a social or professional position, who do not want to be identified as narcotic users, and (4) heroin users who, when necessary, supplement their heroin with nonblocking dosages of methadone, which together achieve the desired high. These four sources of customers assure a more than adequate market for street methadone salesmen. The estimates of enrolled methadone patients who sell methadone on the street in any significant amount is about 85%.

5. Effects of Social Welfare

The functions of welare and Social Security in methadone programs have appeared all through this paper. It is difficult to evaluate the positive or negative effects of their participation. It can be argued that without these easily available funds for the methadone patient, he might be motivated to find legitimate work or prepare himself educationally for a future legitimate position. On the other hand, it can be argued that his past experiences as a drug user, with its necessary concomitant of criminal behavior, have conditioned him beyond the possibility of turning his way of life around. It is an open question at this time.

6. Return of Heroin

If heroin, as is widely predicted, returns to the street in good quantity, quality, and price, there is overwhelming evidence from our data that it will again become by far the drug of choice for street users. As one subject put it:

> If a guy can really get "zonked" for $10 or $15, the methadone programs will be in serious trouble, because a guy won't take methadone if it's going to block his high.

Although the possibility of heroin reappearing is widely predicted, the present writers are more skeptical than most observers that this is going to happen, at least in the near future. In spite of the many reports in the media and in the professional literature that it is already here, we have no hard evidence that this is the case.

In a recent paper that appeared after the above observations were prepared for publication, Dole and Nyswander (1976) commented on some of the shortcomings and failures of methadone maintenance programs. They attributed the failures to two main causes: (a) the relative lack or inadequacy of social and psychological rehabilitation as adjuncts to the medication program and (b) the stringent controls imposed upon methadone programs by government agencies, notably the U.S. Food and Drug Administration. It is our view that these conditions are far less important than the subcultural changes which have occurred among drug users with the widespread distribution of methadone.

Two recent anecdotes regarding the experiences of two of our research subjects will serve as a passing comment on the Dole-Nyswander observations. With regard to rehabilitation services, one subject was asked if counseling was available to him at his program. He answered that it was and that once in a while he would "give the social worker a break" and talk to him for five minutes. As for the "stringent controls," another subject was recently arrested for buying methadone on the street in front of his program's building, just after he had legally acquired his dosage of methadone. Both of the programs involved in these two episodes are highly regarded by professional workers in the field and by methadone patients. These are only two anecdotes, but they are typical.

We want to conclude this paper with a follow-up report on each of the 50 subjects who were interviewed in at least three one-hour, tape-recorded interviews. It may be objected that 50 is not a significant number, but a compensating advantage is that it is possible to get accurate, detailed information on their status at any time.

In Table 1, a note describing significant events and changes in the research subjects' lives follows each subject number. The time period indicates the length of time that had elapsed since the last formal interview with each subject. The follow-up data were obtained either from direct contacts or, where that was not possible, from a panel of eight research subjects who, among them, knew the current status of each subject. The average length of time between the last interview and the follow-up contact was just over seven months. There were 43 males and 7 females, with an average age of just over 27. They are listed with a category number indicating the nature of their drug use: (1) methadone and alcohol, (2) methadone, alcohol, and pills (barbiturates and tranquilizers), (3) methadone, cocaine, alcohol, and pills (barbiturates and tranquilizers), and (4) predominantly heroin. This follow-up study of 50 subjects shows, among other things, the number of subjects who are (1) socially productive, (2) not socially productive, (3) attempting to become socially productive. The breakdown is as follows:

(1) Socially productive: 7 (14%)

(2) Not socially productive: 39 (78%)

(3) Attempting to become socially productive: 4 (8%)

It should be noted that 45 of the 50 subjects (90%) are on either public or private methadone maintenance programs.

These figures correspond very closely with the data (reported earlier in this paper) from the head count and a consensus of the estimates of our subjects regarding drug use in the study area. Although the study so far has not featured the criminal activities of our subjects during the follow-up period, 18 (36%) have been arrested one or more times.

In addition to the objections which may be raised about the relatively small number of subjects reported on, it may also be objected that an average length of elapsed time between the last formal interview contact and the follow-up contact—an average of just over seven months—is too short a time period. Such an objection may be justified, but at least the follow-up data reveals how a street drug user's life can change significantly, in some cases dramatically, over a short period of time.

With the mixed drug use patterns that exist today, at least in our study area, it is difficult but not impossible to draw any generalized conclusions regarding the current street drug scene. The hustle and the high are still the two most important phenomena in the users' motivations to use drugs, although the hustling has decreased since the days, 10 years ago, of predominantly heroin use. This is especially true for those who limit themselves to methadone and

Table 1. FOLLOW-UP STATUS OF
METHADONE MAINTENANCE PATIENTS

	No. of Months since Interview	Drug Use Category*	Sex	Age	Present Activities or Status	Socially Productive
1	10	1	M	21	Salesman, less drinking	Yes
2	7	1	M	24	No significant change	No
3	10	3	F	32	Under psychiatrist's care	Yes
4	2	3	F	32	Separated from husband	No
5	7	1	M	26	Drinking heavily, disorderly arrest	Attempt
6	7	1	M	14	Disorderly arrest, no change	No
7	11	1	M	33	College student, off methadone	Yes
8	10	1	M	31	Drinking heavily, two felony arrests	No
9	9	1	M	19	Drinking. Robbery, assault, and rape arrests	No
10	11	2	M	29	Selling marijuana and pills	No
11	7	2	M	33	Five-year sentence for robbery	No
12	7	1	M	36	No significant events	No
13	10	3, 4	M	33	Burglary arrest, 5½-month sentence	No
14	8	1, 4	M	30	No significant events	No
15	5	3, 4	M	25	Married pharmacy worker	Yes
16	9	3, 4	M	30	Burglar, two narcotics arrests	No
17	7	2	M	15	No significant events	No
18	9	1	M	35	Arrested for methadone sales	No
19	10	2	M	40	Using cocaine	No
20	9	1	M	33	Drinking heavily	No
21	9	2	M	28	Dead from drug overdose	No
22	7	3	M	29	Burglary and robbery arrests	No
23	2	1	M	32	Beaten to death by subject No. 33	No
24	7	1	M	15	No significant events	No
25	10	1, 4	M	29	No significant events	No
26	2	1	M	27	No significant events	No
27	5	4	M	25	No significant events	No
28	11	1	M	34	In psychiatric ward	No
29	8	4	M	31	Drinking, burglary arrest	No
30	9	3	F	32	Purse-snatching arrest	No
31	8	3	M	23	Drug pusher	No
32	2	1	M	39	Babysits four stepchildren	Yes
33	11	1	M	31	Four arrests, on murder charge	No

Table 1 (continued)

No. of Months since Interview	Drug Use Category*	Sex	Age	Present Activities or Status	Socially Productive
34	9	2	M	25	Has married and had child	Yes
35	8	2	F	29	No significant events	No
36	3	2	F	18	No significant events	No
37	6	2	M	24	No significant events	No
38	9	2	M	30	Heavy drinking, four felony arrests	No
39	9	3	M	22	Enrolled in college	Attempt
40	6	2, 4	M	23	Three burglary arrests	Attempt
41	7	2	M	17	Heavy drug user	No
42	8	3, 4	M	32	Employed as doorman	Yes
43	9	2	M	36	No significant events	No
44	9	4	M	21	Police informer, drug arrest	No
45	8	1	M	39	No significant events	No
46	8	2	M	19	Hustling homosexuals for drug money	No
47	2	1	M	19	Armed robbery arrest	No
48	6	4	F	30	Prostitute	No
49	3	3, 4	M	21	Furniture refinisher	Attempt
50	8	1	M	22	In jail for burglary	No

*1, methadone and alcohol
2, methadone, alcohol, and pills (barbiturates and tranquilizers)
3, methadone, cocaine, alcohol, and pills (barbiturates and tranquilizers)
4, predominately heroin

wine. But for them the high is still important, which most of them cannot achieve on methadone alone. The effects of prolonged use of alcohol along with methadone results in physical, psychological, and social deterioration for this type of user, but at relatively little social cost to the community.

With the other mixed patterns involving various combinations of methadone, heroin, cocaine, barbiturates, tranquilizers, and alcohol, the user and society are still paying a high price—a price which the user is willing to pay but which society is forced to pay. In these cases, methadone maintenance has not realized its goal of promoting social productivity and has been only partially successful in reducing the criminal activities associated with drug use.

REFERENCES

DOLE, V.P., and NYSWANDER, M.E. (1965). A medical treatment for diacetylmorphine (heroin) addiction: A clinical trial with methadone hydrochloride. Journal of the American Medical Association, 193:80.

——— (1976). Methadone maintenance treatment—A ten year perspective. Journal of the American Medical Association, 235(May 10):19.

GEARING, F.R. (1970a). Evaluation of methadone maintenance treatment program. International Journal of the Addictions, 5:517.

——— (1970b). Methadone maintenance treatment program: Progress report of evaluation through March 31, 1970. Unpublished manuscript, May 8.

——— (1971). MMTP: Progress report through March 31, 1971—A five year overview. Unpublished manuscript, May 14.

——— (1973). "Report." P. 452 in Proceedings 5th National Conference, Methadone Treatment, Napan, New York.

——— (1975). Personal communication, September 16.

GEARING, F.R., and SCHWEITZER, M.D. (1974). An epidemiologic evaluation of long-term methadone maintenance treatment for heroin. American Journal of Epidemiology, vol. 100.

HURDLE, E. (1975). Personal communication from his office, New York City Department of Health, August 27.

International Journal of the Addictions (1971). Methadone: A bibliography, 1929-1971 (2 parts, June, December).

PREBLE, E., and CASEY, J.J., Jr. (1969). "Taking care of business: The heroin user's life on the street." International Journal of the Addictions, 4(1):1-24.

11

A NEIGHBORHOOD HISTORY OF DRUG SWITCHING

In May 1968, when I first began my field study among Italian-American street males in the fictitiously named community of East Highland, Sergeant Clarence Clancy of the Coastal State Police told me emphatically that when he began specializing in narcotic arrests 17 years earlier, East Highland had no drug problem. "Then," he claimed, equally emphatic, "I watched it grow. First, they began with marijuana, and, when this didn't give the user the bang he was looking for, he went on to the cough syrups. Now, they're on the hard stuff."

The notion of a natural progression from milder drugs to increasingly more potent ones, usually beginning with marijuana and concluding with heroin, has been a commonly accepted proposition among the general public for approximately three decades. Like Sergeant Clancy, proponents of the escalation argument have usually

AUTHOR'S NOTE: The data for this paper was taken from a four-year research project officially entitled "The Career of the Lower Socioeconomic Drug User," which was funded by the National Institute of Mental Health (MH 15 281). I would also like to acknowledge the contributions of the Drug Abuse Council, Washington, D.C. It was during my tenure with the council's fellows program in 1972-1973 that the bulk of this paper was written.

selected marijuana as the villianous initiating substance that introduces innocent youth to a world of wonderous sensations, which after prolonged use eventually become dulled. From this point of view, individual experimenters, titilated by the effects of lesser drugs, are launched on an evitable pursuit of more potent substances until they find a kind of grand satisfaction in the overwhelming joy of heroin, the monster narcotic that mysteriously enslaves and then transforms the experimenter into the kind of criminal only the sleaziest adjective could describe.

The stepping-stone proposition has been losing advocates recently, not because heroin has lost its mystification but because marijuana has come to be more commonly accepted and has been decriminalized in at least eight states as of this writing in the spring of 1976. Jerry Mandel (1968), a social historian, has documented the history of the stepping-stone theory, showing that its creation in the middle 1940s was connected to a developing hard line among federal law enforcement officers toward heroin addiction. Mandel would appear to be one of the few drug researchers to connect the invention of social theory to the political thrust of developing public policies, a theory in this case which acquired currency not because it had empirical documentation but because of the authoritative position of the proponents. Later, John Ball et al. (1968) dignified the stepping-stone proposition by blurring the sequential aspect and by stating rather than illustrating that a scientifically determined causal connection had linked marijuana smoking to eventual addiction to heroin. Ball suggested that marijuana smoking may be viewed "as a predisposing influence in the etiology of opiate addiction in the United States" and claimed that opiate use is commonly preceded by the smoking of marijuana, especially among residents of the eastern and western states. The findings were derived from a sample of 2,213 opiate users in the U.S. Public Health Service hospitals in Lexington, Kentucky, and Fort Worth, Texas.

In more recent days, now that the issue of decriminalizing marijuana has become a political issue, the arguments over the stepping-stone proposition have become a barometer that distinguishes the liberal from the conservative, liberals naturally renouncing the proposition and conservatives supporting the theory and seeing it as one of the more serious negative consequences of permissiveness. Whichever side an advocate chooses to argue, the conceptual tendency has been to view the drug user in social isolation, where the only important variables that account for drug-using behavior have been the individual user and the drug with which he has experimented, as though all decisions connected to a career in drug use were dependent on the user's emotional and physiological response to chemical substances. One serious consequence of this narrow perspective has been to neglect those neighborhood relationships of a youth in his street system, relationships which not only tend to influence the selection of drug-using activities but also may shape his life chances in education, employment, and other important social roles that sum up his identity. In viewing a youth in social isolation, one screens out those aspects of his street corner relationships. Further, the impact of the interrelationship of the collectivities of young men in the street system with the law enforcement officials who carry out the mandate of a prohibitionist public policy is hardly recognized. In East Highland, these relationships—long-standing friendships with other street participants and the exciting interplay with police and other representatives of the criminal justice system—established the social context in which the history of drug switching could be studied, not as an individual phenomenon but as an historical evolution that moved from a condition of limited drug use in the middle 1950s to a recent period in the early 1970s when some 35 different substances had become the staples of everyday street activities.

In East Highland, there was a clear history of drug switching; and, if escalation meant the eventual use of heroin by some members of the street system, then there was limited but definite evidence that supported the stepping-stone proposition. The movement, however, from a point in history when only limited drug use took place to a community condition in which a large number of youths experimented with a wide variety of mood-altering chemicals did not have the simple linear development that Sergeant Clancy claimed with such knowing emphasis. Rather than each individual drug user coming to an individual determination that less potent drugs grew increasingly dissatisfying, the movement toward different and more socially menacing drugs like heroin grew from the interaction of groups of young users *discovering* new ways of getting high and the official responses aimed at denying them that pleasure. The origins, the spread, and, in some cases, the escalation of drug use in East Highland could best be understood by viewing the phenomenon within an historical context in which the systemic relationships between street groups of drug users and representatives of social control agencies with authority to enforce policies of drug prohibition structured a dangerous game of moves and countermoves that progressively grew in excitement, seriousness, and magnitude. In the East Highland drug scene, the street system and the agents of social control were inextricably bound to one another. Viewed in this interactive framework, the history of drug use in East Highland can be traced as it emerged first as an innocuous activity of a small group to the point some 15 years later when it had been identified as a major social problem in which the use of more than three dozen substances had become the common, everyday knowledge of all street youth.

THE ERA OF DISCOVERERS

Prior to 1957, street drug use other than alcohol consumption was literally unknown in East Highland. Even stories of elderly addicts whose drug use might have begun medically as a result of illness or injury in military service were conspicuously absent. In fact, by 1972, when the study officially ended, the oldest living heroin user was only 33 years old. And if older addicts existed outside the scope of the study, their influence on the emergence and spread of drug use in the street system was negligible. Essentially, by 1972, the nonmedical use of illicit substances among male street corner groups was a practice that existed for no more than 15 years.

Although the exact incident when the first East Highland youth experimented with an illicit drug is historically clouded, what appears overwhelmingly clear is that the first wave of drug users was a small group of high status "solid guys" with local reputations as either "crazy" or "tough."[1] In 1957 these young men were in late adolescence or in their early twenties. By street standards, they constituted a top-level corner group whose individual and collective behavior had been built on supremacy in fighting, heavy drinking, carrying (and using) weapons, and pursuing other activities admired in the street system of East Highland. They had freed themselves of the constraints of traditional institutions of socialization, often dramatically and irrevocably. They had either dropped out of school or been suspended, and their military careers were marked by court martials and discharges under less than honorable conditions. Geared to action and daring behavior, they needed few inducements to experiment with a foreign substance that held promise of producing a new and different kind of intoxication.

In East Highland the first illicit substance reported to be used by street youths for the sole purpose of getting high was not marijuana, as Sergeant Clancy had indicated, but a cough medicine called Tussar, which, according to some of the old-timers, contained a heavy component of codeine.[2] The transition from alcohol to cough medicine seemed natural enough since both were ingested orally. In drinking a new substance whose chemical makeup was unclear, young men could avoid identifying the activity as drug taking and view it only as a new way to enjoy a different kind of high which did not produce the negative effects connected to alcohol. When they were introduced to Tussar, each solid guy in his own separate way made a social-psychological-physiological dis-covery: the disquiet that a reputation of tough or crazy created could be magically silenced and converted into a warm, lazy comfort unknown before. As one old-time user of Tussar stated in reflection over his first experience with Tussar, "I didn't know I could feel that good." The dramatic altering of feelings induced by the cough medicine had beneath it a comparative analysis. On the one hand, the solid guy had been emersed in a life-style in which a high level of tension was so pervasive that it could not be articulated in terms that he could communicate. On the other hand, a bottle of cherry-tasting syrup could remove the tension and replace it with an ease unknown before. The important aspect of the discovery was not that codeine could soften a condition of chronic anxiety but that anxiety itself could be artificially managed and that a state of repose could supplant the tension that building a street reputation entailed.

Built into the relaxed state was a correlate of the pleasure, an aftermath of the relaxation that could be enjoyed simply by concentrating on the feeling itself and allowing a free flow of imagery. Called the "nod" or "nodding," the feeling state was a new experience in the emotional-physical enjoyment that street youth associated with adventure. This "awake dream" as another respondent called the nod, a twilight state between sleep and a softened reality, was in fact a major discovery in East Highland. Achieving it in those early days of drug experimentation was connected exclusively to Tussar.

When compared to alcohol, the only other substance used for intoxication, drinking cough medicine had a number of advantages. While alcohol frequently acted as incentive to violence, Tussar was an antidote to the inner preparedness for challenge. The relaxing effects washed away the desire for fighting, although previous reputations of either tough or crazy could be mobilized against anyone who intruded on the high and disturbed the hazy relaxation which the early discoverers reserved for an evening's activity. Rather than an evening of restless hanging around, when the accumulation of a day's disappointments and irritations frequently culminated in a search for action, there would be an evening in which Tussar would wash away the belligerent edge of irritability so that the urge for action could be confined to sitting in a car, listening to music, and concentrating on the nod. Jack Bando, a self-identified crazy guy with a penchant for guns, observed the remarkable change in his own behavior during a nine-month period of drinking Tussar:

> It's a very passive drug. In other words, if they legalized it and forced every criminal to take a bottle a day, there wouldn't be any crime. The only period of nine months in my life where I never got in a beef [fight]. I got six years of my life in jail, probably got 40 convictions . . . all kinds of trouble. And that's probably the only nine-month period where I haven't got arrested.

In the early days of Tussar, when its use was confined to only a handful of groups, street youth seldom connected drinking it to the illegal activity of drug taking. Although they may have viewed getting high on Tussar as wrong in much the same way that they believed getting drunk on alcohol was wrong, the practice was hardly ever conceived of in the terms usually associated with opiate consumption. Self-identification as drug users awaited official efforts to curtail use of Tussar as an intoxicant. Jack Bando underscored the absence of labeling the behavior as drug-taking until law enforcement agents gratuitously began to intervene:

> To us, [Tussar] was like drinking a different kind of booze. In all the time we used it, I never heard it referred to as a drug by any of us until the cops stepped in. The closest it came to being a drug to us was we had to get it in a drugstore. I never thought of myself as a drug user until the police began warning the druggists as to our purpose of using the stuff. Then the druggists started yelling at us to get out of their stores or they would call the police and tell them we were trying to buy drugs.

Although speculating on whether street youth in East Highland would have confined their drug taking to Tussar if the activity had never been intruded upon may be nothing more than toying with historical "ifs," the self-limiting nature of drinking Tussar suggested that the later explosion in drug use might have been avoided. The old-timers who had experienced Tussar and then later become chronic heroin users consistently expressed their preference for Tussar. Their preference was stated usually with regard to the superior quality of the feeling state that it produced, and they spoke of Tussar with a loving nostalgia. As Ducky Barrett, one of the tough guys from the original group of Tussar experimenters, claimed, "If you put a bottle of Tussar and a street bag of heroin in front of me, I'd take the Tussar every time." Other negative features usually connected to heroin addiction—increased amounts, high cost, and the sordid procedures surrounding illegal purchases—were all conspicuously absent.

In the early days of experimentation with cough medicine, before there was a need for sophisticated group strategies to obtain and use other drugs and narcotics, the young men who drank Tussar permitted the suppliers of the product to structure its distribution. Since legal reputations limited the amount of purchase, the young men involved adapted easily to the limitation and bought a single bottle per day which was usually reserved for evening use.

In the early days of Tussar, few people outside the street system (with the probable exception of druggists) understood enough about the emerging fad to recognize a coherent sequence of activities sufficiently to identify it. Not only could the users enjoy the fun that accompanied participation in quasi-legal activities, a kind of in-group secret accomplishment, but they could accrue some prestige from admiring younger solid guys whose own group status could rise through association with older, tested neighborhood heroes. And even during the earliest days of Tussar experimentation, the discoverers realized that they had moved into fertile territory and that future recruits would somehow upset the stability of operations.

THE ERA OF EXPLORERS:
MARKET SATURATION AND DRUG SWITCHING

Being high-status solid guys, the discoverers acted as well in the role of pacesetters whether they wanted to or not because their achieved positions on the street thrust them into the leadership of a new drug revolution. Two factors eventually disrupted their romance with Tussar: (1) as new recruits entered the practice of drinking cough medicine, demand began to outweigh the sources of supply, and (2) once the use of Tussar became widespread, keeping the practice secret from legitimate society was increasingly difficult.

The growth in new users occurred without proselytizing. The proximity of established solid guys to younger street aspirants provided a natural inducement. And younger men with ambitions in the street world valued whatever tidbits of information and recognition that they could garner from older established solid guys.

With the growth in the number of users, the demand on suppliers in the legitimate market place increased proportionately. It seemed evident from the reports of the old-timers that, once the use of Tussar became widespread in East Highland, druggists could be recognized in either of two categories: those who unwittingly sold Tussar as a cough medicine, and those who understood that the product was used for its intoxicating effects. "You could always tell," explained one respondent, "by the price." When certain drugstores became known as sources of easy purchase, they soon were inundated with East Highland youths trying to buy their bottles of Tussar before others bought up the supply. As the practice spread, first as a single ripple and then like a rain of concentric circles, the competition for supply increased. The younger adolescents added a gamelike excitement to securing cough medicine. An evening's activity for some groups consisted of drag racing to a known supply before it was exhausted.

As the practice spread, law enforcement became aware of the new development. And according to all the old-timers, the state narcotics police "would investigate any druggist who put in for a large supply." Between 1959 and 1960, Tussar became difficult to buy. In the meantime, some of the older users, now in their twenties, had arranged with a druggist in a distant community for a more steady supply. But even he was unable to stretch his limited amount and feared police investigation if he sold it excessively. Jack Bando explained how he and his group met the enforcement policy of limiting the supply of cough syrup by negotiating a business arrangement with a druggist:

> We were doing business with a druggist named Fleece; he liked our money and rather than lose it he asked us one day how Tussar made us feel, that if we described the effect maybe he could make something up for us with a similar effect. We described it and he said he had just the thing. Seconals and Nembutals. We were soon taking Seconals with the small quantity of Tussar we could purchase.

While the inclusion of barbiturates as a "booster" to the Tussar high may have been an outgrowth of drug users' motivation for intoxication, it developed as a consequence of the official effort of trying to limit what was perceived as an abuse of cough medicine even though the purchase and use of Tussar might not have constituted an actual violation of the state's drug laws at that time. While the effort to manage the nonmedical use of codeine cannot be called the "cause" of drug escalation, it was an important contributory factor in the early history of switching from cough medicine to barbiturates.

When Tussar could not be purchased, barbiturates, especially

Seconals, became the drug of choice among street experimenters. From 1959 to 1961,[3] "popping pills" not only changed street behavior but created a different social order among street groups and brought into existence new social roles that were specific to drug-using activities and which were new to the Italian-American community of East Highland.

Unlike Tussar, which had a quieting effect on the inner tensions of street youth, Seconals were an aid to violent behavior. The unexpected result of increased action rather than sedation could be achieved simply by fighting off the drowsiness that the barbiturates usually induced and then enjoying a relaxed state free of anxiety, guilt, or remorse.

As Joe Gulf called Seconals: "Them's hate pills."

In a neighborhood like East Highland where fighting was such an important activity in determining a youth's street status, barbiturates, much like alcohol, could blur judgment and permit even frightened youth to step fearlessly into dangerous situations. And top-level solid guys who periodically might regret the injuries that they inflicted upon victims could in a state of groggy indifference unleash violence free of concern and with only a partial memory of the incident. When looking back on the days when barbiturates were the principle drug in use, some heroin users believed that times, rather than worsening, had improved. Randy Lang, a heroin user at the time of the study, made the comparison between the heroin situation of the present day and the fighting days of 1959-1962:

> You know how people in East Highland say heroin, heroin. . . . Heroin quiets you right down, Harvey. Honest to God. I remember even when I wasn't taking barbiturates. I remember the older guys used to take it. You think we're nutty. You should have seen these older guys.

Billy Caesar, a self-identified "crazy guy," concurred when he said, "Compared to the way East Highland used to be, this place would win the Nobel Peace Prize or something."

The switch from Tussar to barbiturates brought important changes in the social organization of corner groups involved in drug taking. With Tussar, the method of purchase and use tended to reinforce group cohesion. Since obtaining Tussar was on a day-to-day basis and was carried out as a group activity with the automobile as the means of transportation, drug use was a kind of recreational activity, reserved for the evening, in which each member, with the possible exception of the driver, had equal standing. Some respondents claimed that frequently one person from the car would go into the drugstore and purchase five or six bottles of Tussar for the total group, but the role of purchaser was an arbitrary selection that did not require specialization. In other words, the use of Tussar provided no basis for status distinction among members of the group; status was determined by behavior other than the practice of drinking cough medicine.

When East Highland users switched to barbiturates as their new intoxicant, the egalitarian status system was disrupted and gave way to new techniques of achieving prestige and control over others, techniques which for the first time were directly related to drug taking. And when users were required to bypass the medical profession as the only legal intermediary between them and a supply of barbiturates, their drug-using activities stopped being merely a recreational pastime. It brought them squarely into acts that were in violation of the state drug and narcotic laws. Drug use itself shifted from being a legitimate adventure to being a higher risk involving violations of criminal statutes.

Arrangements for the purchase and distribution of barbiturates accounted for changes in the local status system among users. With cough medicine, each individual user could carry out his operations autonomously and remain relatively independent even though his pleasure was enjoyed in a group setting. Each day could be viewed as a discrete unit in which a user would buy one bottle of Tussar, drink it, and enjoy the effects. With barbiturates, where two to six Seconals would produce a high, access to a supply required a different arrangement. A single user could not purchase barbiturates in small amounts for only a day's use. The nature of the product itself and the conventional method of its distribution acted against the usual procedures that Tussar users had known. With Tussar, the illegality of purchase may have been questionable, but the shift to barbiturates removed any masquerade of legality. As a protective device for the legitimate seller, wholesaling became the system of supply and distribution. Ducky Barrett explained how the demand for Seconals led to the emergence of middlemen:

This guy I'm talking about, the druggist we did business with, we were with him for a period of about maybe four years off and on. There was a period there where for about three months, he shut us off. He says, "Look, things are getting too hot, too many guys are coming by." . . . So for about three months he shut us off. . . . So we waited three months, went back, and we hit him. But this time we went back, we gave him something like, I remember it was $350. And we bought a lot of stuff. . . . When we told him we had three-fifty, he says, "Well, we'll do business." And from then on, he would only do business with us as far as selling thousands of Seconals. Like we couldn't go in and buy a hundred. We hadda buy a thousand.

In addition to arrangements with pharmacists, some older users learned techniques for forging prescriptions, and "banging scripts" became a speciality in itself. With the abundance of Seconals, the older users had sufficient supplies for themselves and enough to distribute among younger action-seekers. There was little evidence that these early middlemen sought out the role for profit. In fact, reports indicated that in 1959-1961, the cost of purchase from the pharmacist was approximately the same as the sale on the street. Seconals were bought and sold for only 10 cents apiece. Rather than financial profit, Seconals were a form of social currency, favors to be passed to friends where the price was measured only to maintain a supply.

The emergence of the middleman with a large supply of Seconals had significant consequences in the street life of East Highland. It created for the first time a social role whose high status was connected exclusively to drugs. Further, and perhaps most important, it brough illicit drug products directly to the street and within easy reach of prospective experimenters. With the proliferation of middlemen, many with sustained connections to pharmacists and some with developed skills in prescription writing, barbiturates literally flooded the streets of East Highland. Joe Gulf remembered the days when "Seconals were like candy." Middlemen, for the most part, were older solid guys who had already achieved street status through their participation in other forms of action behavior. When they became key figures in accumulating large supplies of Seconals, they were able to achieve and maintain some mastery of the local market. The sheer audacity of being in possession of thousands of Seconals made their behavior, according to street standards, an achievement to be admired. In a sense, the middlemen became bankers in drugs, and their affluence made financial profits unimportant compared to the influence that they could wield among peers simply through the distribution of barbiturates. Because of the abundance of their supplies, they introduced competitive features of drug taking that displayed their physical capacities and daring. The huge amounts that they consumed showed their fearlessness of death—some users came miraculously close—and separated them qualitatively from the usual run of solid guys who enjoyed their highs on lesser amounts. One middleman user explained his excessive consumption in what seems to be retrospective exaggeration:

> I'll tell you the thing that ruined me. I think the thing that might even have cost my marriage. I got these 3,000 Seconals. You know, in the drugstore. And I started taking, this is when I really got bad. I'd take 20 and wait half an hour. Then I'd take another 20. And BOOM, I'd go right out. I'd drop for 14 hours. All 14 hours, out. I wouldn't know where I was, who I was with, whose car I was in, how I got up the house.

Once the middlemen made Seconals available on the street, younger and more reluctant solid guys could experiment with small amounts if they could neutralize their stereotypical fears that pill taking began an inevitable development into addiction. Neutralizing these stereotypical fears came about through everyday observation, a kind of street inductive reasoning and through the belief that addiction was connected to the use of opiates, a spinoff from the antidrug propaganda of the time. A youth needed only to take his own survey of Seconal users to note that addiction to heroin or other opiates was either so rare or nonexistent at the time that the truth of the propaganda was mitigated by the slimness of evidence. In fact, the heavy users of Seconals at this time stated a fear of heroin. Jack Bando claimed, for example: "It [heroin] was like going all the way and we didn't want that."[4]

Even though barbiturates taken in large amounts and over an extended period of time have the potential for producing physical dependence, there were few reports that drug habits were consciously recognized. Fear of physical dependence was subsequently neutralized by young experimenters as being the result more of the personal characteristics of the users than of an inherent quality of the drug. Since the manner of recruitment took place within the corner group—friend to friend—a youth, seeing his close friends or boys slightly older taking small amounts with few apparent negative effects, could feel with some assurance that addiction was more myth than reality.

Once over the hurdle of fear, the more typical solid guys, especially ones who had never experienced Tussar, tended to compare the Seconal high from moderate amounts to the familiar effects of an alcohol drunk. The resulting slurred speech, staggering, and general grogginess were symptoms that could be related to previous experiences with alcohol; and the familiarity of the sensations tended to lessen fears about barbiturates. Within the comparison with alcohol, some features of Seconal made it for some youth a superior choice. There were no telltale odors, and a youth could conceal taking drugs from authorities and parents, who, at that time, had few suspicions and little knowledge of the emerging drug-taking pattern. The hangover syndrome was absent; and on the following morning, the user frequently experienced a pleasurable afterglow, a kind of subdued continuation of the previous evening's high. At 10 cents apiece, the cost was congenial to lower socio-economic youth whose income from work or family was often limited. And perhaps even more important, the use of small amounts of barbiturates permitted youth from all levels of the street hierarchy to participate in a new form of risk-taking activity that was both emotionally pleasurable and status enhancing.

As news of the enjoyable effects of barbiturates spread from corner to corner, use of them became ubiquitous among members of the East Highland street system. While higher status young men began to devote greater amounts of time to acquiring and ingesting them, the run-of-the-mill solid guy could cut the costs of a weekend bender by consuming Seconals as a substitute or as a companion to the usual Friday and Saturday drinking. The positive rationalizations of their benefits served to mask the fact of their illegality and their physical dangers. In the action orientation of the street, however, these concerns, rather than acting as a deterrent to use, were transformed into incentives for daring behavior. Unless users consumed unusually large amounts or became involved in extremely violent behavior, "popping pills" within the context of street behavior was seldom viewed as deviant even though the larger society defined barbiturate use outside the boundaries of medical prescription as both deviant and criminal.

INTRODUCTION OF
HYPODERMIC NEEDLES AND RECRUITMENT

Before 1960, drug use among action-seekers in the East Highland street system was sufficiently secret from legal authorities so that arrests of users were either for violent assaults, which may, in some cases, have been carried out while high on barbiturates, or on mistaken charges of drunkenness. Even though some policemen were aware of the emerging use of barbiturates—one local officer caught his younger sister in possession of Seconals—making arrests which would hold in a court of law was difficult. Since internal possession did not constitute a violation of state law, drug users under the threat of apprehension could rid themselves of incriminating evidence simply by swallowing the pills in their possession, a practice that was generally recognized as dangerous.

In the meantime, social control agencies attempted to stop the flow of barbiturates through a policy of investigating pharmacists and alerting them to the developing practice of forging prescriptions. The attempt resulted in the arrest of a small number of middlemen who were often severely intoxicated at the time of their attempted purchase and were easily apprehended. Police activities in the drug field, however, were haphazard. Rather than pursuing drug users under the direction of a plan, police appeared to be the beneficiaries of the blunders that barbiturate users made as they staggered under heavy sedation into fights or in slovenly attempts to cash illegal prescriptions. These few but easy convictions brought a small collectivity of East Highlanders into the county jail at Bucks Island. While serving short sentences, usually about six months, they met drug users from other neighborhoods of Coastal City where drug and narcotic use was endemic. In comparison, the Italian youth of East Highland discovered that they themselves were neophytes in the broader drug world. Under the tutelage of more experienced drug users, they heard the details of a broader range of drug use, particularly the hypodermic injection of heroin.

Around 1961, the street supply of Seconals was slowed temporarily. In the same year, Tussar was legally removed from the market. Some drug users, after sampling the pharmacopoeia of cough medicines, discovered that Robitussin AC produced effects similar to (but weaker than) those of Tussar. But the more daring users of barbiturates, who had already suffered the social stigma of arrest and/or jail sentences, began to inject Seconals with a hypodermic needle.

The introduction of the hypodermic needle had an important consequence on the changing social organization of drug users: it separated the casual experimenters who used Seconals as a way of avoiding the negative effects of alcohol from the drug users who were more seriously preoccupied with heavy sedation and greater risks. The needle provided a concrete status distinction between the truly daring and the marginally committed solid guy. In 1961, the numbers of solid guys willing to chance injecting Seconals was small; and, since they were predictably from the ranks of the tough and crazy guys with local prestige, they became within the realm of drug users an elite group.

Injecting Seconals had a number of disadvantages, however, which drug users soon learned. If they missed a vein, the subsequent swelling was painful and far too visible. Even if they were successful in intravenous injections, many of them reported a siege of chills and shivering; and, too frequently, users would fall into extended states of unconsciousness. Once a sizable number of drug users had experimented with the injection of drugs, they soon found one that had more congenial results, a drug that they could connect with a high that they had already experienced and one that kept them from viewing themselves within their own stereotype as "dope fiends," a phrase that East Highland drug users reserved for heroin addicts. Sometime between 1961 and 1962, injecting paregoric (PG) replaced injecting barbiturates among many of the top-level drug users.

At the same time, the use of Robitussin AC had become a common practice among younger users, partly in imitation of older solid guys, partly for the sensation of relaxation that the codeine induced. With the older or more intent solid guys involved in needle injections, younger and lower status youth could reason that drinking AC, usually on weekends, was after all not a serious step into drug use when compared to injecting other drugs. For the solid guy eager for a more prestigeful street reputation, use of paregoric and the hypodermic needle provided instant entrée into high status street groups.

With the introduction of paregoric, the requirements of purchase and complicated preparation made it a group activity. Users learned that, to achieve the desired effects of relaxation and a nod, several eyedroppers-full were needed. They learned, as well, that between three and five eyedroppers could be extracted from one bottle of paregoric. To acquire paregoric in sufficient amounts, one had to make several purchases from different drugstores. Further, to avoid serious and potentially fatal consequences, one had to burn off the alcohol in the solution before injecting it. This procedure required the privacy of an apartment.

Unlike drinking cough medicine, where each participant independently secured and drank his own bottle, the use of paregoric demanded some measure of interdependence where key contributions of money, transportation, purchase, preparation, and privacy were necessary components for a group to carry out the activity successfully. Where one component was absent, providing a replacement led, for the first time in East Highland, to recruitment efforts.

Recruitment efforts were not necessarily calculated to lure unsuspecting victims into eventual drug dependence. They were simply searches for some missing segment in the drug activity in much the same way that three bridge players would seek out a needed fourth hand. Selection was based on the person's ability to provide the missing component, maintain secrecy, and be generally impressed with the adventurous nature of the sequence of events. The more typical reason for a recruit's willingness to become initiated to the needle injection of paregoric was his previous trusting friendship with the recruiters. From the recruiter's perspective, the understanding of a neophyte's concern for maintaining peer status or avoiding a drop in peer status accounted for the relative ease with which new users could be enlisted into meeting the challenge of a needle injection and the illegality of the total activity. Cookie Delgado, an ex-marine, explained that the constraint of peer respect blocked his retreat from experimenting with paregoric:

> *Cookie:* No one likes to blame anyone else for turning them on, but it was Joey Sordello who turned me on. That was the first time I saw how PG was done. I was with him and some other guys one night . . . helped them buy a couple of bottles. And then I watched them shoot up. After they were all through, Joey said to me, "Well, it's your turn now."
>
> *Author:* What did you do?
>
> *Cookie:* I didn't want to look like no asshole, so I let Joey do it.
>
> *Author:* Were you afraid at first?
>
> *Cookie:* Yeah, I was probably more afraid of looking like a jerk in front of my friends. When I got the feeling, a high, not a real good high though, I liked it.

Paregoric as a preferred drug had a number of features which made it superior to the previous substance. Injected intravenously, it was quick acting and provided, according to users, a "better nod" than Robitussin. It did not have the side effect of chills and shivering that injecting barbiturates caused. And its cost of 40 cents a bottle (available at the time without a prescription) made it the choice drug for the top-level solid guys until 1964-1965, when heroin use replaced it and sent it into extinction.

POLICE RAIDS AND PUBLIC ATTENTION

With the introduction of the hypodermic needle, a new era began in the relationship between police and the drug users of East

HARVEY W. FELDMAN [267]

Highland. During the four- to five-year period between 1957 and 1962 in which cough medicines and barbiturates were used almost exclusively, arresting users depended on fortuitous circumstances. In consuming both substances orally, one reduced the risk of arrest to only the time that it took to purchase and swallow the substances. When intravenous injection of Seconals and paregoric became popular among a small but important segment of drug users, the indisposable nature of the hypodermic needle provided the basis for organized attempts to curtail drug use in East Highland by arresting drug users. Even though the switch to heroin was still a few years in the future, the appearance of the hypodermic needle aroused suspicions among local detectives that heroin had moved into the community. With the explanation that an epidemic of heroin addiction could be avoided by diligently pursuing traffickers, police launched a new era by carrying out planned raids on drug users. Since illegal possession of a hypodermic needle, according to state law, constituted a felony, convictions could be secured with the concrete evidence of a needle. Users could no longer rid themselves of incriminating evidence to avoid arrest. As Jack Bando ironically explained, "You can't swallow a spike."

When an individual is arrested, a remarkable alteration in his social relations and concept of self takes place. Kai Erikson (1964), a sociologist in the field of deviant behavior, stated that

> The community's decision to bring deviant sanctions against an individual is not a simple act. It is a sharp rite of transition, at once moving him out of his normal position in society and transforming him to a distinct deviant role.

To take Erikson a step farther, the status of that "distinct deviant role" will vary according to the audience that judges it. While conventional society may view arrested drug users with leperous distaste, the boy on the street saw them quite differently. Rather than pariahs to be avoided, arrested drug users, especially the heavy users of paregoric and Seconals at the time, were cast as leading protagonists in a drama of prosecution rivaled only by the fiction of Hollywood. The manner in which raids were carried out made the group use of paregoric and Seconals seem as sinister and conspiratorial as the gangland meeting at Appalachia. Ducky Barrett described one of his early drug-related arrests when the police, acting without search warrants, raided an apartment of paregoric users:

> It was 12 cops in on it. Two detectives and 10 uniform cops. . . . They hit from the front and backdoors, you know. . . . They were waiting for us. They blocked up the streets. . . . When my car came down the street, we seen . . . you know, put up them wooden horses in back of our car. As we went by, they put wooden horses in the street, "Do Not Enter." We didn't get wise to it. . . . So we went in the house. Three minutes after we were in the house, BANG, BANG. They hit both the doors. BOOM, come right in. Caught us with everything right on the table.

What about the local adults whose experience with narcotics had been confined to fictional accounts or who held automatic stereotypes (usually connected to racial minorities)? The raids shocked them into a discovery that the publicized horrors of the "dope fiend" were dangerously close to home. The manner of the arrest, with its striking squad of a dozen or more men who staked out and charged an assembled group of young men, was sufficient reason to believe that the objects of the raids posed a serious threat to public safety.

For the youth on the street who knew the arrested drug users and respected their street reputations, the raids served to solidify a view of them as bold, reckless, criminally defiant—qualities that elevated and secured their street reputations. For the drug users to become the central foci of such high adventures placed them alongside fictional and real criminal heroes like Little Caesar, Trigger Burke, Crazy Legs Diamond, Baby Face Nelson, or John Dillinger, criminals whose reputations commanded similar police activities. Like top-level gangsters, the local drug users caught in neighborhood raids had their names printed prominently in the *East Highland Gazette* or in the *Coastal City Daily News* so that newspaper publicity certified their local importance.

In this dual view, the arrested drug user developed a double status. Among nonusing adults, his conventional image was seriously damaged—and for some arrested users irrevocably, since a narcotic felony conviction would remain a permanent fixture on almost all future legitimate social roles. While his conventional image was negatively transformed, his street image was enhanced. Conventional defeat and street triumph were complementary components, both tarnishing the user's image among adult nonusers but making him an enviable hero among other street youth who were potential candidates for similar treatment.

For the arrested drug user, the simultaneous reward of high-status criminal recognition among peers and the stigma of official punishment inspired a self-view that tended to elevate the importance of the street role at the sacrifice of conventional ones. On the street, he could gain prestige from the notoriety of his experience, pass negative judgments on the lack of knowledge and sophistication of his oppressors—arresting officers, judges, probation staff, etc.—and generally transform his punishment into a framework of victory. After a period of time, he could even begin to state (and perhaps believe) that the conventional roles no longer open to him were boring and uninviting.

HEROIN: "THE ULTIMATE"

When heroin became the drug of choice for a minority of drug users in East Highland, the development grew for two sets of reasons: (1) the convenience of preparation and (2) the sales value of heroin for young, aspiring solid guys seeking elevation of status within the local drug scene.

Among drug users in East Highland, the dividing line between higher or lower status in the context of daring drug activities was symbolically determined by an individual's fear or willingness to use the hypodermic needle. Prior to 1963-1964, the largest segment of drug users who chanced needle injections were partial to paregoric.[5] As paregoric users noted, the amount of time required to purchase paregoric from several drugstores, the elaborate preparation of burning off the alcohol, the telltale smells of the cooking, the need for cumbersome equipment (i.e., a stove, a frying pan or pot, eyedroppers, and needles), the requirement of four to 10 or more eyedroppers of the drug to achieve a desired high, all made the use of paregoric problematic. And when police began to stage raids, being bound to a house—or, more specifically, a kitchen—made users of paregoric easy targets for arrests.

Switching to heroin simplified procedures. In order to inject heroin, users needed only a hypodermic needle, an eyedropper (obtained with almost any commercial eyewash), a bottle cap (called a "cooker"), a small piece of cotton to strain out impurities, and water to heat the drug into liquid solution. This "set of works" could easily be packaged into a handkerchief, tied together with a rubber band and stored in any number of secret places: behind pipes, in the brush of an open field, or under rocks. Unlike the equipment needed for preparing paregoric, "works" for heroin injections were portable and permitted the users to expand the number of potential locations where heroin could be secretly prepared and injected. Although most users preferred the comfort and apparent safety of an apartment, the options for privacy were greatly expanded; and places like gasoline stations, automobiles, cellars, restrooms, and even school yards could be converted temporarily into "shooting galleries." Because heroin could be heated into solution rapidly and unless special circumstances arose—clogged needles, collapsed veins, etc.—the whole procedure could be completed in no more than 10 minutes.[6]

Heroin came into public visability not as a result of its being introduced by older pacesetting solid guys who had discovered Tussar, switched to barbiturates, and then pioneered paregoric. Instead, it developed among a younger crowd of action-seekers whose push for top status within the street system was linked to exploring drug adventures that even older, time-tested solid guys like Jack Bando viewed as "going all the way." In the intergenerational competition of street groups, it was the "younger guys" who, growing up around drug-using role models, launched the heroin revolution. While the older crowd may have edged into drug use by clouding the definition of narcotic intoxication as just another way of getting high, the younger crowd had adopted drug taking and transformed it into one of the key activities around which street reputations developed. It should be remembered that, by 1964, drug use in East Highland had existed for approximately seven years, so that a number of street corner generations had been exposed to the drug use of succeeding, older groups. In 1964, a young man of 19 would have been exposed to drug information as early as 12 or 13 years old. His fear of drug dangers would have been mediated by his observations of the local users whom he knew, as well as by his own experimentations with cough medicines and barbiturates. In brief, the younger crowd of drug users were the beneficiaries of the drug knowledge and discarded fears of older users. By moving into heroin use, they could issue a status assertion of the first order, since even the most daring solid guy among the older crowd had reservations about experimenting with heroin. Their move toward heroin was calculated to elicit responses of admiration from older drug users and peers for daring to challenge a narcotic whose reputation placed it at the extreme of risk-taking behavior and pleasure. One of the heroin users from the 1965 era explained his satisfaction with the achievement as measured by comparative drug use:

When I first started shooting dope, I did the same thing [bragged]. I used *heroin*, you know. Seeing a kid drinking cough medicine, I'd say, "I wouldn't take *that* shit. I graduated, man. Heroin is great. It is fabulous." . . . Like I tried the ultimate.

Heroin in its beginning days had a ready-made market of users among two sets of potential candidates: (1) young, aspiring solid guys whose curiosity and daring moved them enthusiastically into reckless fads and (2) older users of paregoric who had come to enjoy its cozy effects. For the young guys who had not experienced the remarkable transformation of moving magically from a state of tension to a relaxed nod the way the older pioneers of Tussar had, the first use of heroin provided evidence that a gratifying state of well-being could be produced instantly. For the paregoric users, the switch to heroin was less enthusiastic but still strongly positive. As Ducky Barrett noted in comparing heroin to paregoric:

It's like drinking a good whiskey and a bad whiskey, you know. . . . They both give you the same feeling eventually. The heroin is going much smoother, you know.

With the movement of young users into heroin and the blanketing in of paregoric users, the sudden upsurge in numbers made it appear as though a heroin volcano had erupted, even though the acutal number of heroin users never exceeded 1% of the youth population.

MARIJUANA: AN ALTERNATIVE TO HEROIN

By 1967, boys entering into the street life of East Highland recognized that use of drugs, like fighting, had become one of the key activities in establishing reputations among peers. Failure to use drugs was not necessarily a cause for censure. It merely limited entry into most corner groups, since the chief requirement for informal membership was participation in group activities. And increasingly, especially on weekends, the core activity of many groups centered around getting high, which implicitly meant use of one of the many drugs available. For an East Highland adolescent who desired nothing more than a modest street reputation, use of opiates was a risk beyond his capacity to manage. His fear of dependence, arrest, or the harsh punishment of his family made the ordinary solid guy skeptical of heroin. By the middle 1960s, he found that cough medicine, mainly Robitussin AC, was a lesser risk; but, with the active law enforcement surveillance of pharmacists, it had become difficult to buy. In fact, a street youth could not purchase Robitussin locally without a prescription and frequently discovered that even drugstores in the rural areas of adjacent states had been alerted to the use of cough medicines by young people. As the supplies of Robitussin and other codeine-based cough syrups became more limited—East Highland youth called the development "burning out drugstores"—the purchase of what East Highland youth considered lesser risk drugs, which were usually acquired through diversion from legitimate channels, became difficult. By 1967, the street price of barbiturates had risen to 50 cents a pill, and they were generally available only through street specialists in forging prescriptions. When they had difficulty in cashing them or when they were arrested, the street supply of barbiturates correspondingly decreased. In addition, use of barbiturates had become less appealing to the lower-level solid guy because of their association with fighting, although they continued to be used heavily by many young people who preferred their effects to the displeasures of alcohol. Too frequently they caused irritability that led to fighting. And the extreme state of intoxication—getting "whacked out"—was not always the kind of high that many lower-ranked solid guys sought and enjoyed.

In the summer of 1968, some three years after heroin had taken hold among a minority of street youth, marijuana came into popularity. By then, drug use had become not simply an acceptable street activity but one that was considered almost necessary as a demonstration of allegiance to the street system. For the middle-range and more lowly ranked solid guy who hesitated about stepping into drug action that chanced arrest, physical dependence, or censure from family, marijuana permitted the kind of minimal status assertion which kept the user within the expectations of the street. Although the risks associated with marijuana were significantly lower than the risks of any of the other drugs that had come into fashion, marijuana still had an association with illegality. The fact that it was listed as a legal equivalent to heroin—possession of either was a felony in the state—provided sufficient risk to make its use a worthy, although lower status assertion. By 1972, when the study officially concluded, marijuana had become the most popular intoxicant in East Highland and was smoked so widely that Carl Modesto, primarily a heroin user and constantly alerted to police activity, stated one evening in almost disbelief of the openness of marijuana smoling by younger street users, "They act like it's legal."

One of the major benefits of the use of marijuana was the way it added rather than undermined the social cohesion of street corner groups. Rather than moving individuals into distrusting relationships in which mutual exploitation was the anticipated norm, such as heroin had done, or inducing a sleepy state of individual enjoyment, such as cough medicines had produced, marijuana was ideally suited to a group project. Each member of the group would pitch in small amounts of money for the purchase of a $5 bag, which was often enough to accommodate 10 to 12 experienced smokers. It was usually smoked in a cheap pipe, and the activity was carried out with egalitarian participation, each person getting an equal number of puffs as the pipe was passed around, regardless of financial contributions. The activity itself and the subsequent actions were usually carried out with such hilarity and uncontrollable laughter that young men who were made the butt of verbal assaults seldom interpreted their situation in the negative ways that they might in sober conditions.

With marijuana as the core substance, other drugs were soon introduced which provided similar sensations that were described in terms of direction: "downs" were known as drugs that subdued and relaxed, and "ups" were drugs that activated behavior so that life could be carried on with a greater sense of zest. Although many marijuana smokers periodically experimented with a variety of downs, usually steering clear of those narcotics that required needle injections, they were most favorably impressed with those substances that energized rather than inhibited social interaction. Along with marijuana, some of the corner boys favored diet pills and enjoyed the nervous energy that they produced. "Black Beauties," as one brand of diet pills was called, were viewed as aids to conversation, so that users reported a discovery of dialogue and the pleasures of conversation while under their influence. For the young men who enjoyed ups in preference to the down sensation of opiates and barbiturates, experimentation with LSD provided the kind of risk taking that was comparable in the opposite direction to heroin. Among the street youth of East Highland the belief existed that permanent damage to mental functions—"fucking up your mind" was the expression commonly used—was a potential outcome from overuse of LSD. Even some higher ranked heroin users who claimed to have avoided LSD because of its alleged capacity to trigger psychosis were impressed, albeit negatively, with the risks taken with the human mind at stake.

With the latter-day involvement with marijuana and other energizing substances, a new set of social arrangements were established among drug users. On either extreme were the street participants who preferred the sedation of the downs or the energizing lift of the ups. In between, the majority of users sampled drugs cafeteria-style, some with a preference in either direction, others using drugs strictly according to what was available in the local marketplace of street sales.

During the four-year period of my study, drug activities had become a natural and acceptable form of street corner behavior in which the social consequences may well have been viewed as less antisocial than other behavioral possibilities. Reno Bernini, a drug sampler who had experimented with all the licit and illicit drugs that became even mildly popular in East Highland, was a product of a street generation that had become socialized into viewing drug taking as a natural alternative to more socially damaging, risk-taking activities. For Reno, drug activities, particularly recreational marijuana smoking, provided a channeling of restlessness, a way to avoid rather than participate in serious crime:

> I don't know what I'd do. I don't know what anyone would do around here if all drugs stopped. I think all the kids'd go crazy. Like they wouldn't know what to do at night. Like I don't think we could just hang around. . . . I don't know. I think they'd probably be getting into trouble.

CONCLUSIONS

The single theme that runs through almost all ethnographic studies of drug users in the natural environments of their home communities centers around the themes of risk taking and action (Preble and Casey, 1969; Sutter, 1966, 1969, 1972; Feldman, 1973, 1974; Waldorf and Reinarman, 1975). In this study of Italian-American corner groups, the history of drug taking was a direct outgrowth of a male-dominated street system in which the guidelines for behavior were based on a set of values and beliefs that emphasized risk taking as a strategy for acceptance and prestige. Within that context, large numbers of young men gravitated to drug use. The history of drug switching in East Highland, however, was not simply a phenomenon of the street system alone. Although the early history indicates that consumption of cough medicines was in itself a pleasurable pastime, the activity did not take on a tempo of excitement until the behavior itself was defined both by the street groups and by representatives of legitimate society as deviant and criminal. In defining the nonmedical use of drugs for intoxicating purposes as criminal and in pursuing users as though they were, in fact, comparable to criminals in other spheres of law-breaking, public policy makers provided the framework for rule-violating excitement. The total activity became symbolic of the life-style of the more sophisticated criminals in organized rackets and crime, where the solid guy motif acted as the role model for youthful imitation.

The interplay between a public policy which defines drug use as criminal and its attraction to street youth as a form of excitement was hinted at but not explored by Chein and his research team as early as the 1950s:

> We saw the law as setting the framework for the problem, but we did not start with any suspicion that the law might be in some way contributing to the existence of the problem. . . . It did not occur to us to ask how much drug-taking behavior would not take place were it not for the challenge of the risk. [1964:6]

Any attempt to develop a causal explanation for the rising interest and experimentation with a wide variety of drugs by young people cannot be separated from the public policies upon which the societal response is based, since the policies and the ways in which they are carried out are the substance of the excitement and risk.

The spread of drug use and the phenomenon of drug switching are by their nature a social process. It is important, for example, to underscore that the early users of cough medicines in East Highland did not define the activity as drug taking until social control agencies attempted to intervene. The process of selecting drug-taking activities and viewing them as grossly illegal, so that youthful participants became the objects of official pursuit as though they were dangerous criminals, brought the role playing of solid guys into a new reality in which the trappings of imitation became the genuine product. Being the objects of police raids, receiving high bail on felony charges, serving time in correctional institutions, facing the hardships of an ex-convict—these and other experiences with the machinery of the criminal justice system were the crucial contingencies that shaped drug careers in East Highland. Once drug use was selected for special consideration, it was elevated to a higher order of risk within the context of street life. The interaction of the social control system and the street system set in motion a chain reaction that progressively magnified the criminality of drug taking so that its social importance swelled within each of the systems. And once drug use was raised to a high level of importance within each system, young men found that their behavioral tactics for achieving prestige, or even simple acceptance, became linked to drug use in one form or another.

NOTES

1. All males who had gained even minimal acceptance into the street system were referred to as "solid guys." The hierarchy of solid guys could be charted on a continuum from high to low status with the roles of "faggot," "asshole," and "jerk" having very low status and the roles of "tough guy" and "crazy guy" having highest status. Tough guys and especially crazy guys were looked upon as local heroes and admired for their feats of daring and adventure. See Feldman (1973).

2. There were several reports that the use of benzedrine preceded cough medicines, but its use was almost never a primary activity performed for its own sake. Rather than using benzedrine and enjoying the high as a discrete activity, the young men took the drug for the lift it provided for other, more valued street activities in which alertness would be required for long periods of time, such as all-night card games. The use of an illicit drug as a primary activity carried out and enjoyed for the drug effects themselves evidently did not occur on a group basis until the discovery of Tussar.

3. According to reports from the old-timers, Tussar was taken off the market in 1961.

4. At the time, a street bag of heroin, which could only be bought in the black ghettos of Coastal City, cost $10. As consumers, the drug users who had explored the heroin market recognized that for the same amount of money they could buy a month's supply of Seconals.

5. For a short period of time, just prior to the introduction and rise in heroin experimentation, use of prescription opiates such as Dilaudid, morphine, and Panapon (but especially Dilaudid) was popular among the young men who chanced needle injections. Use of these opiates, however, never became widespread except by a small group of users who developed superior skills in writing and cashing prescriptions.

6. The hypothesis of shifting to heroin because of its convenience has some historical precedence. Terry and Pellens (1928:74) noted a similar trend in the switch from opium smoking to use of other opiates in the early 1900s: "The equipment required, the odor of the burning drug and later its cost all combined to make relatively easy the closing of the places [opium dens] where the drug was used in this form once public opinion and police activities were awakened.

" . . . It is not inconceivable that taxation and police and other activities had less to do with the ultimate near-control of the practice of smoking opium in the United States than had the popularization in the underworld of the hypodermic and sniffing of heroin, forms of indulgence that were cheaper, more convenient, more adaptable to many surroundings, and far more easily concealed from friends, public and authorities."

REFERENCES

BALL, J.C., CHAMBERS, C.D., and BALL, M.J. (1968). "The association of marihuana smoking with opiate addiction in the United States." Journal of Criminal Law, Criminology, and Police Science, 59(2):171-181.

CHEIN, I., GERARD, D.L., LEE, R.S., and ROSENFELD, E. (1964). The road to H: Narcotics, delinquency, and social policy. New York: Basic Books.

ERIKSON, K.T. (1964). "Notes on the sociology of deviance." In H.S. Becker (ed.), The outer side. New York: Free Press.

FELDMAN, H.W. (1973). "Street status and drug users." Society, (May/June):32-38.

——— (1974). Street status and the drug researcher: Issues in participant-observation. Washington, D.C.: Drug Abuse Council.

MANDEL, J. (1968). "Who says marihuana use leads to heroin addiction?" Journal of Secondary Education (May).

PREBLE, E., and CASEY, J.J., Jr. (1969). "Taking care of business: The heroin user's life on the street." International Journal of the Addictions, 4(March):1-24.

SUTTER, A. (1966). "The world of the righteous dope fiend." Issues in Criminology, 2(2):177-222.

——— (1969). "Worlds of drug use on the street scene." In Delinquency, crime, and social process. New York: Harper and Row.

——— (1972). "Playing a cold game." Urban Life and Culture, 1(1):77-91.

TERRY, C.E., and PELLENS, M. (1928). The opium problem. New York: Committee on Drug Addictions, in collaboration with the Bureau of Social Hygiene.

WALDORF, D., and REINARMAN, C. (1975). "Addicts: Everything but human beings." Urban Life, 4(1):30-53.

ABOUT THE AUTHORS

MICHAEL H. AGAR is an Associate Professor of the Department of Anthropology, University of Houston. He has worked in both academic and applied research settings, including the University of Hawaii and the University of California, Berkeley, and the National Institute of Mental Health Clinical Research Center in Lexington, Kentucky, and the Drug Abuse Control Commission in New York City. His publications include a book-length study of heroin addicts, *Ripping and Running,* as well as several journal articles.

HARVEY W. FELDMAN received his Ph.D. from Brandeis University and is currently a research associate at the Berkeley Center for Drug Studies, Wright Institute, Berkeley, California, and a general consultant. He was formerly Associate Professor at St. Louis University from 1974 to 1976. From 1972 to 1974, he was a Fellow of the Drug Abuse Council, Washington, D.C. He worked as a Project Director of a Public Welfare Study at Brandeis University and was co-Principal Investigator (with Irving K. Zola) of a "Neighborhood Drug Study" supported by the National Institute on Drug Abuse. He has written many articles and two monographs on drug addiction.

JAMES A. INCIARDI is currently Associate Professor and Director of the Criminal Justice Program, Department of Sociology, University of Delaware. He received his Ph.D. from New York University and has more than 14 years of experience in the clinical and research areas of substance abuse and criminal justice. He worked directly with criminal offenders and drug users while a member of the New York State Division of Parole and was Deputy Director of Research of the New York State Narcotic Addiction Control Commission. His major work is *Careers in Crime,* and he has coedited four other books on social issues and crime.

JENNIFER JAMES is an Assistant Professor of Psychiatry and Behavioral Sciences at the University of Washington and is one of the very few scholars who has done extensive ethnographic research in the field of prostitution, addiction, and other female offenses. She has been an advocate for the revision of statutes involving "victimless crimes" and for the removal of sexual discrimination in arrest, conviction, and incarceration procedures. She received her doctorate in anthropology from the University of Washington in 1972. Her major publications include *The Politics of Prostitution* and a number of journal articles.

CARL B. KLOCKARS is currently Adjunct Associate Professor of Sociology at the University of Delaware. The author of *The Professional Fence*, a life history of a major dealer in stolen property, he is now working on a two-year ethnographic study of detective-level police work. The study is sponsored by the Twentieth Century Fund and focuses on the use of informants. In addition to his work on police, professional crime, and, particularly, the trade in stolen property, he is editing a collection of essays on the ethics of research with deviant subjects which will be published in 1978.

CHARLES W. LIDZ is currently Assistant Professor of Psychiatry and Sociology at the University of Pittsburgh. He received his Ph.D. in sociology from Harvard in 1974. He has published articles on heroin, police, and the theory of intelligence and is coauthor of *Connections: Notes from the Heroin World*. A second volume on heroin and its social control is currently undergoing final revision. He is currently doing research on the legal regulation of psychiatry.

THOMAS MILLER was born and raised in Yorkville, one of the two study areas in Manhattan. He works full time as a community research worker and is affiliated with the New York State Office of Drug Abuse Services. His main employment has been in the construction field as a tractor-trailer truck driver and sandhog. He has been active in youth activities programs in Yorkville, mainly in the fields of sports and athletics.

EDWARD PREBLE is currently Professor of Anthropology at the New York School of Psychiatry and Principal Investigator of a neighborhood drug study program affiliated with the New York State Office of Drug Abuse Services. He has had wide experience in the areas of narcotics addiction, crime, and delinquency and has published in these areas. He has had much street ethnographic experience as director of several research projects in crime and delinquency. He also coauthored (with Abram Kardiner) *They Studied Man*.

HARVEY A. SIEGAL is Assistant Professor of Medical Sociology, School of Medicine, and Assistant Professor of the Department of Sociology, Anthropology, and Social Work at Wright State University. He received his Ph.D. from Yale University and has worked in academic positions in both Miami and Mexico. He has coedited three books on drug addiction and crime and has authored the forthcoming *Outports of the Forgotten: Lifeways of Socially Terminal People in Slum Hotels and Single Room Occupancy Tenements.*

IRVING SOLOWAY is a member of the graduate faculty at the Medical College of Pennsylvania. He is an urban ethnographer who had done ethnographic fieldwork, since 1970, among active heroin addicts in Philadelphia, as well as ethnographic fieldwork in a methadone maintenance program, of which he was the director of research, and in a therapeutic community treating addicts and alcoholics. His publications include articles on methadone treatment. In addition, he is currently completing a taxonomic analysis of the cognitive orientations of amphetamine abusers, a study of territory and social identity, and an ethnography, *Pimping the Program: The Culture of Patients at a Therapeutic Community.*

JAMES P. SPRADLEY received his Ph.D. from the University of Washington and is currently Professor of Anthropology at Macalester College. He has done fieldwork among the Kwakiutl Indians and the subculture of tramps in Seattle. He has published many articles on urban phenomena, ranging from drinking behavior to using dope, has coauthored three books, and edited several others. His major works are *Guests Never Leave Hungry: The Autobiography of James Sewid, A Kwakiutl Indian* and *You Owe Yourself a Drunk: An Ethnography of Urban Nomads.*

JOAN H. TRUE received her Ph.D. from the University of Florida, where she studied anthropology and educational administration. She studied education and linguistics for an M.A. at Stanford University. She worked as Academic Director of a private school in San José, Costa Rica, following several years as a classroom teacher. She now is an educational consultant for the *Miami Herald* and has finished writing (with Elizabeth Eddy) a book about desegregation in Florida schools.

WILLIAM R. TRUE received his Ph.D. from the University of Florida and now is an Instructor in the Division of Addiction Sciences, Department of Psychiatry, University of Miami. He was field office coordinator for a study of chronic marijuana use in Costa Rica (sponsored by the National Institute of Drug Abuse) and served as a Peace Corps volunteer in rural Peru and as a Navy officer on a cruiser. He has published articles on Costa Rican social structure and drug use.

ANDREW L. WALKER is currently Assistant Professor of the Department of Social Science at Stephens College. He is coauthor of *Connections: Notes from the Heroin World* and has written articles on drug addiction and ethnographic methodology.

JAMES WALTERS is a graduate student in the Department of Psychiatry at the Medical College of Pennsylvania. He was a member of the Philadelphia Police Department for several years and has published articles in criminal justice and drug abuse.

ROBERT S. WEPPNER is Associate Professor and Director of the Division of Addiction Sciences of the Department of Psychiatry, University of Miami School of Medicine. He received his Ph.D. in anthropology from the University of Colorado. He was Director of the Social Research Center (Federal Narcotics Hospital) at Lexington, Kentucky, for four years and taught at the University of Kentucky Medical School. He was also Director of Research and Evaluation for the Dade County Division of Rehabilitation Services. He has published articles in the areas of urban problems, drugs, crime, and adjustment of American Indian migrants.

NAME INDEX

Adams, R.N., 23, 48
Adler, F., 22, 49
Agar, M.H., 22, 23, 31, 32, 33, 47, 48, 143, 151, 156, 162, 163, 177, 179 184, 193, 198
American Law Institute Model Penal Code, 172-175, 177
Argyris, C., 25, 48
Aswad, B.C., 197, 198
Aydelotte, F., 75, 76

Ball, D., 91, 101
Ball, J.C., 250, 278
Ball, M.J., 278
Banton, M., 39, 48
Barber, B., 42, 48
Barnett, H.G., 197, 198
Bateson, G., 146, 156
Becker, H.S., 26, 28, 43, 48, 89, 97, 101
Blum, R.H., 179, 198
Blumer, H., 96, 101, 193, 198
Bohannon, P., 47, 48
Bowen, C., 34, 50
Branzburg, P., 175
Buel, J.W., 75, 76
Byrnes, T., 10, 63, 75, 76

Caldwell, E., 175
Campbell, D., 116, 122
Campion, D., 75, 76
Carey, J.T., 38, 48
Carroll, E., 17, 47
Carter, W.E., 140
Casey, J.J., Jr., 23, 44, 50, 145, 156, 159, 177, 184, 193, 199, 229, 230, 236, 248, 275, 278
Caudill, W., 37, 47
Chambers, C.D., 23, 49, 278
Chandler, F.W., 75, 76
Chein, I., 159, 177, 276, 278
Cleckner, P.J., 21, 47, 48
Cloward, R., 159, 169, 177
Coggins, W.J., 140
Cohen, A., 159, 177
Cohen, R., 104, 113, 122
Cohen, Y.A., 191, 199
Comitas, L., 21, 50, 125, 141

Conrad, H.T., 51
Cook, S., 123
Costello, A.E., 10
Crane, L., 24, 49
Crapsey, E., 63, 75, 76
Cressey, D., 27, 28, 50
"Crying Phil," 66, 67
Cunningham, P., 75, 77
Cutpurse, Moll, 206

Davis, A., 168, 177
Dearden, R.L., 75, 76
Denzin, N., 94, 101
Despres, L.A., 29
Deutsch, M., 123
Dickson, W.J., 25, 50
Dole, V.P., 232, 244, 248
Doughty, P.L., 140
Douglas, J., 24, 26, 28, 30, 35, 48
Dressler, D., 75, 76
Dunn, J., 116, 123
Durkheim, E., 122
Duwars, R.E., 86, 101

Earle, C.S., 10
Eckerman, W., 47
Eddy, E.M., 29, 48
Edgerton, R.B., 179, 199
Egnal, J.D., 177
Erikson, K.T., 91, 92, 99, 101 267, 278

Fabrega, J., Jr., 14, 16
Feldman, H.W., 21, 24, 29, 47, 48, 104, 122, 145, 156, 193, 199, 275, 278
Feldstead, S.T., 75, 76
Feyerabend, P., 202, 225
Finestone, H., 193, 199
Fischer, C.S., 29, 31 49
Flexner, S.B., 56, 177
Frake, C.O., 188, 199
Freilich, M., 34, 49, 86, 101
Furnivall, F.J., 75, 77
Furst, P.T., 125, 141

Gans, H., 97, 101
Garfinkel, H., 113, 123
Gearing, F.R., 233, 234, 248
Gerard, D.L., 278

Wild, J., 206, 212
Willard, J.F., 75, 77
Williamson, H., 27, 51
Willmoth, P., 97, 102

Wilson, J.Q., 179, 199
Wolfgang, M.E., 48, 51

Yablonsky, L., 159, 170, 177

SUBJECT INDEX

UNIVERSITY COLLEGE LIBRARY CARDIFF